You Can Have What You Want

Michael Neill

HAY HOUSE, INC.
Carlsbad, California
London • Sydney • Johannesburg
Vancouver • Hong Kong • New Delhi

Published and distributed in the United States by: Hay House, Inc.: www.hayhouse.com • *Published and distributed in Australia by:* Hay House Australia Pty. Ltd.: www.hayhouse.com.au • *Published and distributed in the United Kingdom by:* Hay House UK, Ltd.: www.hayhouse.co.uk • *Published and distributed in the Republic of South Africa by: Hay House SA (Pty), Ltd.:* orders@psdprom.co.za • Distributed in Canada by: Raincoast: www.raincoast.com • *Published in India by:* Hay House Publications (India) Pvt. Ltd.: www.hayhouseindia.co.in

Editorial supervision: Jill Kramer • Design: Charles McStravick

Library of Congress Control No: 2005939084

ISBN 13: 978-1-4019-1183-6
ISBN 10: 1-4019-1183-8

09 08 07 06   4 3 2 1
1st Edition, November 2006

Printed in the United States of America

To Nina, Oliver, Clara, and Maisy—
without you none of this would have been worthwhile
or anywhere near as much fun.
I love you more than words (even these words)
can express. . . .

"I'm not a teacher:
only a fellow-traveller
of whom you asked the way.

I pointed ahead—ahead
of myself as well as you."
— George Bernard Shaw

CONTENTS

FOREWORD

*'Give a man a fish and he'll eat for a day;
teach him how to fish and he eats for a lifetime."*
— Lao Tzu, Chinese philosopher, 6th century B.C.

THERE ARE VERY FEW PEOPLE in the human-potential movement these days who impress me. Unfortunately, I have come to realize that many of the biggest names are better marketers than agents of change. Michael Neill is different. He has a truly original message and a wonderfully lighthearted style of delivery. This is partly a product of his high level of skill, but also an indication of who he really is as a person.

I first met Michael back in the late '80s when he was working in a New Age book shop in Camden, and I was a DJ at Capital Radio in London. We both went on to become Neuro-Linguistic Programming (NLP) trainers and stayed in touch on and off over the years. Then several years ago, I was in L.A. and we met up again.

When I asked him what he was doing, he told me he had become a "success coach." He explained that this is different from therapy, where the emphasis is on what happened in the past and on "fixing" what's broken. In coaching, his job is to assist people in enjoying the present and creating the future. Instead of just giving his clients what they say they want, he teaches them how to get it for themselves.

Then he asked me if I'd consider having some coaching with him. I almost said no—things were going well for me, and I wondered what he could teach me about change—but I was curious, so I hired him for a month to see what he could do.

What I didn't realize at the time was just how exceptional a coach Michael really is.

According to a brand-new research study (reported in the UK publication *The Guardian*, happiness, rather than working hard, is the key to success. Cheerful people are more likely to try new things and challenge themselves, which reinforces positive emotions and leads to greater success at work, stronger relationships, and better health. This echoes what Michael has been demonstrating for years, and is one of the primary messages of this wonderful book.

Scientific or not, I can only talk from personal experience. Since using Michael's approach to creating inner and outer success, I have become happier in myself, more successful, and to be blunt, I have simply made a lot more money! This book contains many of his techniques that I can personally attest are powerfully life-changing.

In recent years I have recommended to many of my closest friends that they hire Michael as their coach, and I have watched their lives transform beyond all recognition. They too have become happier, wealthier, and perhaps, best of all, more inspired and alive than ever before. I will tell you the same thing I tell them if they are skeptical or hesitant about getting started: Working with Michael will help you to get more of what you truly want out of life.

For the small investment in time and effort it will take you to read this book and do the experiments, you will experience a profound and positive life change. Do it!

— **Paul McKenna, Ph.D.**

ACKNOWLEDGMENTS

WERE I TO MAKE A FULL LIST of the people to whom this book and I are indebted, it would be longer than the book itself. Therefore, with a huge "Thank-you" to everyone who has contributed to the accumulation and sharing of experience represented by this book, here are a few of the people I would particularly like to acknowledge:

- Stuart Wilde for pushing me out in front of a group of people before I had any idea that I could: I came, you pushed, I flew!

- Richard Bandler for his support and for developing the field that saved my life and launched my career.

- Paul McKenna for dragging me out of premature retirement kicking and screaming (and for being a great friend along the way).

- Gay and Kathlyn Hendricks for convincing me that sticking my head above the parapet would be much more fun than living in an eternal crouch.

- Sacha Gervasi for encouraging me to write this book "before I was ready."

- Sue Crowley—my angel of serendipity—without whom this book would have languished on the bookshelves of my mind.

- Robert Kirby, Jacqui Clark, and Angela Torrez for helping me deal with the numerous people who asked, "Who the hell are you and why should we care?"

- Michelle Pilley, Joanna Lincoln, Jo Lal, Megan Slyfield, Reid Tracy, and the whole Hay House team for giving me the chance to share what I do with a wider world.

- The "Magnificent Seven," who let me bounce my early drafts off them and bounced them back to me better than before.

- Mike Meakin and Jill Kramer for helping me to dot my 'i's, cross my 't's, and mind my 'p's and 'q's.

- Bill Cumming and Peter Fenner for playing midwife to the emergence of my spiritual self.

- Mandy Evans and Michele Lisenbury Christensen for continually encouraging me and assisting me in living what I teach.

- All my teachers, coaches, and clients past and present: Your contributions to my life and to this book have been immense!

I would also like to especially acknowledge the children's "Uncle Father David" for being my best friend, confidant, teacher, and fellow- explorer. I'm grateful to have met you so young that I never had to find out what a rare gem our friendship is. . . .

INTRODUCTION

"There are no rules here—we're trying to accomplish something."
— Thomas Edison

LET'S BEGIN OUR TIME TOGETHER with a little experiment . . .

I'd like you to put the book down and swap shoes with the person nearest you. Now, if you're in the bathroom, or reading this all alone in the middle of nowhere, I understand that might be a little bit difficult. But otherwise, go for it. Take off your shoes, go up to the person nearest you, and ask them to swap.

Done?

Okay, let's talk about it.

Nobody questions the fact that your feet are different from other people's. Different size, different shape, different appearance. There may be people you know with similar feet, but no one with ones identical to yours. And the reason you almost certainly didn't do what I just asked you to do (and if you did, for goodness' sake, swap back!) is because you understood immediately that it was ridiculous.

The chances of someone else's shoes fitting your style and taste (or, more important, your feet) are slim at best. Yet to them, their shoes might be the most wonderful ones in the world—comfortable, practical, attractive, and with great memories attached as well.

What's less obvious to most of us is that the same principle holds true of our beliefs and practices in the world. Setting goals, meditating for thirty minutes twice a day, doing the latest diet or practicing yoga might be as painful, uncomfortable, and inappropriate for you as trying to squeeze into your favorite movie star's underwear—but you might still try to do it because it looks so good on them!

What if you don't need to do things someone else's way in order to live a happy, successful life? What if everything you've ever learned about success was just wrong?

This book is about what happens when you use your head, listen to your heart, and follow your bliss. It's about what happens when you stop doing all the things you think you should be doing and start doing what you really want to be doing—when you stop listening to everybody else and instead turn up the volume on the still, small voice within.

By the time you've finished reading, you'll know beyond a shadow of a doubt that you can have whatever you want in life: more money, better relationships, a new job, or anything else that makes your heart sing and your soul come alive. The only question you'll be left with is whether or not you really want it!

Let's face it—most people spend their lives chasing someone else's dreams, then wind up being disappointed that they never achieved them or even more disappointed that they did.

As you explore the ideas in this book and put them to the test in your one and only life, you will get back in touch with your own dreams. You will discover what actually works for you, regardless of whether or not it works for anyone else. And best of all, you will finally be able to truly enjoy the journey every bit as much as the roadblocks along the way.

Debunking the myth of the experts

'The great enemy of the truth is very often not the lie, deliberate, contrived and dishonest, but the myth—persistent, persuasive and unrealistic."
— John F. Kennedy

Having grown up in a family of scientists, I was thoroughly immersed in the myth of the experts, which can be summed up in the phrase "Follow the advice of the experts—they know best."

The idea is that there are these people out there called "experts," and what they do is study everything there is to study about a field, and they find the best ways of doing things. Then they tell you what they've learned, and even if it feels wrong to you, you should do what the experts tell you—because they're experts.

Makes sense, right?

Well, it made so much sense to me that I grew up and became an expert in my area of psychology called Neuro-Linguistic Programming, or NLP. I've studied hundreds of books and worked with thousands of people over the past fifteen years, including a foreign prince, numerous millionaires, and famous (sometimes infamous!) members of the Hollywood elite. I'm an unquestioned expert in the field of human behavior.

Yet I'm not going to give you a single bit of advice about what you should do with your life.

Why?

Because even if what I say is true in my experience, it may not be in yours.

In theory, I may know better than you, but in practice you know best (or at least you have the potential to know best) what will work for you.

In fact, I'll go so far as to say this:

You are the expert on you.

But here's the catch . . .

Most of us have never claimed our expertise—we've never made a study of ourselves. And if you're going to step up and be your own best expert, one of the most useful things you can do is to begin tapping into your own inner senses and inner genius on a regular basis.

While no one can teach you exactly how to do that, it is something that can be learned—and I've designed every sentence in this book to act as a catalyst in the process of bringing your genius to life.

The idea of "genius" being a measure of intellect is actually fairly recent. In its original form, the word had two primary meanings. The first refers to that natural inclination that we all seem to have that draws us toward some things more than others. This is different from cultural conditioning, which would make us all want the same things and agree that only certain things are "good" and "right," while everything else is bad and wrong.

The second root definition of "genius" is *djinn*, or "genie." And like the genie in the magic lamp, when you learn to unleash your inner genius, you will find your "wishes" to the universe are granted more easily and effortlessly than you may have ever thought possible.

How it all works

In Part I—Creating a Life That Makes You Go "Wow!"—I will share with you the same stories and techniques I use with my clients to help them unleash their own inner genius and put it to work in creating their lives. You will learn the keys to knowing yourself, trusting yourself, inspiring yourself, and even loving yourself—what I call the "four pillars of an extraordinary life," because each one provides a core structural element in supporting you on your journey, and together they form an unbreakable foundation for living the life of your dreams.

You'll also learn some of the foundational secrets of effortless success—that kind of success where it seems as though you got what you wanted without even trying. We often think about these experiences as anomalies—happy accidents while we're getting on with the "real" business of working to create what we want in our lives. In fact, your experiences of effortless success are the keys to finding and walking along what I like to call "the path of inspiration"—that unique blueprint for success, happiness, and fulfillment that is being drawn on your heart and in your life each and every day.

In Part II—An Obstacle Course to Success—I'll walk you step by step over, around, and through the nine key life obstacles that people use to stop themselves from having everything they want in life. This section is packed with simple tips, techniques, and proven action strategies for getting unstuck and moving forward with your dreams.

Throughout the book, you'll also find a number of boxed sections called "*From theory to practice . . .*" These are based on a simple but important idea:

The difference between theory and practice is that in theory, there is no difference between theory and practice— but in practice, there inevitably is.

Each of these sections will contain an experiment or two that you can do for yourself to find out if what I'm saying works for you—if it enhances the quality of your life and moves you closer to having more of what you want.

You do not need to do all of the experiments in this book in order to succeed!

Instead, I'd like you to think about each one of them as an invitation to learn more and have fun doing it. As with any invitation, you don't have to accept it—but if you don't, you might just miss the party.

How to NOT change your life

One of the core skills of NLP is learning to use language "hypnotically." I have put these skills to use and have written this book in a way that your life will change for the better just by reading it.

Despite this, there are still a few ways you could avoid making your life better if you really want to. . . .

1. Dismiss it all as New Age happy-clappy bubble-gum pop psychology

If you're already thinking about hiding this book inside a porn magazine so you don't have to be embarrassed about people seeing you read it, there are a couple of things in here you may find difficult. . . .

First, there are times when I use words like *love, happiness,* and even *God* (gasp!).

Second, I tell the occasional "little bunny FuFu" story. You remember little bunny FuFu, don't you? The one who went hopping through the forest, scooping up the field mice and bopping them on the head?

You don't have to work out exactly what these stories are supposed to mean consciously. They're written for another part of your mind—the part that keeps your heart beating and your body breathing, even as you're reading this book right now.

2. Turn the ideas in this book into a new set of "rules" for how you're supposed to be in the world and what you "should" and "shouldn't" be, do, have, or want

In the famous story of the blind men and the elephant, each of the men in turn mistook the small part of the elephant they were able to grasp in the moment for the true nature of an elephant. Therefore, the man holding the tail thought the elephant was like a snake, the man who grabbed an ear described the elephant as being like a bat, and the man who got hold of one of the legs thought the elephant to be very like a tree.

In the same way, it's the easiest thing in the world to turn any one perspective on life into "the whole truth" and then expound on it as if it really were the "right" way to be.

But if you read this book as a manual for how you *should* be and what you *should* do if you want to be happy and successful, you will find ways of turning every positive possibility into a limiting straitjacket.

Know this: No matter how well things are going for you or how badly you may be suffering right now, you're almost certainly doing the best you can to take care of yourself, moving toward happiness and away from sorrow in the best way you know how. And as Oprah Winfrey is fond of saying, "When you know better, you'll do better."

3. *Override your inner wisdom by listening to me instead of yourself*

The reason why I focus so heavily on experimentation is that until you actually try things out for yourself, you won't know where, when, and how they will make the biggest positive difference for you.

Here's an experiment we'll be playing with throughout the book . . .

It is very easy when reading to get "lost in thought," particularly if something I say doesn't seem to fit in with what you have learned about happiness, success, or life. But if the ideas most people had in their heads about what it takes to live their dreams were accurate, there would be no point in my having written this book, and even less point in your reading it now.

Therefore, whenever you see this symbol:

check to see if you have disappeared off into your own head. If so, pat yourself on the back for noticing and bring your attention back into your body by closing your eyes and taking a slow, gentle breath in as you focus on your physical heart. You can use these checkpoints as an easy way to reconnect with yourself and your inner wisdom. We'll talk more about why this makes such a difference in Chapters 5 and 6.

So . . . what do you want?

I'm hoping that you picked up this book because there are all sorts of things in your life that you want and you'd like some help in getting them. Maybe you want to make more money, improve (or even change) your career or start up a company of your own. Perhaps you are looking for a new or improved relationship, better (or even any!) sex, different friends, or a more enjoyable social life.

What you want may be even more personal—more intimate. You might be wanting to save your marriage or get on better with your resident teenager. You might have a health condition you are hoping to overcome. You may even be saying to yourself, I just want to be happy or peaceful or loved.

The good news is, you can have what you want, even if right now it seems too remote a possibility to even wish for. That's not to say that just because you want to go out with your favorite movie star, you automatically will (although one of my clients did—her story is in Chapter 2), but rather that you will come to realize over the following pages that the universe runs on a fundamental and oh-so-wonderful principle:

When you get really clear and honest about what you want, everything in the universe conspires to help you get it.

I call this the principle of effortless success, and it's at the heart of everything you'll be learning in this book.

Along the way, I'll share dozens of stories of how people just like you and me have overcome traumas, achieved "impossible" goals, and made improvements in areas of their lives where they had abandoned all hope. In fact, I'll be sharing with you the best of what I've learned from over 15 years of coaching and teaching thousands of people to have what they want, catalyze their genius, and live a life that makes them (and often everybody around them) go "Wow!"

But there is a catch . . .

You're going to have to allow this to be easier than you think, faster than you expect, and more fun than you can imagine.

Are you ready to begin?

———❦———

PART I

Creating a Life That Makes You Go "Wow!"

CHAPTER ONE

MASTERING THE HAPPINESS/ SUCCESS CONNECTION

The happiness priority

*"Happiness is the meaning and the purpose of life,
the whole aim and end of human existence."*
— Aristotle

MOST PEOPLE'S GOALS IN LIFE are made up of the things they believe will "make" them happy. But as one of my business partners once said to me, "If the bottom line is so important, why is it at the bottom?"

In other words, if what we really want is happiness, why don't we start there?

Having now asked this question of thousands of people, the answers generally come down to what I consider to be the greatest myth in Western civilization . . .

I'll be happy when I get what I want.

This idea has been with us for thousands of years and is endemic throughout all mythology, ancient and modern—that when you battle with a dragon and win, you get the princess and you live happily ever after. Or if you *are* the princess, you just need to be patient long enough and someday your prince will come and *then* you'll live happily ever after.

In fact, people are often willing to endure great hardship on the way to success because they just know there's a pot of gold at the end of their rainbow—and they plan on using that pot of gold to buy the feelings of happiness and fulfillment that they really want.

To give yourself a sense of how this myth might be active in your own life, think about three or four ways you could finish this sentence:

I'll be happy when . . .

- . . . I've got enough money.
- . . . I'm in a loving relationship.

3

- . . . I get a better job.
- . . . my boss/co-worker/friend stops being such a jerk.

Whatever you're putting between you and being happy in this very moment is a by-product of the myth of happiness: the idea that when you finally sort out your outer life, your inner life will take care of itself.

But the truth beyond the myth is simple yet profound:

**If you're doing things in order to be happy,
you're doing them in the wrong order!**

When you make happiness your number one priority and allow yourself to follow your "happy wanting," success is not only more likely, attaining it is much more fun. As Albert Schweitzer said:

*"Success is not the key to happiness.
Happiness is the key to success.
If you love what you are doing, you will be successful."*

Which brings up an important question: What exactly is "success"?

The origins of "success"

Success (noun)

First appeared (in print in English) in 1537:

1. An outcome or result.
2. The attainment of wealth, favor, or eminence.
3. One that succeeds.

Isn't it amazing that the first recorded success didn't happen until 1537? What did they call people who attained wealth, favor, or eminence before then?

I mean, sure, Ben Hur "did well" in the chariot race. Richard the Lionheart "rocked" the crusades, and Genghis Khan "achieved some very impressive things" in the plains of Outer Mongolia, but the first recorded use of the word *success* wasn't until 1537.

(Personally, I like to think the first person written up as a "success" was a Renaissance barber named Bob who increased his business by two score and ten when he introduced bloodletting as one of his services.)

Here's my problem with the dictionary definition of the word *success*—linguistically speaking, it describes something that doesn't actually exist.

The word *success* belongs to a category of words called "nominalizations." And nominalizations are words that describe an activity as if it were an actual thing. Think about words like *love, happiness, relationships,* and *joy.* You can't stick them in a wheelbarrow, yet we talk about them as if they are things that exist outside ourselves.

Why is that significant? Because if we're spending all our time trying to become successful and there's no such thing as success, we're all doomed to failure!

What this means is that if our pursuit of success is going to be a meaningful one, we need to start by defining success for ourselves. To begin exploring how that definition might look, let's take a look at the two categories of things that people talk about as "success." . . .

1. Outer success

"I always wanted the trappings of great wealth, but instead I've got the trappings of poverty. I've got hold of the wrong trappings— and a rotten load of trappings they are too."
— Peter Cook

The trappings of outer success are the things we're used to seeing on TV and reading about in magazines—the money, the cars, the homes, the husbands/wives/mistresses/toy-boys, the servants, and so on. Status symbols may change from generation to generation, but in the world of outer success, he (or she) who dies with the most toys nearly always wins the game.

2. Inner success

"Finding inner success is the best, easiest and, in fact, the only way to achieve and enjoy everything else in life."
— Spencer Johnson

Inner success is the ongoing experience of love, happiness, fulfillment, and well-being—the experience of joy in your everyday life. And most people would say that given the choice, inner success is by far the more important.

Yet why do we have to choose?

What if you didn't have to give up the taste of a really great steak for a taste of enlightenment?

What if you didn't have to give up the scent of eternity for the smell of a rose?

Happy success, and what I'm convinced most of us are really after, is the combination of the inner with the outer—a truly fulfilling life that is a combination of authentic happiness and really cool stuff.

For example:
- A wonderful experience of working at a wonderful job.
- A fantastic sense of well-being within the context of a fantastically loving relationship.
- Peace of mind and a nice piece of real estate overlooking the ocean.

From theory to practice . . .

What Happy Success Means to You

1. Imagine you're out near the end of your life. In your mind, notice a future you, looking happy and content. What is it about that person that lets you know they are happy and content?

2. Go say hello! Ask them what it is they have done with their life to make them feel so good. What were the key actions, attitudes, choices, and accomplishments that led to it being a wonderful life?

3. Before you go, be sure to ask for at least one piece of advice they could offer you with the benefit of hindsight. Don't forget to thank them for their time!

4. Based on what you've learned, what does "happy success" mean to you?

Happy success for me is . . .

_____

_____

_____

The secret of happy success

If the greatest myth we are up against in our pursuit of happy success is the idea that "getting what we want will make us happy," the secret of happy success is simply this:

Your happiness does not depend on getting what you want.

Now, at first glance that may seem innocuous enough. After all, you've probably heard similar things before, ranging from "Happiness is a choice" to "Happiness is an inside job" to "Would you rather be right or happy?" (a question to which my answer has always been a resounding "Both!").

But what if it were *really* true? In other words, what would you want if you didn't have to be unhappy about not getting it?

When I ask this question in my seminars, I often have to repeat it several times before people can even hear it, so here it is again:

What would you want if you didn't have to be unhappy about not getting it?

We are so used to connecting up our pleasurable feelings with getting what we want and our unpleasant feelings with "failure" that many of us have never questioned the idea that happiness and success are intrinsically linked.

This apparent link is the source of nearly all our fears about failure and success. Think about it—are you afraid of failing, or are you afraid of failing and feeling bad about it? Are you afraid of losing all your money, or are you afraid of losing all your money and feeling bad about it? Are you afraid of ending a relationship, or are you afraid of ending a relationship, feeling fine about it, but feeling bad that you don't feel bad about it? (Complex, aren't we?)

For example, I have a client who was involved in a difficult break-up with a woman he had seriously considered marrying. During our session one day, he said to me, "The thing is, I just don't love her anymore."

This struck me as a bit odd because everything I'd ever seen or heard him express about her was deeply loving.

"Yes, you do," I said.

"No, I don't," he replied, seemingly trying to decide whether to be annoyed or confused by my response.

"Yes, you do still love her," I continued. "You just don't want to be with her anymore."

He went quiet for a minute or two as he considered it for himself.

Finally, he said, somewhat tentatively, "Can both of those things be true at the same time?"

Several days later, I was speaking with a friend who was complaining about how much she hated her work and how she wished she was able to make enough money doing what she really loved to quit her job immediately.

After listening to her go on for a while, I was struck by something neither of us had ever really considered before.

"What if you could absolutely love the work you're doing at the moment and STILL leave to do what you really want as soon as it makes sense to you to do so?"

This time it was only a few moments before she replied.

"Am I allowed to do that?" she asked, her voice filled with wonder.

The theme running through both these dialogues was the idea that it was necessary to be unhappy in order to change.

Bruce DiMarsico, the creator of the Option Method, posited a simple but powerful theory about why people experience unhappiness in any form, be it fear, anger, sadness, depression, or misery:

**The only reason why you are ever unhappy
is because you think you should be.**

In other words, when you feel bad, it is because in that moment you think "bad" is the best way to feel—that there are some important and positive benefits to it.

These benefits generally fall into one of two categories:

1. We feel bad because we think it will motivate us (or are afraid that we wouldn't act in our own best interests if we weren't):

2. We feel bad because we think it means something good about us (or are afraid that it would mean something bad about us if we didn't).

I will always remember the man who challenged me during an NLP and Happiness workshop I was giving in London with a somewhat provocative question over whether I was advocating that he should feel happy about the recent death of his wife.

After quickly pointing out that that was NOT what I was saying, I went on to explain that for me, the question was not whether or not he "should" be happy, but simply if he was willing to be. That is, would it be okay with him if he felt at peace with what had happened?

He shook his head no, so I went on to ask him:

"What are you afraid it would mean about you if you were not unhappy about your wife's death?"

He looked at me aghast. "What kind of a monster would I be if I was not unhappy about that?"

"So are you saying," I asked, "that your feeling unhappy now is your way of expressing your love for your wife?"

He softened immediately and nodded.

"Is that how you want to express your love for her?" I asked.

"No," he acknowledged, "but won't other people think there's something wrong with me if I'm not miserable?"

Rather than venture forth with my own opinion, I asked him how he would answer his own question.

"I suppose," he said slowly, "that if they did, that would be okay with me. Because if there's one thing I know for certain, it's how grateful I am for our time together and how much I will always love her."

Is it really true that we are only unhappy because we think we should be?

Honestly, I don't know. But whether we have learned to use sadness to express our love, anger to signify our caring, or fear to motivate ourselves to go for what we want, the point is this:

Whatever you can do with unhappiness, you can do better when you're happy.

From theory to practice . . .

Happy Success in Action

1. Think about something in your life that you are unhappy (angry, sad, fearful, etc.) about.

2. If I could wave a magic wand and you would be instantly happy in that situation without anything else changing, would you want me to wave it?

   In other words, would it be okay with you to be happy in that situation, exactly the way that it is?

   (Remember, this is not saying you shouldn't be unhappy about whatever you are unhappy about—it is just a sincere and curious question from you to you.)

3. If your answer was no, ask yourself either or both of the following questions:

   – What am I afraid would happen if I wasn't unhappy about _____?

   – What do I think it would mean about me if I wasn't unhappy about that?

4. Whatever you came up with, pick out the positive intention behind it, i.e., the "very good reason(s)" you have for getting and staying unhappy.

5. Finally, imagine yourself feeling comfortable and peaceful in yourself and handling the situation elegantly and well. Come up with at least three ways that you could fulfill that positive intention without the "unhappy" emotion.

The three types of happiness

A few years ago, I participated in a vanguard program training coaches in using the distinctions from the relatively nascent field of Positive Psychology. As a part of the training, Dr. Martin Seligman, a well-known author and researcher, shared his notion of the three types of happiness and how to experience more of them in your life. As you review the following introduction to the three "happinesses," think about which of them are most and least developed in your own life.

1. Pleasure

"All the money in the world is spent on feeling good."
— Ry Cooder

The thought that "whole-body aliveness" or "background bliss" could be a place to live from, not just a mountaintop to occasionally visit during a particularly deep meditation or wonderful sexual experience, may be a real stretch for you. And yet, what if it were possible?

What would it be like to live in a space of vibrant energy in which feelings could arise and dissipate against the gentle background hum of your whole-body aliveness?

For that matter, how good do you feel in your body right now on a scale from 1 to 10? Not how happy or sad or angry or fearful, but how wonderfully, pleasurably alive?

I remember that the first time I felt really, really alive in my body was when I was 15 and watching a rerun of *I Dream of Jeannie*. As it happened, I was sitting cross-legged with my spine straight, a position it turns out facilitates an easy flow of energy through the body. I felt such an overwhelming sense of peace and well-being (what I now recognize with my scientific mind as an endorphin release) that I thought I had died and gone to heaven.

So significant was this experience for me that I spent much of the next five years trying to re-create it by sitting in the same posture, studying meditation, experimenting with drugs, and watching reruns of classic 1960s television. (See, Mom, I told you it was research!)

As I moved into my 20s, I temporarily gave up my quest for inner delight to focus on my career and family. After all, I reasoned with myself, who has time for bliss and a mortgage? But the memory of the possibility never really went away, and since reawakening my search a few years back, I've learned some wonderful ways to access ease and well-being in the body on a regular basis.

Here is one of my favorite techniques you can use to experience more life in your body and more aliveness in your life.

From theory to practice . . .

A Warm, Fuzzy Practice

1. Take a few deep breaths and become aware of your whole body, from head to toe.

2. Now, find a part of your body that feels especially nice. This might be a warm tingle in your hands or a soft, "fuzzy" feeling in your heart.

3. As you tune in to that good feeling, keep part of your attention with that part of your body. Imagine the feeling as a color, and let it spread up to the top of your head and down to the bottom of your feet.

4. Next, look around the room you are in, keeping part of your attention on that good feeling inside you. If you notice that the good feeling starts to fade or you suddenly become aware that you've stopped focusing on it as you're looking outside yourself, then just return to the good feeling. You can close your eyes as long as it's safe and appropriate to do so. When you have that good feeling back, start to look around again.

5. As soon as you get comfortable looking around and holding that good feeling inside you, go ahead, stand up, and walk around the room you are in. Again, if you notice the good feeling start to fade, go back to your body until you're reconnected.

6. When you can walk around and still hang on to the good feeling in your body, find some other people to interact with, either in person or on the phone. Remember, part of your attention is staying with that good feeling in your body; part of it is focused on the person you are with.

   Anytime you notice the good feeling start to fade, just pull back enough to get back to it. Reconnect with the warm fuzzy, wherever it is in your body. When you're ready, you can once again engage with other people and the world.

2. Satisfaction

"If all the year were playing holidays,
To sport would be as tedious as to work.
But when they seldom come, they wish'd-for come."
— Prince Henry in Shakespeare's *King Henry IV*, First Part, I, ii

Perhaps the simplest way to grasp the distinction between pleasure and satisfaction is to think about it as the difference between those things that feel good in the moment and those things that we feel good about afterwards.

Here are some common pleasures my wife and I have been known to enjoy on the odd occasion:

• Eating chocolate cake
• Receiving a full-body massage
• Shopping for clothes (one of us)
• Drinking beer while watching football on a large-screen TV (the other one of us)

Here are their equivalent satisfactions:

• Making a chocolate cake
• Giving a full-body massage
• Making or designing clothes
• Playing football (probably without the beer!)

Pleasures give our bodies, well, pleasure; satisfaction nourishes our souls.

Does this mean satisfaction is better than pleasure?

Not at all. But the pursuit of pleasure for its own sake will rarely lead us to the type of lasting happiness that so many of us seem to crave. Like the root of the word itself, the path to satisfaction is invariably paved with action, and the more challenging the action, the more satisfying the journey.

Here are some questions that will help you bring more satisfaction into your daily life:

• What are some things that bring you pleasure? What are their equivalent satisfactions?
• What new challenge could you give yourself today?
• What would you need to do today to be able to look back and feel great about what you've done?

3. Meaning

*"It is better to allow our lives
to speak for us than our words."*
— Mahatma Gandhi

There's a story about a journalist who pursued Mahatma Gandhi through a train station, hoping to get an interview for his newspaper. Despite his persistence, Gandhi politely but repeatedly declined to respond to the man's questions.

Finally, as the train was pulling out of the station, the reporter called out, "Please, give me your message for the people!"

Without hesitation, Gandhi shouted back, "My life is my message!"

When I first heard that story, I was struck by a persistent question of my own:

If my life were my message, what would the message be?

I tried on a bunch of noble-sounding ideas, ranging from "Help yourself by helping others" to "Joy is the pathway to success," but nothing seemed to quite fit. Finally, I decided to get real and look not at what I would have liked the message to be, but what it really was. After some uncomfortable soul-searching, the answer became clear. The message my life at the time was giving out was this:

*"Set big goals and then half-ass your way toward achieving them,
and blame everybody but yourself so you don't have to feel bad when you fail."*

I realized then that it's not enough to follow the Quaker admonition to "let your life speak"—you also need to put some real thought into what it is you'd like your life to say.

From theory to practice . . .

Letting Your Life Speak

1. If you haven't already done so, ask yourself the Gandhi question:

   "If my life were my message, what would the message be?"

Remember, this is not "What would you like the message to be?"—that comes later. Begin first by taking a long look in the mirror. Even if you don't like what you see (and it's fine if you do), there's no better place to start than right where you are sitting now.

Examples:
- *"Do unto others as much as you can get away with."*
- *"It's never too late to blame someone else for your life."*
- *"Make resolutions and never follow through on them, then hate yourself for it."*

If you can, resist the impulse to reject the "real" message in favor of a more positive one. The more you are willing to take ownership of the message, the easier it will be to make changes in your life.

2. Now, what would you like the message of your life to be? What message would you like people to take away from experiencing your presence and being a part of your time here on Earth?

Examples:
- *"Always do your best and your best will always get better."*
- *"The fastest way to future rewards is by following present joy."*
- *"The question is irrelevant; love is the answer."*

3. Next, brainstorm any changes you would need to make to bring your life in alignment with this new message.

Examples:
- *Life message:*
  - *"Always do your best and your best will always get better."*

- *Changes to make:*
  - *Seek to do my best, even when part of me wants to just "get away with it."*

  - *Focus on continual improvement, particularly in my relationships.*

  - *Choose to participate fully in everything I do.*

4. Finally, ground your new life message by choosing one concrete action you can take in the next 24 hours.
   Examples:
   * *Life message:*
     – *"The question is irrelevant; love is the answer."*

   * *Changes to make:*
     – *Focus on my heart more than my head.*
     – *Don't spend so much time trying to "figure everything out."*
     – *When in doubt, love it!*

   * *Grounding action:*
     – *While I'm on the way home from work today, I will silently send loving energy to every person I see.*

To Seligman's three categories, I would like to propose a fourth, which for me lives out above and beyond pleasure, satisfaction, and meaning because it exists as a pure choice available to us in any moment. . . .

The art of contentment

*"You can resent your bald spot
or be glad you have a head."*
— Timothy Miller

One of the myths of modern living that keeps so many people running full-speed on a treadmill of their own creation is the idea that if they allow themselves to feel happy and content before their lives are perfect, they won't have a reason to get out of bed in the morning.

In my own experience, something very different happens the instant I choose to be content—to declare that I have enough (for now) of whatever it is that I want. Rather than leading to apathy or indifference, I find myself energized and enthusiastic. I feel *more* instead of just trying to feel *better*. I begin to enjoy what *is* instead of trying to make it into what *isn't*.

In Buddhism and Hinduism, contentment is revered as a worthy goal in its own right, based on an understanding that "All there is is all there is, and all there is is enough."

In the traditional Passover ritual, Jews the world over sing the thousand-year-old song *Dayenu,* a word that translates roughly as "That would have been enough." The song is a reminder that although we can content ourselves with any one of God's blessings, the blessings will keep cn coming.

In Christianity, Jesus describes the abundance of contentment in his Sermon on the Mount, when he says, "For whoever has, to him more shall be given and he will have an abundance; but whoever does not have, even what he has shall be taken away from him."

In other words, all the world's major religions recognize that when we cultivate contentment (by taking the time to really be present with what we already have), we get to have more and more and more.

So . . . what do you still need to change before you would be willing to feel content?

Do you have to earn a million dollars? End world hunger? Marry the man or woman of your dreams? Create world peace?

How much enough will be enough for you?

Webster's Unabridged Dictionary defines contentment as "Rest or quietness of the mind in one's present condition." This gives us a clue as to how to be content.

First, we focus on our present condition: on experiencing things exactly as they are. Second, we focus on resting or quieting our minds in the present moment.

While there are many practices that can enhance your experience of contentment, here are three of my absolute favorites. . . .

1. Be where you are and do what you are doing

I once had a teacher who defined meditation as "the practice of keeping your mind in the same time and place as your body." If our minds really wanted to go somewhere else, we were encouraged to take our bodies with them.

By consciously choosing to be present to where you are and what you are doing, you demonstrate your contentment—your recognition that at least in this moment, there is nowhere else you need to be and nothing else you need to be doing.

2. Breathe deeply

If you were under attack, your breathing would become rapid and remain shallow in your chest, enabling maximum oxygenation to your heart to help pump the adrenaline you needed to mount a mighty battle or hasten a speedy getaway. By purposely breathing slowly and deeply into your belly, you trigger your body's natural endorphin response, allowing your felt sense of contentment to deepen along with it.

3. Saunter

According to Jungian psychologist Robert A. Johnson, the word *saunter* comes from the Middle Ages, where everything was considered sainted including the earth (St. Terre). Therefore, to saunter is "to walk on the earth with reverence for its holiness." By taking the time to live life in the slow lane, we quickly experience a deeper, more profound experience of contentment.

In other words:

To be fully present with what is is to be content,
and to be content is to be blessed by everything that happens in life.

A final thought on the happiness/success connection

"Now and then, it's good to pause in our pursuit of happiness
and just be happy."
—Guillaume Apollinaire

As we have already discovered, many of the things people go for in their pursuit of success are really being chased in pursuit of happiness—a kind of happiness that is already within your reach once you know how to grab hold of it.

And as you explore the happiness/success connection more closely, you can find subtler and subtler ways in which you have been limiting yourself, and in so doing, free yourself up to feel happy with your life as it is even as you go for and have what you want.

Try this premise on in your own life and see how it fits:

When you're unhappy, you want to be happy.
When you're happy, you want what you want.

The more you live *from* happiness instead of *for* happiness, the sooner you realize that changing the world is the worst possible way to change how you feel.

So let me ask you one final question:

**If you already had all the happiness and love in the world
right now, what would you still want?**

We'll be exploring your answers to this question in the very next chapter. . . .

CHAPTER TWO

THE POWER OF "WOW!"

A Room in Heaven

One day a human went to heaven in the way that humans often do. Upon arrival, the human was greeted by a host of angels and given a tour of all of heaven's wonders. Over the course of the tour, the human noticed that there was one room the angels quickly glided past each time they approached.

"What's in that room?" the human asked.

The angels looked at each other as if they'd been dreading the question. Finally, one of them stepped forward and said kindly, "We're not allowed to keep you out, but please believe us—you don't want to go in there."

The human's mind raced at the thought of what might be contained in that room. What could be so horrible that all the angels of heaven would want to hide it away? The human knew that one should probably take angels at their word, but found it very hard to resist temptation. "After all," the human thought, "I'm only human."

Slowly walking toward the room, the human was filled with dread and wonder at what horrors might be about to be revealed. But in fact, the room was filled with the most wonderful things imaginable: a beautiful home; nice things; great wisdom; a happy family; loving friends and riches beyond measure.

Eyes wide, the human turned back to the angels. "But why didn't you want me to come in here? This room is filled with the most amazing things I've ever seen!"

The angels looked at each other sadly, then back at the human.

"These are all the things you were meant to have while you were on earth, but you never believed you could have them."

Why S.M.A.R.T. Goals aren't always so smart

> *"You want what you want whether or not you think you can have it."*
> — Robert Fritz

The number one reason people don't already have what they want is that they have learned not to let themselves want what they don't think they can have.

In order to avoid disappointment, or "be realistic," or even "to be a good person," they systematically cut off from the natural flow of wanting that lives inside their hearts and resign themselves to either "take what they're given and like it" or to create "realistic" goals that they think they might be able to attain. But there are two main problems with setting "realistic" goals.

The first is that our own views of reality are so skewed by our hopes, fears, and beliefs that by the time we make our goals "realistic," they may no longer bear any resemblance to what we actually want. The second is our tendency to approach "realistic" left-brain goals with a realistic left-brain plan, and life's annoying lack of cooperation in creating results that can be explained with simple left-brain cause-and-effect thinking.

In fact, your goals may actually be in the way of your having what you want. By setting goals based on what you think you can have instead of what you really want, you will often wind up without the inspiration necessary to fuel your journey.

I was working with a client once who was feeling stuck in her pursuit of Hollywood success. When I asked her what she most wanted, she trotted out a list of practical-sounding goals, targets, and action steps for the next year or so.

"No," I responded. "What do you *want*?"

She looked a bit befuddled, then began repeating her list.

"Okay," I continued, "but what do you *really* want?"

She then expanded on her original list, talking about what she thought might happen if she were a little bit more successful than she thought was possible.

At that point, I explained to her what I believe to be the most important thing you will ever learn about setting goals. After about five minutes more of questions and answers, I asked her: "What do you want so much that it brings a big smile to your face just thinking about it? What would make you go 'Wow'?"

She went quiet for a few moments, then began smiling from ear to ear.

"Oh," she admitted. "I want to win an Oscar."

From that moment on, our conversation changed from a "sensible" discussion of what would be S.M.A.R.T. (specific, measurable, action-oriented, realistic, and time-specific) to a passionate, inspired exploration of what would be wonderful.

From theory to practice . . .

What You "Should" Want

1. What do you want? Make a wish list of the first dozen or so things that come to your mind. If you can't get to a dozen, try harder!

2. Now, imagine you are going to show this list to a cantankerous old father figure who has the power to either grant your wish or punish you for wishing it if he disapproves. What would you leave on the list? What would you take off before he sees it?

3. What "should" you want? In other words, what would the people around you approve of you for wanting?

4. What are some "logical next step" wants in your life? *Examples:*
   - *I'm a middle manager, so I want to be a senior manager.*
   - *I have two kids, so I want a third.*
   - *I earned $50,000 this year, so next year I want to earn $60,000.*

5. What did your parents want for you? What do your friends want for you? Do you want any of these things for yourself as well?

A Millionaire's Guide to Goal Setting

"The great danger for most of us is not that our aim is too high and we miss it, but that it is too low and we reach it."
— Michelangelo

One of the perks of my job as a genius catalyst and coach is that I get to work with a lot of people who've scaled the heights of what most people think of as success. This not only means I get taken out to some very nice restaurants, it also gives me the chance to learn about what people used to having what they want *really* do to get it.

For example, I once asked one of my most financially successful clients, a multimillionaire "super salesman," whether or not he set goals. He told me that he did, and in fact always had, but not in the way that most people do.

Traditional goal setting encourages us to think big and reach for the stars, but also to keep our target constant while we do whatever it takes to achieve it. My client didn't do any of that. He would sit down once or twice a year over a good meal and a nice glass of wine and ask himself, "What would be fun and exciting to make my life about over the next year?"

He would then take as long as he wanted to write down his ideas until he had a list that totally inspired him. As the year unfolded, he would check in with his "goals" every now and then and adjust them up or down depending on how things were going in his life.

When he saw how horrified I looked (didn't anyone ever tell him you're not allowed to change your goals once you've written them down?), he told me something I have never forgotten:

*"The only real purpose of a goal is to inspire you
to fall more deeply in love your life."*

The dream confessor

I was once on a weeklong winter retreat with a group of people who had come together to learn more about ourselves and what we really wanted in our lives.

On the night before the first day, we all met up in a cabin on the mountain property for hot chocolate and a chat about why we were there. Everyone shared their dreams, and each story seemed more exciting than the last.

But one of the participants (I'll call him "Alex") snorted at each story and rolled his eyes at each dream. He was an outwardly successful businessman in his mid-50s, and he spoke of himself with an odd mixture of arrogance and contempt.

"I'm here because of my wife," he muttered. "I sent her up here to sort herself out . . . and somehow she did. When she came back, she was like a different woman." He glared at everyone, especially me. "But I don't have any problems!" he roared.

Every time Alex spoke from that moment forward, he revealed something else about himself that I didn't like, from the way he screwed people over to make his millions to the disdain he had not only for my dream, but for anyone who dreamed of a better future.

During an exercise where we were supposed to tell each other the truth about what we thought and felt about each other, I made the interesting choice to do exactly that.

"I think you're a real jerk," I told him. "I hate the way you talk about your wife, I hate the way you take pride in your violent tactics, and I'm grateful that you live so far away and have never had the opportunity to get anywhere near me or my family."

When it was his turn to talk about me, he didn't say anything—just glared his now-familiar glare and moved on to the next participant.

On the third evening of the retreat, I had wandered off to phone my wife from one of the few pay phones on the property, conveniently located down a narrow passageway between two empty cabins. When I hung up the phone, I turned to find the exit to the passage blocked by Alex.

"I want to talk with you," he said in a voice straight out of a 1940s film *noir*. "Let's go for a ride."

The theory of relativity explained

Einstein once explained relativity using this analogy:

"When a man sits with a pretty girl for an hour, it seems like a minute. But let him sit on a hot stove for a minute and it's longer than any hour. That's relativity."

Well, during the few seconds it took for me to decide whether to follow him into his car or attempt to push him over and run like hell, I somehow had time to consider all of the following:

1. My family was safely back in England and there was no way I could think of that Alex could hurt them.

2. However much I had managed to annoy him, it struck me as unlikely that he wanted to kill me.

3. He might actually just want to talk—and if he did, that would be a conversation I did not want to miss.

The most plausible scenario to me was that Alex had paid some locals to beat me up, a favorite tactic he had shared in an earlier session. I figured if he really wanted to have me beaten up, he could probably find a way to do so whether I followed him or not.

After a 30-minute car journey in the direction away from the nearest town, we finally pulled into the parking lot of a fairly deserted looking roadside bar, affirming both my fear that I was about to get hit repeatedly in the stomach by large men named Moose and Judd and my hope that I might have the opportunity to numb the pain with alcohol before, during, or after the event.

I followed him as he strode purposefully across the empty room and we took two seats at the end of the bar. As we knocked back our first beer, Alex turned to me and said, "I brought you here so I could tell you why I hate you. Normally, I wouldn't bother with someone like you. But I guess I came on this retreat to learn a little bit more about myself, so I'm going to give this a try."

He continued, "This morning I looked at myself in the mirror and said, 'Alex, you haven't known this guy long enough to hate him this much. What's going on?' And then I realized why I hated you. You're going for your dreams. And I gave up on mine."

For the next hour, he told me the story of how he had come from a wealthy, powerful New England family who didn't understand his youthful obsession with writing and in particular, the life and work of James Joyce. When he was 17, he ran away to Europe to write stories, meet women, and walk in the footsteps of his idol. Two years later, his parents sent a private detective to bring him back, told him to grow up and get a job, and put him to work in the family business.

He got married, had children and prospered—in short, did exactly what was expected of him. And until his wife sent him on that retreat, he had managed to hide from his big dream.

Finally, when he finished his story, he looked me in the eye and said, "Now why do you hate me so much?"

The answer came to me almost immediately and in the spirit of confession, I shared it openly. "Because you're what I'm afraid I'll have to become in order to live my dream."

Alex and I got along just fine after that. We stayed in touch for a few years, exchanged Christmas cards, that sort of thing. Last time we spoke, his dream had changed, as dreams often do once we see them in the cool light of day. He was still making time to write every day (a practice he began after that night in the bar), and he was now in the process of tracking down every person he screwed over on his way up in order to make amends. His marriage was going well, and to his own amazement, he was finally and genuinely happy.

From theory to practice . . .

What Do You Really Want?

1. What's the biggest "Wow!" you can imagine? Not the "logical next step" if you follow the path you're currently on, but the thing that would really make your heart sing? Here are a few "dream starters" to help you if you're feeling stuck:

   Imagine you got to retire to a tropical island with unlimited wealth and the sex symbol of your choice. Now imagine you've been doing that for five years and you're bored out of your mind.

   – What do you want to do next?
   – What did you want to do before you "grew up" and "got real"?
   – What would you do if no one else would ever find out?
   – What would you do if it was really entirely up to you?
   – What would you do if nobody minded?
   – What would be even better than that?

2. What would "Wow!" look like in the different areas of your life?

   – work/career_____

   – finances _____

   – family _____

   – friends _____

   – contribution _____

   – spirituality _____

The golden rule of goal-getting

Have a look at each of the goals and dreams you are now aware of. On a scale from 1 to 100 (where 100 is the biggest "Wow!" you can imagine), where is each goal now?

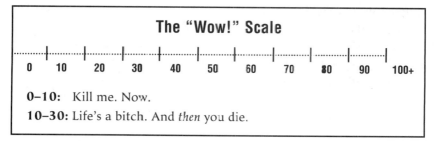

The "Wow!" Scale

| 0 | 10 | 20 | 30 | 40 | 50 | 60 | 70 | 80 | 90 | 100+ |

0–10: Kill me. Now.
10–30: Life's a bitch. And *then* you die.

30–50: What can I do? I have a family to feed.

50–70: If I can just do this a few more years, then I'll have enough money/status/power to do what I *really* want!

70–80: Why not?

80–90: This could be fun. I could really see myself enjoying/doing well at this.

90–99: Absolutely as good as I can imagine it.

100+: WOW!!!

I did this exercise with a friend once who scored each of his goals at 95. When I asked him what that was all about, he said, "Well, I want to leave room for something better to come along." This sounded great, but completely untrue. Something either makes you go "Wow!" or it doesn't. And just because you have one "Wow!" doesn't mean you can't have a dozen more.

What my friend was suffering from was a case of what I call "premature practicality." While part of us is genuinely excited at the idea of focusing in on what we would really love to be, do, and have in our lives, the rest of us is busy trying to figure out how on earth we're going to get it. We calculate the odds, decide that it is unlikely at best, and put it out of our minds as best we can.

"After all," we say to ourselves, "I can't have what I *really* want. But this will be okay."

And of course, it is okay. Your happiness does not depend on getting what you want. But that doesn't mean you don't want it, and it certainly doesn't mean you can't have it. In fact, I call this the golden rule of goal-getting:

It's easier to have what you *really* want than what you think you can get.

One of my favorite examples of this happened when a client of mine was visiting Los Angeles from London. Rebecca is beautiful, intelligent, and strong, but she had spent most of her life pretending that she wasn't so she wouldn't upset anyone.

During a session where I shared the golden rule with her, she actually laughed in my face. "If that were true," she said, "I'd be going out with a sexy movie star this evening instead of back to my hotel room alone."

Although she was joking, I could feel the energy in the room lighten up as she confessed to an authentic if unlikely desire. Here's what happened . . .

When she got back to her hotel, she decided to lay out by the pool. Suddenly, she overheard two people talking excitedly on some nearby sun loungers. "Isn't that . . . oh my God, I think it is!"

She looked up and sure enough, a sexy movie star (in her humble opinion) was walking toward the pool, looking for somewhere to sit. And there just happened to be an available lounger right next to her. While I have no idea what happened next, she phoned me the next day sounding as though she was awakening from a wonderful dream.

"It really happened," she said excitedly. "Just imagine what it would be like if I let myself do this with the rest of my life!"

Which is exactly what I encouraged her to do.

The second half of your goals

Something that is often overlooked when people work on setting goals is the context in which they are setting them. For example, I got an e-mail from someone who had been listening to my radio show and who was very concerned as to whether or not he was wording his key financial goal "correctly." He had read and been taught conflicting things in books and seminars about how to word goals for maximum effectiveness, and asked me to assist him in choosing the best way to think about them.

Here was his short list, phrased in some of the many ways he had learned in the various goal-setting systems he had studied:
• I want to be a millionaire.
• I want to attain a net worth of a million dollars.
• I am a happy, healthy millionaire.
• God wants me to be rich—a million dollars is mine by divine right.
• I live in a beautiful home surrounded by wonderful things that I easily afford with my million-dollar-plus net worth.

What I pointed out to him is that in my experience, how we phrase the first half of our goal statements is nowhere near as important as the content of the second half—the usually unwritten, unspoken, and underlying conditions, consequences, or conjectures that motivate us even more strongly than our desire for the achievement of the goal.

Let's take a look at some of the different "second half of the goals" he might have been tacking on to his seemingly simple and clear desire for more wealth.

1. Conditions

Sometimes we want what we want, but only under certain conditions.

For example:

- I want to be a millionaire (as long as I don't have to work more than 8–10 hours a day).
- I want to be a millionaire (providing I don't have to do anything too scary).
- I want to be a millionaire (by doing exactly what I want to do when I want to do it).
- I want to be a millionaire (as long as I don't have to do anything illegal).

Note that while some of these conditions are more socially acceptable than others, they all limit what we will or won't do to be, do, or have what we want.

2. Consequences

Occasionally, the second half of our goals are to do with what we think the consequences (positive or negative) of attaining the goal will be:

- I want to be a millionaire (so that I can make a real contribution to the planet).
- I want to be a millionaire (and then I'll be happy).
- I want to be a millionaire (so I'll never have to worry about money again).
- I want to be a millionaire (and that will prove my parents/teachers/friends wrong once and for all).

In these examples, the second half of our goals reveals what we *really* want: the goal behind the goal. When we discover what we really want, we often find that there are easier and more effective ways of getting there than the pathway we originally planned on taking.

3. Conjectures

The third category of limitation we put on our own goals is the conjectures and assumptions we make about *how* or even *whether* what we want will come to pass:

- I want to be a millionaire (but it's never going to happen).
- I want to be a millionaire (and that means I'm going to have to work 18 hours a day at something I don't really enjoy).
- I want to be a millionaire (but I don't want to miss my kids growing up).
- I want to be a millionaire (but I want everyone to like me for myself).

The good news is that the minute you become consciously aware of what the second half of your goal sentence is, you have the opportunity to change both halves of the goal to more accurately reflect what it is you truly want.

In the end, the man worked through the first and second halves of his goal until he arrived at the following statement, which he recently e-mailed to tell me he has happily and easily kept at the forefront of his mind every day since:

> *I have an abundance of love and money to share
> with my family, my friends, and the wider world.*

From theory to practice . . .

The Second Half of "Wow!"

1. Make a list of your top five "Wow!"s for the year (or whatever time-frame feels appropriate).

2. For each of the five items on your list, write in the hidden "second half of the goal." Make a note of whether it is a condition you are placing on how you are going to achieve the goal, a consequence you are hoping the goal will bring you or a conjecture about what it will mean to go for and get what you want.

3. If you don't like what you discover, change it! Experiment with three or four different "second halves" until you find one that looks, sounds, and feels wonderful to you. Here are some of my favorite things you can change it to:

   . . . *as a part of my wonderful life.*
   . . . *and enjoy the process.*
   . . . *for myself and others.*
   . . . *for the highest good of all concerned.*
   . . . *as a natural consequence of living my highest values.*

> 4. Finally, rework both halves of your goal until just reading it brings a smile to your face and a warm, fuzzy feeling to your body.

But what if I just can't make it happen?

"All dreams appear impossible until someone makes them happen."
— Barry Neil Kaufman

The fact is, many of the "Wow!" goals you set for yourself will appear impossible to you when you first set them. Fortunately, it's not your job to make them happen. The problem is that in a culture that encourages us to become self-sufficient, celebrate our independence, and even "empower ourselves," the very idea of admitting that we can't handle something on our own often feels worse than the prospect of failure.

It's a bit like the old story of the mountaineer who was trapped in a snowstorm at the edge of a cliff on a high mountain. Knowing that he only had a few more minutes to live, he gathered all of his remaining strength and called out into the storm, "Is there anybody there?" Immediately, he heard an angelic voice whisper in his ear, "I am here. Step off the edge of the cliff and I will carry you safely through the storm." The mountaineer thought for a moment, then called out, "Is there anybody else there?"

Yet for all that, you can probably think of at least one experience in your own life where you hit absolute bottom and asked for help from a higher power (even if you didn't believe in one). Somehow, miraculously, help came. The trick to setting goals that make you go "Wow!" is that you don't wait until you hit bottom. You deliberately dive in over your head, knowing that allowing yourself to be out of your depth is a master key to accessing the higher power that awaits your call in any moment.

Alcoholics Anonymous (AA) and the related 12-step programs have assisted hundreds of thousands of people in achieving the "Wow!" goal of living lives free from the effects of debilitating addictions. In AA, the first three of the 12 steps are as follows:

1. We admitted we were powerless over alcohol—that our lives had become unmanageable.

2. Came to believe that a power greater than ourselves could restore us to sanity.

3. Made a decision to turn our will and our lives over to the care of God as we understood what God is.

If we translate that into layman's language, you can read it as a formula for setting and achieving any of your "Wow!" goals:

1. Admit that you've bitten off more than you can chew; that you've set goals for your life or business or career that are beyond your personal capacity as you currently experience it.

2. Open up to the idea that a power greater than yourself could enable the goal to be achieved anyway.

3. Make the decision to turn the goal over to the care of that higher power.

There are essentially two ways to do that:

1. Intend and release.

2. Invite and allow.

When we "intend and release," we hold the intention of what it is we want to do, be, or have and release the doing of it to a higher power, whether we believe that power to be God or the highest and best we have within ourselves.

To "invite and allow," simply imagine you are sending out invitations for whatever it is you most want to come join the party of your life. Of course, when it shows up, you will need to allow it in the door.

We'll explore more about the mechanism behind releasing, allowing, and letting go in the next chapter. For now, let's finish off this discussion of goals with one final experiment. . . .

From theory to practice . . .

Intend, Invite, Release, and Allow

1. Review your list of "Wow!" goals. If you haven't made a list yet, just choose one or two things you know you want to play with for the purposes of this experiment.

2. For each item on your list, decide whether to intend or invite it into your life.

   I intend . . .

   I invite . . .

3. Create a mini-ritual for yourself around releasing and allowing. *Examples:*
   - *Write down everything that you want on a piece of paper, stick it inside a helium balloon, and release it up into the heavens.*
   - *Print out invitations and send one to each of your goals.*
   - *Stick your goals in a time capsule to be opened in a year's time. Alternatively, stick them in a book or drawer where you know you're unlikely to find them again until long after you've consciously forgotten about them.*

4. Be on the lookout for any "inspired actions" that occur to you to take in support of your goal. You'll know which actions are inspired rather than from your limited mind because (a) they'll seem a little bit strange; and (b) they'll feel right anyway, like something you wouldn't normally think to do but which kind of makes sense when you think about it now.

CHAPTER THREE

THE SECRET OF LETTING GO FOR IT

Take it easy for a change

"Angels fly because they take themselves lightly."
— G. K. Chesterton

HAVE YOU EVER WATCHED people suffer at the gym?

I remember one particular man whose workout routine always reminded me of a medieval priest self-flagellating in punishment for his sins. Driving himself into his 16th set of 85 repetitions at a weight three times his own, he seemed to take a perverse pleasure in torturing his body on a daily basis. Every time I saw him, he was wearing a new knee brace or elbow brace or neck brace. At one point he showed up with his leg in a cast to work his upper body!

The myth of "no pain, no gain" is pervasive in our society. Whether it manifests in your life at the gym, the office, or in your relationships, most of us find ways of punishing ourselves with the best of all possible intentions: to help us grow and to motivate ourselves to become "better" people. The only problem is it doesn't work. Oh, it might work for an hour, a day, or even a month, but over time the pain fades and we find ourselves right back in the old pattern of behavior. Or worse still, we punish ourselves, feel bad, and then eat cake and take drugs and do things we'll regret later in order to make the bad feelings we've just created go away.

Allow me to share my personal philosophy on the subject. I can sum it up in a simple phrase:

No pain, no pain.

It's not that I believe pain must be avoided at all costs or that we should give up on something we know we want to do as soon as it gets difficult. It's just that I've become aware that when we are pursuing our goals and living our dreams, some of what we do is painful and some of it isn't. You don't get any extra points for suffering, unless you make up the rules of the game that way.

Hootlessness

"You can have anything you want, providing you first let go of wanting it."
— Lester Levenson

Many years ago when I was an out-of-work American actor living in London, I got a call from my agent asking if I wanted to go on an audition in Wales. Being relatively uninformed as to the geography of the UK, I asked him where it was. He replied, "Go west to the edge of England and just keep going." Well, this sounded terribly exotic to me, so I grabbed my passport, picked up a train ticket, and set off on my adventure.

Eventually, I arrived at my destination: a small, prefabricated office building in the middle of nowhere that housed an architecture firm. In the back, beside a picture of Daniel J. Travanti from *Hill Street Blues* dressed somewhat incongruously as a cowboy from the old West, was the office of a production company that was creating a pilot for a radio series about, of all things, a New Age American's travels in the Welsh valleys.

Now, one thing that nearly every auditioning actor comes to realize is that you most often get the jobs you care about the least. Lester Levenson, creator of The Sedona Method, called this phenomenon "hootlessness"—that inner state of Zen-like detachment when you genuinely don't give a hoot whether you achieve a particular goal or not and therefore often do.

I was so caught up in the adventure of the day (and convinced that a sitcom launched from the backroom of an architect's office in the Rhondda Valley would never come off) that I was completely relaxed and consequently was at my best in the audition room. Ultimately, I found out they chose me for the role less because of my (obviously) stunning acting ability than because in my state of complete ease I poked my head into the casting "office" and asked if anyone wanted a cup of tea, a genuine question that they found so incongruous they decided it was exactly the sort of thing the character would do and hired me on the spot.

(The rumor was that the BBC only wanted two changes for the transfer to television: they wanted to replace my girlfriend on the show with a young up-and-coming Welsh actress named Catherine Zeta-Jones, and they wanted to replace me with a hot-but-not-yet-*Matrix*-sized American actor named Keanu Reeves. Fortunately, both Catherine and Keanu got the crazy idea they would do better to pursue their fortunes in Hollywood, and the rest is history.)

Hootlessness is freedom, but it is not the same as apathy. In fact, one of the most misunderstood tenets in both Zen Buddhism and New Age religion is that we need to cut off from all of our feelings in order to be free.

An acting-coach friend of mine once explained to me the following disappointingly accurate way he spotted people who were on a "spiritual path":

"There are some people who come in to audition for me who are essentially dead from the neck down—that is, they are stuck in their heads and utterly unresponsive to life. I always ask them if they are on a spiritual path and invariably they say 'yes,' proudly assuming I can tell from their 'peaceful demeanor' and 'spiritual vibe.' In fact, it is their complete lack of energy, presence, and aliveness that gives them away."

Of course, this lack of aliveness has nothing to do with authentic spirituality. Doc Lew Childre, founder of The Heartmath Institute, describes this distinction as being between apathy, care, and "overcare."

- Apathy is that inner deadness that usually comes about as a reaction to the pain we think we will feel if we set a goal and fail to achieve it.

- Care is genuine, ungilded affection for a person, place, or outcome.

- Overcare is what happens when that affection is distorted by our attempts to control the person, place, or outcome and "make things happen."

Imagine that what you want is like a beautiful butterfly in your hands. If you squeeze too tightly, the butterfly will be crushed; if you hold your hands too loosely, the butterfly will simply fly away. The secret is to hold it gently. The same is true in almost any area of our lives:

- If you focus too intensely on money, you will squeeze any sense of prosperity or abundance out of it; too loosely, and what little of it you have will slip through your fingers.

- If you hold on to your partner too tightly, he or she will feel stifled and the joy will be crushed from the relationship; too loosely, and there will be no relationship to crush.

- If you obsess about your business or your work, you may succeed, but at the cost of your health, relationships, and well-being; if you leave it to take care of itself, chances are someone else will wind up taking it away from you.

A gentle, consistent focus in any area of your life will lead to gentle, consistent results. By releasing your attachment to making things happen without cutting off from your authentic desire for them to happen, you release the best in yourself—and in so doing, make the space in which what you want can come into your life more easily.

In order to create a bit of breathing room between your intention and your longing and find the "butterfly point" between apathy and obsession, do the following experiment:

From theory to practice . . .

Finding the "Butterfly Point"

1. Make a list of three to five things that you "really, really, really, REALLY" want to have happen in your life.

2. Write down one of these goals or fantasies at the top of a sheet of paper, then divide the paper into two columns. Head the left-hand column "Why this would be amazing" and the right-hand column "Why this might suck."

3. Write down at least five things in each column. If you're having trouble coming up with reasons why having your heart's desire might suck, ask a more cynical friend to help you out!

4. Continue balancing pros and cons until you find the "butterfly point": a state of balanced care without overcare, desire without attachment, and intention without tension.

The hard way to succeed

One of the problems with teaching concepts like "hootlessness" and "happy success" is that it is in fact possible to get what you want on the outside without experiencing any pleasure whatsoever on the inside. Here's the magic formula:

Tension (Stress) + Continual action = Success

If you think about such type-A overachievers as Donald Trump, Attila the Hun, and any sports coach who has ever burst a blood vessel, they are all believers in the bigger, better, faster philosophy of life, success, and achievement. Consequently, they are always on the lookout for more efficient and effective ways of driving themselves and their charges ever onward and upward into an endless sky of personal achievement, glory, and success.

While stressful action can unquestionably be effective in the short term, it is ultimately self-defeating, as it destroys the goose (that's you!) in pursuit of the instant gratification of more and more golden eggs. It brings about outer success (nice stuff) at the cost of inner success (the quality of your experience).

Imagine a kettle filled with water. As we increase the heat under the kettle (take more action, push ourselves a little harder), the water begins to heat up. But if we take too much action and push ourselves too hard, the kettle itself begins to melt and the water inside evaporates into thin air.

The reason so many people continually return to attempting to succeed the hard way is they think their only other choice is what I call the simple way to failure:

Tension (Stress) + Continual inaction = Failure

When we tie ourselves up in knots without taking any action toward what we want, we generally experience frustration, hopelessness, and even self-loathing.

In traditional learning theory, this corresponds to the stage of Conscious Incompetence. We've suddenly become aware of how ineffectual we are at whatever it is we are trying to learn how to do and consequently generate unresourceful feelings that make us even more ineffectual.

This is the stage where it is most common for people to give up on a project, goal, or dream, as it feels virtually impossible to make anything happen. It is also the stage where the inner voice of the "should" goes into overdrive, attacking us with seemingly well-meaning advice like "You should just do it." "This should be easier," or "I should be better at it."

Fortunately, when you're ready to stop "shoulding" all over yourself, there is an easy way out. . . .

The easy way to success

Easy (adjective/adverb)

First appeared (in print in English) in the 14th century:

1. marked by peace and comfort
2. not hurried or strenuous

---

3. free from pain, annoyance, or anxiety
4. without undue speed or excitement
5. in or with moderation
6. without worry or care
7. without a severe penalty
8. without violent movement
   or my personal favorite:
9. to proceed calmly and in a relaxed manner.

The Easy Way to Success is not always without difficulty, but it is without any undue effort or stress. It is not without work, but it is by definition without hard work because it teaches us to approach that work with a sense of joy and inner ease. And while it may not always be without pain, it is invariably without suffering. (As the saying goes, "Suffering is optional, but you have to provide it for yourself.")

Here's my four-part formula for taking the Easy Way to Success:

Ease + Focus + Action + Inaction = Success

1. Ease

I remember when I was first learning to drive, as long as nobody attempted to communicate with me, there was no ambient noise and I didn't need to breathe, I would do fine. While I did get where I wanted to go, I generally arrived exhausted.

When I started playing comedy tapes in my car (Steve Martin, Monty Python, and Bob Newhart), I relaxed enough to begin enjoying the process. Not only did I still get where I wanted to go, I arrived refreshed and ready to play.

You can increase your sense of ease as you go for what you want by physically relaxing your body, breathing deeply, being present with whatever it is that you're doing, and finding a way to enjoy it even more than you already are.

From theory to practice . . .

Cultivating Ease in Action

1. Crumple up as many pieces of paper as your environmental conscience will allow. Get a wastebasket or similar receptacle and place it about five feet away from you.

2. Get your body into a relaxed state. A simple way of doing this is to hold your breath and tense all your muscles for a moment, then let it all go on an exhale, shaking your body out as you breathe. Put a gentle smile on your face as you do it.
3. When you are feeling relaxed, begin throwing the crumpled-up paper balls into the basket. The key here is that regardless of where the balls wind up, you stay relaxed and easy in your body. A nice way to test is to imagine someone watching you. If you've "got it," they would probably assume from watching you that you meant to throw it over there!
4. Keep practicing your toss until you can do ten in a row with your body relaxed and easy. If you accidentally start putting the balls in the basket, that's okay, too—but if you can stay relaxed and open as you miss ten out of ten, you're in the advanced class.

2. Focus

The power of focus works on a simple principle: the more you focus on something, the more of it you get. Physiological, psychological, and metaphysical theory abound as to why things work this way (the reticular activating system, psychological vestment, and the law of attraction being three of my favorite explanations), but for our purposes let it suffice to say that it's pretty darn important to focus on what you want.

How do you know if you're focusing on what you really want? It feels good

If thinking about what you want is causing you to feel bad, it probably means you're actually focused on how far away it is, or the problems you're having along the way, or on why you'll never get there. Focusing on what you *really* want feels good. That's one of the ways you know you really want it.

3. Action

I sometimes like to do a little reality check when it comes to my goals by asking myself:

"If affirmation, visualization, and all that other mind stuff was all a load of crap and the only way to get stuff was to do stuff, am I putting in the hours and doing enough of the right things to get where I want to go?"

Note that I'm not saying that those things aren't extremely valuable, just that by themselves they're rarely enough to take us all the way to our goals.

What's an "easy action"? Any action that you find intrinsically rewarding—i.e., which isn't dependent on your achieving a specific result for it to seem worthwhile. While the specifics will vary from person to person, here's an example of the two different types of actions I might choose to take if I were pursuing the goal of losing weight.

Success-only actions (only worth it to me if I reach my goal)
Giving up my favorite foods, not going out for dinner anymore, saying no to sweets, taking aerobics classes (a personal dislike).

Intrinsically satisfying actions (worth it to me whether they "work" or not)
Drinking more water, going for long walks in nature, stretching, creating my own training program based on swimming and water-based weight-training (a personal delight).

As always, be sure to personalize your action plan until you find those actions that are intrinsically satisfying to YOU!

4. Inaction

*"It is necessary to be slightly underemployed
if you are to do something significant."*
— James Watson, Nobel Prize-winning scientist

Inaction is important in the attainment of success for at least two reasons:

a. Quality recovery time
Sports-training specialists universally agree that the harder you train, the more important it is to take deliberate breaks to allow your body, mind, and spirit to recharge. The more frequently you build quality recovery time into your schedule, the less dramatic these breaks need to be. If you're someone who feels like you need a month off just to catch your breath, start building mini-breaks (I recommend three minutes an hour to begin with) into your day and notice how quickly you reconnect with your natural enthusiasm.

b. Allowing the universe to catch up
What's the difference between a good salesman and a great one? A good salesman sells and sells until he makes a sale; a great salesman sells only up to a certain point and then allows the client to sell themselves the rest of the way.

Similarly, if you push and push and push to reach your goals, you may be trampling all over the seeds before they have a chance to flower. As one of my coaches once asked me, "What might God be able to do if you took the day off?"

The 110% Solution

There once was a seeker who was eager to reach his goal of enlightenment as soon as possible. He traveled long and far to find a Zen master who had a reputation for quickly guiding people to their highest potential.

After three agonizing days of waiting, the seeker was finally granted an audience with the Zen master. He explained the intensity of his desire and asked how long it would take for him to succeed. The master looked deeply into the seeker's heart and said, "Twenty years." The seeker was horrified.

"What if I really apply myself? I will willingly work twice as long and hard as any other student in your monastery!"

The Zen master looked bemused. "Ah, I did not realize the ferocity of your commitment. Then it will take you at least 30 years to succeed."

Now the seeker was confused.

"Perhaps you did not understand, oh Great One," the seeker continued, "I am willing to push myself to the limits, go the extra mile and give 110% in order to achieve my goal—I am desperate for enlightenment!"

"In that case," replied the Zen master. "it will take you no less than 40 years to get what it is you are seeking."

I remember getting a call from an investment banker in Singapore who was desperate to be coached by me. When he gave me the history of everything he had been doing to try and "make things happen" in his career and why I was his "last chance," I noticed my body tensing up in sympathetic resonance with the pressure he'd been putting on himself to succeed.

Before agreeing to take him on as a client, I gave him the following task: For the next two weeks, give up completely on attempting to reach your goals. Take them off the calendar and remove them from your to-do list.

If he took even one action to make things happen, I said, I would refuse to take him on as a client.

He thought I was nuts, but I knew that at least one of three things would invariably happen:

1. He would recharge his batteries and return to his goals and projects refreshed, energized, and ready to make a fresh start.

2. Everything he'd been working so hard for would suddenly happen "all by itself." I've lost track of the number of times I've watched someone's career take off in the first month after they "quit," or seen them meet the perfect partner within days of giving up the search.

3. He would realize that the only thing that was keeping him moving forward was momentum and he'd give up for real. This often happens when the goal is either something you never really wanted (but thought you "should" have) or when you've outgrown the goal, but just didn't notice in the whirlwind of your own activity.

He fought like hell for the right to keep working himself into an early grave, but finally agreed to his enforced holiday. Here's what happened . . .

When I spoke to him again two weeks later, he sheepishly admitted that he had intended to keep on attacking his goals and just tell me that he'd taken a break so that I would agree to work with him.

A sudden illness had laid him out for a few days so he decided to take advantage of that and give "not doing anything" a try. To his amazement, several deals he had been pursuing for months came through while he was flat on his back in bed. But by the time his body was ready to get back to work, he had realized that despite the financial rewards, his heart just wasn't in it anymore.

I worked with him over the next six months to transition out of investment banking and into the art world (a secret "Wow!" for him), and he now runs a successful import business making more money and having more fun than ever before.

The easy way in action

Okay, so now that you know what it is, how do you actually do things the Easy Way? Why, in three easy steps, of course . . .

1. Tune in (to how you're feeling right now)

I heard a story once about Morihei Ueshiba, the founder of the martial-art discipline of aikido. When praised by one of his disciples on how he lived permanently in balance, Ueshiba thought for a moment. "I do not actually live in balance," he said. "In fact, I am virtually always off balance. But I know what balance feels like, and I am continually in the process of returning to center."

Take a moment now to tune in to your body. Which parts of your body feel tense, and which parts of your body feel especially relaxed?

Tune in to your mind. What are the voices in your head talking about today?

What movies are playing in the cinema of your mind?

Finally, tune in to your heart, your connection with love and joy and spirit. What higher guidance is waiting for you as you focus your attention on peace, love and understanding?

2. Relax (and enjoy finding your natural energy)

One of my mentors, Gay Hendricks, taught me two wonderful questions I use throughout the day to keep myself moving toward deeper levels of relaxation even in the midst of action:

• Could I let this be easier?
• Could I let this be lighter?

Whatever it is you do, chances are you'll do it better when you relax your muscles and do it with ease and lightness. At first, relaxation can seem to drain your energy (ever fall asleep during a massage, yoga class, or even sex?).

However, as tension-based energy sources (sugar, caffeine, and adrenaline) drain out of your system, the subtler natural energy of your body will begin to flow and you will find yourself waking up refreshed and filled with energy.

3. Do less (but do something)

You probably already have a pretty good idea of whether you're pushing too hard or not hard enough, and it's a balance that can change many times within the life of a project, goal, or dream.

If you suspect that you do need to do something, get started with something fun; that is, intrinsically satisfying, whether or not it immediately achieves your desired end result.

If you're already racking your brain to figure out what else you could be doing to push yourself over the edge of success, take some time off from your goals and allow the universe to catch up with you before you succeed in pushing yourself over the edge!

Why is it so hard to let it be easy?

As a kid, one of my favorite musicals was the Pulitzer Prize winner *How to Succeed in Business Without Really Trying*. The show traces the fortunes of a young window cleaner who acquires a book on how to become president of a major corporation and marry the girl of his dreams armed with nothing but self-belief, quick wits, and "the grin of impetuous youth."

I thought the best thing in the world that could happen to me would be to find a real-life copy of that book. But when I first began playing with these ideas and started *actually* succeeding without any sense of really trying, I found that I was left without feeling any sense of accomplishment whatsoever.

Like a lottery winner who loses it all within a few years, when our success comes too easily we tend to hold it too lightly, buying in to the cultural beliefs that belittle the unearned victory. "Easy come, easy go," we tell ourselves, and then set about either hanging on to what we've got for dear life or getting rid of it as quickly as we can.

In fact, not feeling worthy of our own success in life has now got its own name—"Paradise Syndrome"—which describes both the stress that comes from waiting for tragedy to strike (after all, people aren't supposed to have it this good, are they?) and the strain that comes from wondering when people will finally realize that you're a total fraud who doesn't belong where you are and doesn't deserve what you've got.

There are three main ways we discount, disown and hide from our success . . .

1. "But I didn't do anything!"

I remember being congratulated by someone on the occasion of my sister's wedding. "What are you congratulating *me* for?" I asked with my best teenage snarl. "I didn't have anything to do with it." Unfortunately, that's how many of us feel about whatever success we may have experienced in our lives. "What are you congratulating *us* for?" we say to ourselves. "We didn't have anything to do with it."

2. "But I don't know how I did it!"

There is a famous story about Sir Laurence Olivier, who was found storming around his dressing room in anger after a particularly brilliant performance of *Othello*. "But Larry," his friends said, "what's wrong? That's the best it's ever been!" "I know," Olivier replied, "but I don't know how I did it!"

In fact, this is a part of the myth of the experts—the idea that because someone has succeeded in their own career, they know how to help others to succeed. In many cases, not only do successful people have no idea what really led to their success, they're afraid to look, fearing that if they become conscious of what has been a largely unconscious process, they'll somehow jinx it.

This reluctance and/or inability to learn from our success can leave us with no idea of how it is we've come to be where we are in our lives.

3. "We're not worthy! We're not worthy!"

A woman I know was at a dinner party when the subject of children came up. When asked if she and her husband planned on having kids, she replied, "Oh no, I wouldn't want to push our luck. We already have a wonderful marriage, a great home, and a terrific life. I'm sure if we had a child, he'd come out hideously deformed!"

While this is a somewhat extreme instance, there are millions of healthy, prosperous people sitting around waiting for the other shoe to drop—for the universe to suddenly notice how good their life is and kick them out of paradise, sending them back down to earth with a bump!

This sense of unworthiness is perhaps the number one obstacle to having what you want. As we take a closer look at this idea in the next chapter, you will begin to recognize not only that you are already worthy of all the good things life has to offer, but also that the only thing between you and the life of your dreams isn't you—it's the idea that you need to change. . . .

CHAPTER FOUR

YOU ARE NOT THE ENEMY

Why you don't suck as a human being (and why you probably think that you do)

"Argue for your limitations and sure enough they're yours."
— Richard Bach

SO MUCH OF PERSONAL DEVELOPMENT, therapy, advertising, and self-help is built on the premise that there's something wrong with you—that if you just changed your thinking, your behavior, your brand of shampoo, or your personality, then everything would be perfect and your life would finally begin to work the way it's supposed to.

And because it never occurs to most people to question that assumption, they spend much of their time learning new ways to fix what was never broken and resolving with each new year to "try harder" to get it right. It is as if we go through life wearing an imaginary "I'm with stupid!" T-shirt—but the arrow is always pointing directly at us.

Once you become aware of this, you have the option of stopping the battle against yourself, your ego, your shadow, or any other name you have for those parts of your personality that you don't like or wish didn't exist.

You also gain the possibility of taking action in the world from a place of comfort and ease and well-being, where your happiness and self-worth are not on the line every time you choose to have a cheeseburger and French fries instead of salad for lunch.

But one of the saddest or most amusing things (depending on my mood) that happens with nearly everybody I speak to about this possibility is the point at which they begin arguing with me about why they really do need to completely change everything about themselves before they can be happy and have what they want:

- "If you really knew me, you wouldn't be saying that!"
- "There really is something terribly wrong with me!"
- "I do try my best, but deep down I really can't be trusted!"
- "If I didn't keep myself on a short lead, I'd wind up doing something stupid and spend the rest of my life in prison—or worse!"

How did we get such a low opinion of ourselves? You have to be carefully taught. . . .

A (very) short course in unconditional parenting

"To love is to be happy with—no conditions,
no judgments, no expectations."
— Barry Neil Kaufman

My wife's family was over to the house one evening when in the midst of a rollicking post-dinner conversation, one of her brothers accused their mother of "attacking" him. Her mother seemed startled and said quite rightly, "I only raised my eyebrow."

After a few moments' thought, I realized that she had spent so many years loading that eyebrow that every time it raised in the direction of her children it was bound to go off.

Did your parents ever shoot you "the look" when you were growing up? You know, the look that let you know it was time to stop or you were going to be in big—no, BIG trouble? Do they still? Do you ever shoot it at your own children (spouse/co-workers/etc.)?

Time-honored though it may be, "the look" stems from a traditional parenting model that uses our childhood need for security, love, and approval as a primary motivational tool. While none of us would ever put it into such crass terms, it generally works something like this:

"Mommy and Daddy love you very much. As long as you do what we want, we will continue to love you as much as we do; if you don't, we will withhold our love (or at least our approval) until you do what we want, at which point we will give all (or at least some) of it back."

This "parenting as behavior modification" model works up to a point, but unfortunately it works both better and worse than it seems. Better in that no matter how much we may rebel while we are growing up, chances are that as adults we are still making choices and behaving in ways that either seek our parents' approval or "prove" to them that we don't need it. (One of my favorite definitions of maturity comes from Gregory Bateson, who defined it as "being willing to do what you really want to do even if your parents want you to do it as well.")

This reinforces the myth that love and approval are commodities to be earned as opposed to essential aspects of our birthright. But what other option do we have?

A friend of mine told me about a meeting he had been to where the person in front of the room held up a brand-new $100 bill and asked how many people would want it. Of course, every hand in the room went up. Then the person at the front of the room proceeded to do everything you could imagine to mess up that $100 bill: spitting on it, making tears in it, and even crumpling it up and rubbing it on the bottom of their shoe until it was covered in dirt.

"How many of you still want it?" the person at the front of the room asked.

Slowly, but surely, every hand in the room went up once again.

"Each one of you is like this $100 bill," the speaker continued. "No matter what it looks like, no matter what it's been through, how beat-up it looks, or how far from perfect it may appear, its value remains undiminished."

This is the true gift we have to offer ourselves and one another —to recognize our inherent value as human beings, regardless of what we have or haven't done up until this point in our lives.

Here's a story about how that might play out in the not-so-real world. . . .

The Educated Rabbit

In her final year of school, a rabbit from the wrong side of the tracks got a new teacher who told her that he loved her no matter what and that he knew she had the power to choose whatever kind of life she wanted for herself. She challenged the teacher again and again, but no matter how "bad" she tried to be, the teacher balanced appropriate discipline with genuine, heartfelt loving kindness.

Whenever she was upset, he challenged her to look at her part in creating and nurturing the upset, and he encouraged her to take care of herself on a daily basis by doing those things that she loved, like napping, running, and reading inspirational literature. (The Velveteen Rabbit was one of her favorites.)

Eventually, the rabbit learned to trust herself more and to worry less about what other people thought she should be doing with her life. But even though she was popular with the other animals (after all, her daily running and jumping had made her the star of the track team), there was a part of her that still knew she was horribly inadequate, and she felt the loving teacher was wasting his time on a worthless ball of fluff like her. No matter how fast she ran, she still cringed inwardly when she saw the birds who flew with such grace and the fish who swam like, well, fish.

Then one day, the unthinkable happened. She stepped on a thistle and hurt her lucky foot; she could no longer run. What little value she felt she had in the world had been taken away by one tiny thorn. The rabbit cried and cried until she was empty, and it was then that she heard a new yet oddly familiar voice inside her mind—still, small, and as clear as a bell. It whispered, "Your value is not in your speed."

From that moment on, the voice stayed with her wherever she went. As she watched the birds fly high above the playing fields, the voice whispered, "Their value is not in their wings." When she saw the fish swimming laps in the pool, the voice said, "Their value is not in their ability to swim." When the rich old badger who helped to support the school came by, the voice said, "His value is not in his wealth."

And the rabbit could see that it was true—the birds' value was not in their flight, her teacher's value was not in his teaching, and her value was not in her speed or in her ability to hop or even in the way she could twitch her nose and make everybody laugh. And that thought made her laugh and laugh until once again she was empty, and the voice spoke again inside her mind. "Now," the voice said, "we can begin. . . ."

Practically perfect in every way

"Friendship is born at the moment when one person says to another, 'What, you too? I thought I was the only one.'"
— C. S. Lewis

When I was about 20, I read one of the many books written about the impact of our self-image on everything from self-esteem to happiness, success, and well-being. According to the author, by repeatedly imagining myself as I would ideally like to be, I would begin to become more and more like that ideal. In order to facilitate the process, I was encouraged to write out an "ideal scene"—the details of who I would be and how I would live as my perfect self.

Here is a rough approximation of what I wrote:

"I am 6'1" tall. My hair is thick, full, and blonde. I am athletic, muscular, chiseled, healthy, and strong (think Brad Pitt, but more interesting). I am a brilliant teacher, an enlightened sage, and after curing cancer and winning the Nobel Peace Prize, I will go on to live in the jungles of Borneo saving Indonesian children from the white man's diseases.

"I am never angry, always loving, always gentle (yet manly and firm), always kind. I treat all people fairly, regardless of race or creed. I am so far beyond prejudice that I genuinely don't notice the sex or skin color of the people I am

talking to. Children and animals love me; presidents and heads of state call me in to advise them, and women adore me, although I am always faithful to my childhood sweetheart."

While this may sound amusing today (especially to those of you who know me), it sounded great to me, and I eagerly awaited the magical transformations I had been promised as this new self-image took root in my unconscious psyche.

In addition, the book encouraged me to "fake it 'til I make it" and act as if I already possessed the myriad traits I was visualizing. I decided I needed to become as wholesome, well-groomed, and squeaky-clean as my image of perfection. I wore my best suit to work, carefully coiffed my hair, exercised each day, and ate nothing each morning but fresh fruit and juice until my "don't mix foods that fight" luncheon of lean turkey, fresh carrots, and an assortment of water-rich greens that would have made any rabbit in town jealous.

Twenty-one days later (the prescribed duration of self-programming recommended to me), I looked in the mirror and I was crushed. Not only did I still look like me, I seemed so unlike my ideal self-image as to render us incomparable.

It was at this point I had a brief encounter with a male model named Tariq who changed my life. He came into the New Age bookstore where I was working looking every inch the image of perfection I aspired to be. Carefully examining me from head to toe with a look of great concern in his steely blue eyes, he delivered his verdict on the results of my 21-day experiment: "You need to start taking better care of yourself. You look like hell!"

With that bit of helpful advice from the living embodiment of my physical ideal, I realized that I hated suits, lean turkey, rabbits, Brad Pitt, and myself. I gave up then and there on my attempts to be the next Tony Robbins, Albert Schweitzer, and Robert Redford all rolled into one, grabbed a beer and a pizza, and set about getting truly wrecked.

Unexpectedly, in the midst of the destruction of my image of perfection, something wonderful happened: I caught a glimpse of myself as I actually am. And, to my amazement, I liked him just fine. In the ensuing years, I have come to recognize that the real secret of lasting self-esteem (and all of its accompanying benefits) is simply the ongoing avoidance of two things:

1. Comparing your insides to someone else's outside

*"I'm jealous of Ethiopian kids. I'd love to be skinny like them,
except for the flies and death and stuff."*
— Mariah Carey

When we first moved from London to Hollywood, one of the first things we did as a family was to visit Universal Studios. While the kids loved the rides, for me the most magical part of the day was touring the studio back lot and seeing the actual sets where movies like *King Kong, Jaws, Psycho,* and *The Mummy* had been filmed.

The remarkable thing about each one of these sets was that no matter how real they looked from the front, as soon as you went behind the scenes you realized it was just a façade—a false front held up by a few planks of wood and a whole lot of paint.

Having worked with so many people over the years, I have come to realize that even outside Universal Studios most of what you see in the people around you is a façade—the "them" they choose to present to the world.

Nearly everyone I get to know well enough finally admits that they are walking around feeling frightened or inadequate, "faking it until they make it," and wondering why they feel like a fraud.

There is an old notion in psychology that I have found to be true:

If everyone could take all their problems and dump them in a pile in the middle of the street, you would take one look at what's going on in everyone else's life, scoop your own problems back up, and run like hell!

From theory to practice . . .
Comparing Yourself to Yourself

1. Think of someone who's got you "psyched out." You'll know who they are because when you think of them, you feel bitter or depressed or angry or anything other than inspired.

2. Next, think of someone you admire. You'll know them because when you think of them, you feel "aglow" with possibility and enthusiasm.

3. Imagine that the two of them get together and compare notes on what has gotten them to where they are today. You can make this imagining as vivid and detailed as you enjoy doing it.

> 4. Now, join them. Have a conversation out loud, on paper, or in your mind where you express to each of them your feelings about them—their gifts, their success and how it affects you. Let the conversation be as positive or negative as it needs to be to be honest. Carry on until the conversation reaches a natural resolution, usually characterized by a feeling of ease and comfort.

This is a potent exercise, so be kind to yourself and give yourself the time and space to really benefit from it.

2. Comparing yourself as you are to the image of perfection you have created in your mind

"The bottom line is that people are never perfect, but love can be."
— Tom Robbins

In all the years I spent trying to "get it right," it never occurred to me to ask questions like "Get what right?" or more important, "What would happen if I did?" Here's an exercise to begin noticing what exactly you've been trying to live up to. . . .

From theory to practice . . .

The "Perfect" You

1. Describe the "perfect" you. In other words, if you were perfect, how would you be? What would you look like? What type of personality would you have?

2. Finish the following sentence: *To become my "perfect" me, I would have to . . .*

3. Is it humanly possible for you to become this "perfect" you? Why or why not?

4. Does your image of your "perfect" you inspire you to do your best, or does it merely discourage you from even trying?

5. What is your image of perfection for your partner, best friend, or parents?

6. If you have them, what is your image of perfection for your children?

Outer strategies for inner peace

So many of our efforts to "better" ourselves are born out of this conflict—the tension between who we are and who we would ideally like to be. And when part of you wants to look great naked and another part of you wants cheese fries, it can be difficult to be at peace with anything!

I'd like to bring this chapter to a close with two strategies normally reserved for the pursuit of outer peace as they apply to the challenges of the inner life.

Strategy number 1: Negotiate a peaceful settlement

> *"Start out with an ideal and end up with a deal."*
> — Tom Robbins

One of the simplest yet most powerful strategies I use for both outer and inner conflict resolution is what I call "the negotiation ladder." It works like this:

1. Clarify the stated goals on each side of the conflict. You can visualize these goals as the bottom rungs on opposite sides of a stepladder.

2. Identify the goal behind each goal: the higher value the goal is designed to meet. This becomes the next step up the ladder.

3. Continue "climbing" up both sides of the ladder until you reach the step at the top. This is the identification of a shared or mutual goal.

4. Brainstorm specific actions that both sides agree will assist them in achieving their shared aim. You can visualize this step by imagining another ladder that goes directly down from the center of the stepladder. Climb down the central ladder only as quickly as the sense of agreement can be maintained.

Let's take a look at how this might work in the "War of the Cheese Fries."

Step 1: Clarify Your Goals

In our example, one part of us wants to eat cheese fries, the other part wants to look great naked.

Step 2: Identify the Goals Behind the Goals

When we look more closely at our desire to eat the cheese fries, we may discover that what we really want is the comfortable feeling we think eating them would give us. Behind the stated goal of "looking great naked" might be the desire to feel attractive.

Step 3: Climb Up the Ladder Until We Find a Shared Goal

Let's imagine each side of our ladder in turn:

Cheese fries are comfort food for me, so what I really want is that feeling of comfort. What feeling comfortable gives me is the chance to slow down and relax. What I get from slowing down and relaxing is the chance to go inside and really feel my feelings. When I feel my feelings fully and completely, I invariably feel a sense of being at peace in my body.

We can map this side of our ladder like this:

Eating cheese fries → Feeling comfortable → Slow down and relax → Go inside and feel → At peace in my body

On the other hand, looking great naked makes me feel attractive. When I feel attractive, I'm more willing to approach others. The reason I want to approach others is to find a romantic partner, and I want to have a romantic partner because I want to feel loved. Why do I want to feel loved? Because when I feel loved, I feel completely at peace.

So on this side of our ladder, we have:

Look great naked → Willing to approach others → Find a romantic partner → Feel loved → At peace in my body

Behind both seemingly opposite desires is a shared goal—in this case, to feel at peace in my body.

Step 4: Brainstorm Practical Action Steps to Achieve the Shared Outcome

Given that what we "both" really want is to feel at peace in my body, we recognize that in this instance, what we choose to do is far less important to us than how we feel when we do it. After brainstorming various options, we decide to have a guilt-free half order of cheese fries. Later in the evening, we will go to the gym for a quick workout, followed by a relaxing, peaceful Jacuzzi. (Well, we do live in Hollywood.)

Strategy number 2: Make love, not war

"Do I not destroy my enemy when I make him my friend?"
— Abraham Lincoln

I was working with a client recently on his New Year's resolutions around eliminating his negative self-talk. After several minutes of listening to him speak about "finally conquering the voices of doubt," I recognized the screamingly obvious: that as long as we make any part of ourselves into an enemy, we will be engaged in an inner war. And as long as we are at war within ourselves, it will be literally impossible to experience lasting inner peace.

This strategy is as simple as the previous one was complex:

1. Identify whatever it is that you are trying to eliminate from your life.

2. Love it exactly as it is.

Now, you may have already guessed that "simple" is not the same thing as "easy." In the case of my client, when I asked him to explore what it would be like to "love his negative self-talk," he actually burst out laughing. But once he committed to the experiment, his entire demeanor changed. His shoulders relaxed, his breath dropped down into his belly, and a new sense of ease filled the room.

And the real magic of this strategy is still to come. Contrary to most people's expectations, when you love something exactly as it is, it inevitably begins to change all by itself. In some ways you were holding it in place by fighting with it—giving it a solidity and reality it could never have on its own. Love your fat and watch the pounds melt away. Love your ego and feel yourself dissolve into spirit. Love your illness and notice your body become well.

In this sense, the only thing wrong with you is the idea that there's something wrong with you—and the sooner you begin loving and accepting what's here instead of obsessing about what isn't, the sooner you'll become more of who you'd really like to be.

How do you love something you hate?

"My religion is simple—my religion is kindness."
— Dalai Lama

Aldous Huxley was a researcher, novelist, and philosopher who spent the majority of his adult life studying human consciousness and exploring religious and spiritual disciplines from around the world. Toward the end of his life, he was asked by a learned group of professors if he would be willing to attempt to sum up the essence of what he had learned. His response was simple and to the point:

> *"It is a little embarrassing that after years of experience, study, and research, all I can tell you is to be a little kinder to each other."*

All I would add is that my own years of experience, study, and research have taught me that being a little kinder to ourselves is of equal or greater importance. In fact, I would go so far as to say:

Kindness is love made visible.

Yet culturally, "being kind to ourselves," especially for men, tends to be seen as roughly akin to dressing up in women's clothing and calling ourselves Nancy. In fact, I remember an episode of a TV show I was in where the tough local barman told my character that he wasn't going to be kind to himself because he was "a real man— broken and destroyed, but a real man nonetheless!"

If you're willing to buck the trend and give kindness a chance, you can begin by asking yourself some of the following "kindness questions":

- What is the kindest way for me to begin my day today?
- How can I be kinder to my boss or co-workers today?
- How can I express more kindness with my family today?
- What would be a kinder way to say no?
- What's the kindest thing I could do for myself right now?

Here's an example of how asking and answering a "kindness question" made a difference in my day as I was writing this:

It is 1:14 A.M. I did not begin writing until late in the evening when our guests had gone, and I have written and rejected three separate drafts so far this evening. I'm feeling tired and contemplating putting off completing this until morning. I ask myself, "What would be the kindest way for me to proceed?"

I realize I have been sitting in an uncomfortable position and shift in my chair. I recognize that for me now, to continue would be far kinder than to stop, though getting up to make a cup of tea would be a welcome break . . . tea in hand, I carry on with my writing.

If you like this idea, experiment with using kindness as your criterion for as many decisions as you can think of. List the choices available and then ask yourself which feel kindest to you.

What if I still want to change myself?

Ultimately, the key to breaking free from your image of perfection for yourself and for others is permission. You really don't have to work on yourself anymore. You're cooked: it's official. You are enough, exactly as you are.

But remember, our habit as humans is to try to turn everything we think might be fun, positive, important, or "good for us" into a new rule to live by. And that can even include an idea as radical and as wonderful as loving yourself as you are.

If you really want to—if it really, really, really, *really* brings you joy—you can still work on yourself. There are any number of inner rewards that will come your way.

But here's the thing . . .

Even if you win the battle against an inner enemy,
you will always be at war.

If the war goes on long enough, you may find yourself trapped in a prison of your own making. Getting out of that prison and experiencing true freedom will be our task over the next two chapters. . . .

—————∞∞∞—————

CHAPTER FIVE

THE GREAT ESCAPE

The invisible prison

"I'm not sure who discovered water—but I'm quite sure it wasn't a fish."
— Marshall McCluHan

THERE ARE ESSENTIALLY THREE WAYS to go for, get, and have what you want—the right way, the wrong way, and your way. The sooner you find your way (and the more you are willing to follow it), the easier your life gets and the more effortless your success.

What gets in the way of following your own path are all the rules you have collected over the years about how things are supposed to be. These inner rules, described in the work of therapist Albert Ellis as "Ought-ism" and "Must-erbation," quickly become the invisible bars of a mental prison—and like a real prison, for as long as you are stuck inside you will have no idea what is really possible for your life.

A woman came up to me in a break at a seminar to argue with me about the idea that she might be stuck in an invisible prison of her own rules. "After all," she told me, "I can do anything I want to!"

Noticing that she was being extremely polite about arguing with me and was wearing a cross around her neck, I played a hunch and said—"Great. Tell me to go to hell!"

She looked at me, horrified. "I can't do that," she said, looking down at the floor and sounding suddenly like a scared little girl. "That would be wrong!"

Now you may be thinking that you would have no problem telling me to go to hell (or even further), but that's not the point. "Hell" was a wall in her particular prison. No doubt you have your own words that you do not like to hear spoken aloud and a long list of actions you couldn't take without feeling as though you were going to be struck down, either by the person you are talking to or a lightning bolt from the skies.

The reason most of us don't notice our own walls is that we stay so far away from the edges of our world view that we never feel the restriction. It's a bit like a dog on a really long leash: if he never strays too far from home, he'll never notice that he's tied to a stake in the ground.

But if we are in a mental prison, who are our jailers?

This is the most invisible thing of all. You are not imprisoned by your past or by your parents or teachers or children or even society at large. You are kept in a prison of mental limitations by that most transparent of all jailers—the voice inside your head.

Eat "should" and die

"That voice inside your head is not the voice of God—
it just sounds like it thinks it is."
— Cheri Huber

Do you ever say things to yourself like:

- "You stupid, stupid girl—you should have known he was going to do that."
- "Oh no, I can't believe I've done it again. Why can't I just be a little bit more careful?"
- "What are you, a man or a wimp? Stop whining, get back out there and do something about it!"

Although we generally begin our lives by following the flow of our own wanting and inclination, it is usually very clear from the reactions of those around us which of our wants are on the "approved" list and which constitute possible expulsion from the family tribe and exile from the love and approval we have not yet learned it is possible to give to ourselves.

Consequently, we develop at a very early age an inner voice whose job is to keep us "safe" by telling us not to do those things that the big people around us don't approve of.

We internalize those outside voices of disapproval and begin disapproving of ourselves first. It's like a great big game of "I'll get me before you can get me," where the most important rule of all is "Don't let them catch you breaking the rules!"

Why are we so afraid of getting caught?

Well, the worst thing that could happen to you as a child is to be rejected by the particular big people you rely on to care for you, like your parents, teachers, uncles, aunts, and even older siblings and friends. This is actually part of a biological survival mechanism. Throughout nature, any animal who is rejected by its caregivers and forced to live outside the safety and comfort of the family or pack is liable to die, either of starvation or by being eaten by predators.

Like our animal forebears, we are genetically programmed to do whatever it takes to ensure our survival. Therefore, over time you started paying very careful attention to which behaviors got you love, approval, and deeper acceptance into your own personal "pack" or "tribe" and which ones led to anger, rejection, and possible banishment.

Here's an experiment that will let you know a little bit more about which rules are currently most active in your life. . . .

From theory to practice . . .

The Way Things "Should" Be

1. Write down the words "I should . . ." at the top of a sheet of paper

2. Writing as fast as you can for two minutes, complete the sentence as many times as possible. (If you don't have at least ten, keep going until you do.)

3. Read through your list, replacing the words "I should" with as many of the following as appeal:

   a. I would but . . .
   b. I could . . .
   c. I can . . .
   d. I want to . . .
   e. I would love to . . .

4. Rewrite your list again, but only include those statements that you can meaningfully start with the words "I choose to . . ."

Of course, you should stop reading and do this experiment right now, but if you don't want to, do yourself a favor—don't, and feel great about it!

How to Escape from Prison

Part I: The "Right" Way

"Human beings are the only creatures who shit in their own nests
to get themselves to move out."
— Bruce DiMarsico

By now, you are probably champing at the bit, wondering how on earth you are going to get out of this seemingly inescapable prison of our own creation. And it is important to know that as with most things, there are three ways: the right way, the wrong way, and your way.

The "right" way, in the sense that it is the way most often suggested in the canon of personal and spiritual development teachings, is to continually push yourself up against the edges of your so-called comfort zone. "If you're not uncomfortable," the saying goes, "you're not growing."

The origin of this idea is that our nervous systems behave like thermostats, which turn on the heat when the temperature drops below a certain point (let's call it point A) and switch off when the temperature rises above a certain point (point B). The "comfort zone" is the range of temperatures between A and B. So far, so good. But why is the comfort zone the enemy of success?

Because—so our personal-development texts tell us—nothing happens there. The solution we are offered is to "turn up the heat" on our problems until we feel sufficient pain that we are forced outside our comfort zones and things begin to happen. Now I know the argument is that every time we step outside our comfort zone it expands, but if it's such a horrible and limiting place to be, why do we want to make it bigger?

Personally, I think the comfort zone gets a bad rap. I like being comfortable. I have big, comfortable sofas and I love sitting on them while I listen to music or watch TV or play video games or snuggle with my wife and kids. I also like going for what I want. I love the challenge of putting myself on the line and finding out that more often than not, I do have what it takes. The problem may not be that we are too comfortable. It may just be that we inaccurately equate comfort with complacency.

What do you imagine might happen if instead of either pushing yourself through discomfort or avoiding it altogether, you embraced and accepted it as part of the rich tapestry of a fulfilling life? What if you could become comfortable with discomfort and at ease with disease?

If you are willing to try something new, spend some time today hanging out with your "negative" emotions. You could do this by enjoying your anger or wallowing in some self-pity, but here's my suggestion.

Put yourself (safely!) in an uncomfortable situation and instead of "adjusting the temperature" by taking action, just be there. Don't try and make it better, don't try and "adjust your mind," just be there, feeling uncomfortable. (You might want to remember to breathe while you're there!)

If you're willing to do this for a couple of minutes, you'll begin to notice something wonderful: when it's really okay to be uncomfortable, comfort happens. And while I know that may still be an uncomfortable thought, a little bit of comfort may be just what you need.

Part II: The "Wrong" Way

The "wrong" way to escape from your mental prison—in the sense that it simply doesn't work—is to continue to try and come up with better and better rules. Yet left unexamined, your rule-making mechanism can continue operating for a lifetime.

Every time you have an extremely positive emotional experience, the mechanism makes a rule about it in the hopes that you will be able to have it again. Any time you have an extremely negative emotional experience, the mechanism creates a rule with the hope that it will allow you to avoid it in the future.

Similarly, if you encounter someone who speaks with great certainty about a topic you are unsure about or seems to have something you do not have, you may seek to take on what they have said as one of your "new" rules. The rule-making mechanism can even kick in if you see or hear something about "breaking the rules" or "not having any more rules." Instead of actually following the advice, you can turn that into a new rule instead!

The philosopher J. Krishnamurti put it like this:

"As long as you are concerned with mere reform, with decorating the bars and walls of the prison, you are not creative. Reformation always needs further reform, it only brings more misery, more destruction. Whereas, the mind that understands this whole structure of acquisitiveness, of greed, of ambition and breaks away from it—such a mind is in constant revolution . . . its action produces waves and those waves will form a different civilization altogether."

A less optimistic philosopher might describe it as "rearranging the deck chairs on the *Titanic*." But if we neither force ourselves through our discomforts nor rearrange the rules to make our stay in prison more comfortable, how can we escape?

Part III: "Your" Way

For obvious reasons, I can't tell you what your way of discovering more freedom in your life will be. I can, however, point you toward something I will be encouraging you to do again and again throughout this book—take the easy way out!

The following story is based on an ancient Hindu parable. Traditionally, the story ends at the lake, but I think what happens after they live happily ever after is far more interesting, don't you?

Wake Up and Roar

Once upon a time, there was a baby lion who was born into the world alone and afraid. A family of sheep found him in their home in the green grassy valley at the bottom of the mountains one day, and because he was so beautiful and because they were so kind, they decided to raise him as one of their own. It was his sister, who had a highly developed sense of irony, who suggested they name him Leo.

So they taught Leo the baby lion how to walk as a sheep and talk as a sheep and taught him all the ways of sheep, and they loved him with all of their hearts. They taught him to fear what all sheep fear and that whatever he did he must stay away from the mountains, for lions lived up there and no sheep who had ever gone up the mountain had returned.

Eventually, Leo became so good at acting like a sheep that even his own family forgot that he was really a lion. Sure, occasionally some of the other sheep teased him for his unusual size and his bushy haircut. But Leo did what he could to fit in, and he made good friends and eventually became a good, productive member of the sheep community.

The years passed uneventfully until one day an old lion from the mountains came down into the green, grassy valley in search of food. Leo was the first to sense his presence and as soon as he yelled "Lion!" all the sheep began to run in panicked circles. In the midst of the chaos, the old lion noticed Leo.

"Hey, you!" roared the hungry lion.

"M-m-me?" whimpered Leo, terrified, but at the same time fascinated by this magnificent old creature.

"What are you doing here with all these sheep?" the old lion demanded.

"They're my family," said Leo proudly.

At this, the old lion laughed. "Then who are you, young one?"

"I'm Leo, and I'm a sheep," Leo bleated.

Suddenly, the old lion's face turned fierce. "Come with me!" he roared.

Leo didn't want to go with the old lion, but he thought that by doing so, he might save his fellow sheep. So with a last look back at his flock, he followed the old lion off into the mountains.

They walked for many miles until at last, high up in the mountains, they came upon a beautiful crystal-clear lake filled with smooth, blue water. The old lion beckoned for Leo to come to the edge of the lake. By this time, Leo was exhausted, not so much from the climb, which he found surprisingly easy, but from the constant fear that at any moment, the old lion would eat him. So with a final reluctant "Baaa," Leo made his way to the edge of the lake and looked where the old lion's paw was pointing.

To his amazement, he saw not a sheep, but the reflection of a strong young lion. In that moment, he knew who he really was and let out a mighty roar that shook the mountains all the way down to the green, grassy valley.

After the shock of discovering his true identity, Leo realized that he was hungry—really hungry. And grass just wasn't going to cut it anymore. Fortunately, Leo knew where he could get food and plenty of it.

But when he got back to the valley to where his old flock was still grazing, he stopped in shock. For what he saw was not a flock of sheep but a pride of lions, each one grazing and bleating and acting for all the world like sheep. It was his own mother who saw him first, and though Leo could see that she herself was a beautiful lioness, she cowered in fear, not recognizing him and bleating "Lion!" at the top of her lungs.

"Mother!" he roared, but the sound just made the sheep/lioness run even faster among the increasingly agitated herd.

Finally, Leo noticed that his sister was looking at him with a faint hint of recognition, and he knew what he must do. He put on his fiercest face and he roared at her, "Come with me!" And though she was afraid, she followed him on the long journey up to the clear blue lake in the mountains. . . .

The self-aware aristocrat

William Penn was a 17th-century British nobleman who accepted the land that became the state of Pennsylvania as payment for debts incurred to his family by Charles II.

At the age of 22, Penn became a Quaker and was immediately faced with a profound dilemma. As the scion of a proud aristocratic family, it was unheard of (not to mention potentially dangerous) to walk around without a sword. Yet if he was to adhere to the letter and spirit of Quaker teachings, carrying a sword was bordering on blasphemy.

Young Will took this quandary to a Quaker elder, who gave him the following advice:

> *"Wear your sword with full awareness for as long as you can.*
> *When you can't wear it any more, stop."*

The elder knew that by encouraging the young aristocrat to bring his full consciousness to the problem, it would resolve itself in the most natural way possible.

The same is true in our own lives. When we decide to "wake up" and live consciously, bringing as much attention and awareness to each moment as we can, our daily dilemmas fade into the background while the full magnificence of life as it is fills the screen. When we can see that the "bars" of our prison serve our favorite emotional cocktails, life becomes easy, effortless, and fun. When we see that we are the ones keeping ourselves stuck, we can often let ourselves go—just like that.

A parable of table manners

One of the consistent issues in the early years of my marriage was a habit I (apparently) had of eating with my mouth open. While at times my wife seemed able to overlook this aberration in what I will assure you is an otherwise well-domesticated animal, at other times she drove herself to distraction watching the hypnotic up-and-down movement of my masticating jaws, enthralled by the changing color and texture of the food in my mouth and openly disgusted by the entire process.

As for me, I not only denied having this habit (surely I would know if I were eating with my mouth open), but objected to the idea that on the off-chance that just occasionally I didn't completely close my mouth as I ate, what business was it of hers?

Even when I decided to make an effort to chew with my mouth closed, if only to keep the peace, the effort would quickly subside as other, seemingly more important things took its place.

Until one day . . .

I happened to sit at dinner opposite a woman who in every other way seemed the epitome of elegance and grace. When the salad course arrived, I was horrified, driving myself to distraction watching the hypnotic up-and-down movement of her masticating jaws, enthralled by the changing color and texture of the food in her mouth and quite, it has to be said, disgusted.

From that day forth, my mouth has stayed resolutely closed while it goes about its business of tasting my food and preparing it for its conversion to energy and waste.

There are two key lessons we can take from this little parable of table manners, and they are both of great importance when we want to make lasting changes in our lives:

1. Self-observation

"Observe all men—thyself most."
— Ben Franklin

So much of the process of personal and spiritual development is taken on faith. That is, we have faith that whoever is writing or speaking to us must know more than we do (remember, they're the experts, aren't they?), and we continually attempt to modify our thoughts, words and actions to be more in alignment with what they tell us is "good" and "right" or even "useful."

Yet what makes this process of faith-based change so difficult is that it can become little more than an extension of the battle of wills we began fighting in our highchairs. Mommy and Daddy may know best, but we're important little ego-bodies, too, and they're not going to get things their way without a fight (or at least without a damn good caterwauling).

When, on the other hand, the motivation for change comes from our own observation, there is one less battle of wills to wade through. We resist change less, simply because it is initiated out of information, not faith. By the time we reach adulthood, we do not play in traffic because Mommy told us not to, but because we recognize we will almost certainly get hurt if we do.

And this is the gift of self-observation. When you can observe your own thinking, speaking, and action with a degree of objectivity, certain thoughts, words, and actions fall away as if of their own accord simply because they no longer make sense to the machine to do.

Change ceases to be an effort imposed from the inside or outside; it becomes a natural response to the best information available at the time.

2. Self-remembering

"I see through my eyes, not with them."
— William Blake

My first introduction to any form of alternative teaching was a dog-eared copy of Shakti Gawain's *Creative Visualization*. So impressed was I by the simple techniques for creating my life that I vowed then and there to visualize my goals daily for at least 15 minutes a day according to suggestions made in the book.

Unfortunately, I only realized I hadn't actually been doing it about six months later when I chanced across the book again and remembered my vow. This pattern of gaining great insight into what it takes to be happy and successful and then completely forgetting about it for as long as two years at a time continued for many years, and with it my frustration grew.

When I came across the phrase "self-remembering" in the writing of P. D. Ouspensky, I was fascinated by his assertion that the primary reason we are often unable to keep our resolutions or make lasting changes in our lives is that most of the time "we" weren't even there.

Based on his own self-observation, Ouspensky came to see that instead of a constant presence, he seemed to in fact be a collection of different I's, each with its own agenda. His resolutions to make changes in his life were continually being undermined by the ever-changing I's, and each new resolution to change was subject to the whims of what author Guy Finley refers to as TIWIICATM—the "I" who is in charge at the moment.

The more I reflected on this idea, the more I recognized it as the key to understanding my own inability to do what I had resolved to do. After all, it's difficult to maintain an intention when there's no one there to maintain it.

Try this mini-experiment:

While you are reading this book, become aware of the fact that there is someone reading it—that is, someone looking out through "your" eyes and taking in the information on this page. Indeed, that same someone seems to be listening through your ears to the sounds around you, although you may not have been fully aware of those sounds until prompted.

This is the key to self-remembering—dividing your attention in every circumstance between what you are doing and the consciousness of the one who is doing it—being present not only to your experience, but also to the experiencer.

In this way, you begin to create a constant "I"—a true, objective witness—and it is only as that "I" (what Richard Moss calls "the I that is we") that you can truly create change, grow spiritually, and transcend the limitations of your personality and conditioning.

**In other words, before you can change,
"you" have to actually exist.**

From theory to practice . . .

Use the STOP Exercise to Begin Self-Observation

Whatever you are doing right now, STOP!

Do your best to neither increase nor decrease the tension in your body until you have completed a full body scan, as though you were taking a photograph of exactly how you were using your body in the moment that you stopped.

If you like, you can then begin to relax your muscles, allow your breathing to deepen, and carry on with whatever it is you were doing (if indeed it still makes sense to based on your new observations).

Setting your inner alarm clock

*"You have the look of a man who accepts what he sees because he is
expecting to wake up. Ironically, this is not far from the truth."*
— from the movie *The Matrix*

Do you know that wonderful dopey feeling when you first wake up in the morning and are debating whether to get up out of bed and face the day or to hit the snooze button, roll over and go back to sleep?

Well, in every moment of our lives, we are faced with the same choice:

**Do we "wake up" by bringing higher levels
of awareness and consciousness to our lives,
or do we go unconscious and let our lives pass us
by in a haze of half-formed dreams
and imagined torments?**

Here are some of the most common ways we choose to hit the snooze button on our lives. It is important to note that few if any of these things are bad in and of themselves, it is simply that using them in order to go unconscious creates the lives of quiet desperation we so desperately want to go unconscious to escape from:

- alcohol
- drugs
- excessive eating
- gossip
- oversleeping
- overworking
- perfectionism
- procrastination
- sex
- shopping
- surfing the Internet

While it may seem daunting to let go of any or all of these habits, it is also often unnecessary. Instead of struggling to "subtract" these behaviors from your life, you can take advantage of your brain's natural ability to learn new things and add any of these three habits of conscious awareness to your repertoire instead.

Habit 1: Do it like it matters

Karma yoga is sometimes called "the householder's path" because it is one of the few paths to enlightenment that can be followed in the midst of everyday life. The essence of this path is to engage with every activity and interaction, no matter how seemingly mundane, as if it were the most important thing for you to be doing in the world.

How would you read this page if it really mattered? How would you sip your coffee? What quality of attention would you bring to the next interaction you have with a fellow human being if you knew that interaction would really matter to them?

While you may never know which of your actions or interactions ultimately makes a real and lasting difference in someone's life, what you will notice almost immediately is that when you act like everything in your life matters, it makes a real and lasting difference to you.

Habit 2: Take frequent holidays

I have always preferred the British term "taking a holiday" to the American idea of "going on a vacation." When I think of vacations, I think of vacating—literally "to be empty" as in *vacuum*, *vacuous*, and *vacant*. Holidays, on the other hand, were originally "Holy days"—a sacred time to renew, recharge, and reconnect to the highest and best we have within us and around us.

To plan your holiday, identify a time later today where you will take at least five minutes for spiritual self-care: a time for nurturing your spirit by reconnecting to your sacred self. You can spend your holiday reading from a book that has special meaning to you, looking at pictures of the people and things you love, or simply contemplating the mysteries and wonder of being alive. The time you spend "away from your desk" will come back to you multiplied in terms of more energy, increased effectiveness, and heightened creativity.

Habit 3: Face everything

When Socrates said, "The unexamined life is not worth living," he was pointing out that until we face what is real inside ourselves and embrace what is real outside ourselves, we may as well stay asleep. It is not enough to become more conscious of our thoughts, words, and actions. We must also shine the spotlight of our attention onto the beliefs and feelings that lie beneath them.

Fortunately, the prescription is also the cure: whenever you directly confront whatever is going on in yourself and in your life, what is unreal will dissolve in the light of conscious awareness, leaving you face-to-face with your own original Self.

From theory to practice . . .

The Three Habits of Highly Present People

1. Choose at least one activity you normally sleepwalk through and just for today, do it like it matters. For example:
   - *type each word of an e-mail as if it matters*
   - *fold a towel as if it were the most important job in the world*

– say "Hello" to someone as if the energy and enthusiasm of your greeting might be a matter of life or death.

2. Take a holiday in the next 60 minutes. If you think you're too busy, take at least two more before the end of the day. Here's a simple way to do it:

   With your eyes open or closed, begin counting your breaths, letting each complete breath—breathing in and breathing out—count as one. If you're at all stressed, you'll lose count before you get to ten (or give up because it's pointless and you've got a lot to do and people are staring and this is just stupid and you could get to ten if you really wanted to and . . . well, you get the idea). The sooner you lose count, the more stressed and unconscious you currently are and the less effective you're likely to be.

   To feel calmer, more centered, and become more aware and effective in a matter of minutes, start again at one and carry on until you can get to ten. Each time you lose count, begin again.

3. Make a list of the ways you most commonly go unconscious and any rituals or practices you already engage in that assist you in waking up and staying awake.

   A simple test for whether you are doing something because you want to or as a way of distracting yourself is to ask yourself this question:

   Would I enthusiastically recommend this behavior to the five people I care about most in the world?

By now, you have had four opportunities to use this symbolic alarm clock to "wake up" and come back to yourself:

For the rest of the book, you can reset your inner alarm clock using any of the additional strategies you have now learned. Because every moment you spend in touch with your present-moment self is a chance to bring more joy, freedom, and inspiration into your life than ever before. . . .

CHAPTER SIX

LIVING AN INSPIRED LIFE

Are you doing what you came here to do?

"Don't ask what the world needs—ask what makes you come alive and go and do that. Because what the world needs is people who have come alive."
— Howard Thurman

One of the first questions I ask any new or prospective client is:

**"Are you doing what makes you come alive—
what you love and want to do with your one and only life?"**

What kind of a response it provokes varies from person to person, but I tend to notice one of the following:

The big smile

The big smile generally comes from someone who is already living an inspired life. They're thrilled you asked and can't wait to talk about it. Often, you'll find their enthusiasm infectious and get caught up in their adventures as if they were your own. You may find yourself offering the big smiler your friendship, encouragement, and support almost in spite of yourself.

The heavy sigh

The heavy sigh is usually followed by a wistful glance off into the distance, as if the person is taking one last look at what might have been. Heavy sighers are generally feeling defeated by their lives. They may still be fighting the good fight, but if things carry on as they are, they're pretty sure they're going to lose. They have a vague, nagging sense that there's something else they could be doing with their life that would be more fulfilling but they don't know what it is, how to find it, or even if it exists at all.

The glare

The glare, often accompanied by anger in the form of sarcasm, abuse, or even rage, can be frightening if you're not prepared for it. People who glare in response to questions about their lives usually feel like they're struggling so hard to make ends meet that the very idea that there might be a better way seems like a horrible imposition. But in my experience, the angrier someone gets in response to the question, the more brightly a big dream still burns inside them.

A cab driver named Adolf

"All men dream, but not all equally. Those who dream by night, in the dusty recesses of their mind, wake to find it was all vanity. But the dreamers of the day are dangerous, for they may act their dreams with open eyes and make things happen."
— T. E. Lawrence (Lawrence of Arabia)

A few years ago, I was in Chicago as part of a comedy "sketchfest"—comedy troupes from around the country coming together to make people laugh, steal each other's jokes, and generally have a good time playing. Our first show was what could politely be called "less than fully triumphant," and rather than stick around and face it like a man, I went skulking off in a cab to visit a friend.

To my delight, within moments of entering the cab it began to snow—and I *love* the snow. Growing up in New England, snow meant sleds, skiing, snowmen, and on a good day, school being canceled. But when I shared my delight with the cab driver, he glared at me with a look of contempt normally reserved for people you've known for years. After a few moments of silence, no doubt spent considering the relative merits of throwing me out of his cab to enjoy the snow I was so fond of "up close and personal," he began to talk.

His name was Adolf and he came from Ghana. He had come to America in 1991 to make his fortune and take care of his family. Thirteen years later, he was driving a borrowed cab 7 days a week, 365 days a year. The money sent home each month enabled his family to live well. His mother owned her own home; his brother and sister were able to finish the equivalent of high school. But Adolf had not been back.

A few months earlier, his mother asked him to come home to visit for Christmas. He told her he would love to, but it would mean he wouldn't be able to send money for a few months. She never brought it up again. Adolf wanted me to know he was a Christian and the great shame that he was living with was that he had spent Christmas Day out in the snow hustling fares instead of in church giving thanks.

Yet through it all, he had a dignity and pride about him that dared me to feel sorry for him. When I asked him if he was doing what he really wanted to do with his life, I thought he was going to kill me.

He got that look in his eyes people get when they can see their big dream a million miles away in their mind's eye then wipe the slate clean before anyone notices the slight smile forming at the corners of their mouth.

"I don't know what I really want to do," he said firmly.

"I don't believe you," I replied, equally firmly.

By now the snow was beginning to stick to the sidewalks, and Adolf pulled the car over to the side of the road. Any thought of visiting my friend was long forgotten. I was in the back of that cab for a reason. Heck, I had pretty much proven I wasn't in Chicago to make people laugh.

"Everyone has access to the voice of inspiration," I continued. "What the Quakers call 'the still, small voice within.' When you listen to that inner voice, it lays out a path like a blueprint that contains everything you need to know to create a life so wonderful to you it will feel like you were born to live it. But sometimes following that voice is so scary that we won't admit we've got one—not even to ourselves."

He was watching me in his rear-view mirror intensely.

"It usually starts with an inkling—a sense that there must be something more to life than getting up and doing the same things day after day after day."

He nodded his head in agreement, so I carried on.

"Then, if you begin to pay attention, you will notice that there are things you think about that are different from most of the people around you. Things you want that are unique to you; consistent daydreams and impulses that keep coming up, no matter how many times you push them away."

Adolf looked at me a bit suspiciously, as though I had somehow gained entry not only into his head, but into a part of his mind he had all but locked away. He did, however, continue to listen.

"The fact is, at some level you already know what you want to do. The more honest you are willing to be with yourself about it, the more your own unique blueprint for a wonderful life will begin to emerge. The voice of inspiration begins to speak louder and more clearly and your life will get easier and easier. But you've got to at least be open to it. As someone once said, 'There are none so blind as those who will not see.'"

We both went quiet for a few moments, then Adolf spoke.

"I do know what I want to do," he began. "My dream is to learn to build houses the way Americans build them. The houses in Ghana are not strong. I want to go back to Ghana and build houses for my village. Then I would know that I had made a difference. And everything else that I have had to endure would be okay. It would have all been worthwhile."

There were tears in both our eyes—something I've noticed is quite common when someone first acknowledges something they've been keeping hidden from everyone, including themselves. And then he sat a little taller in his seat and we both knew it was time to move on.

What is inspiration?

> ### *Inspiration (noun)*
>
> First appeared in print in English in the 14th century:
>
> 1. The act of inspiring or breathing in.
> 2. The act or power of exercising an elevating or stimulating influence upon the intellect or emotions; the result of such influence that quickens or stimulates.
> 3. A supernatural influence that qualifies men to receive and communicate divine truth; also, the truth communicated.

Thomas Edison was once asked the secret of his prolific creativity, to which he responded: "Invention is 1% inspiration and 99% perspiration." While I have certainly experienced the need in my own life to put in the hours in order to succeed, I think Edison's equation is misleading. It seems to imply that inspiration is relatively unimportant, when in fact if what you want is a wonderful life, I'm not sure that anything is more important!

By way of example, I remember going to my local hardware store to get some burnt-orange paint recently. The man behind the counter took a large tub of pure white paint, added a few drops of yellow dye and a few drops of red, and after a few minutes of mixing I had a whole can of burnt-orange paint.

Here's the point: less than 1% of the content of the can was the source of one hundred of the color.

In my experience, moving forward when you are inspired is like climbing into a canoe and going for a ride down a river. Trying to move forward when you are out of touch with your inspiration is like carrying the canoe up a dry riverbed.

While inspiration without perspiration may be impotent, perspiration without inspiration just plain stinks!

My own definition of inspiration is a bit more prosaic but hopefully a bit more practical:

Inspiration is caffeine for the soul.

Navigating by joy

"The only tyrant I will follow is the still, small voice within."
— Mahatma Gandhi

The only question you need to ask to begin turning up the volume on the voice of inspiration in your own life is this:

What would I love to do right now?

If that seems like a startling question in the context of an almost religious-sounding idea, it's only because it's so unfamiliar. Yet the rewards of asking and answering that simple question on an ongoing basis are phenomenal and life changing.

How about this question:

How would I love to be right now?

Or this one:

What would I love to make my life about today?

Whenever you find yourself caught up in suffering or despair, you can be sure that you're out of sync with your own best interests, doing what you think you should or have to do rather than what would be uniquely right for you. On the other hand, each and every time you take the time to check in with the compass of your own joy, you are reorienting your life toward an ongoing experience of happiness, joy, and well-being.

How do you know when you're listening to the voice of your inspiration and navigating by joy?

1. You are doing what you love and want to do

I remember sharing the idea of living an inspired life with a minister who had come along on one of my Coaching Mastery trainings in order to gain new skills for helping his parishioners. I could see that he was uncomfortable with the idea, so I asked him a simple question: "Do you think God wants you to be unhappy?"

He said, "No, but I do think God wants me to be willing to sacrifice some of my own wants if that would be for the greater good."

I then asked him this: "If you knew that by giving up some of your own comforts you could benefit mankind, would you want to do that?"

"It would be an honor to do that," the minister replied, looking inspired.

"Then when you sacrifice your desires," I continued, "you are doing what you love and want to do in that moment."

2. You feel guided

One of the ways to feel guided is by noticing the synchronicities and serendipitous coincidences that begin to happen when you are following your wanting and joy. My most humorous experience of this came when I was walking through a bookstore, hoping to gain some insight into a challenge I was facing with a client. Before I could get to the self-help section, I brushed against one of the shelves and a book literally fell on my head. When I picked the book up off the floor, the title was *God Winks: A Guide to Coincidence in our Lives*. I opened it up to a random page and sure enough, there was the answer to my question.

While not all coincidences are that dramatic, most people have had the sense of certain parts of their life having been guided, where all they had to do was listen to the whispers and the next step magically appeared.

3. Things seem to unfold as if by design

There is an old story about a monk who teaches his followers that enlightenment is really just a "happy accident." When one of his students asks him why then they have to engage in so much disciplined meditation and practice, the monk replies, "To become more accident-prone."

The same is true of your quest for happy success. The more disciplined you are willing to be in doing what you love (and not doing what you don't), the more "happy accidents" you will begin to experience. When you are really following your inspiration and navigating by joy, your success seems almost effortless. It's not that you are not doing anything; it's just that you are no longer struggling to "make" things happen.

If you're ever not sure whether you're hearing the voice of inspiration or "that voice inside your head," use this simple guideline:

The still, small voice within doesn't think you suck.

If it's that easy, why isn't everyone doing it?

If it's possible to navigate your way through life simply by asking yourself what you would most love to do and doing it, why on earth would any of us ever do anything else?

Reason number one: The "dangers" of joy

"Reasonable men adapt themselves to circumstances, whilst unreasonable men persist in attempting to adapt circumstances to themselves. That is why all progress depends upon the unreasonable man."
— George Bernard Shaw

Many people fear the consequences of doing what they want because at some level they still believe that they are inherently "bad" people. Therefore, what they want would inevitably be bad for themselves or bad for others.

But is it true?

For example, if you always ate what you'd love to eat, wouldn't you get fat and horrible and unhealthy and die and have to be buried in a piano box?

Apparently not, though most people until recently have been unwilling to put it to the test.

In the 1930s, scientists did a study where they let kids choose their own diets over a 30-day period. The result was that every child in the study ate a balanced diet over the course of the 30 days (although I suspect there was an abnormally large number of chocolate éclairs and cream cakes consumed on the first few days of the study!).

In other words, when children were first given the freedom to eat whatever they wanted, they began by sampling the "forbidden foods." But once the thrill of newfound freedom had been put to the test and the handcuffs weren't slapped back on, they began to tune in to their own inner wisdom even more deeply.

The reason most of us have never put navigating by joy and inspiration to the test is that we've never allowed ourselves to do it long enough to get past the initial burst of "naughty wanting" that inevitably follows an extended period of repression, restriction, or (mental) incarceration.

So if you're a bit worried that what you'd love to do is going to involve robbing little old ladies or having sex with the Swedish volleyball team (male or female!), remember that even the voice of inspiration doesn't have to be blindly followed.

Think of each piece of joy-based guidance you receive as a direction to move toward rather than an outcome to be achieved. And let's face it, just because you recognize that true north is "thataway" doesn't mean that the best path to get there is to blindly plough straight toward it.

There's a line in Phillip Yancey's book *What's So Amazing About Grace?* that has stayed with me constantly over the years since I first read it. In discussing his personal interpretation of the Christian gospels, Yancey sums up the notion of unconditional love as follows:

> *"There is nothing you can do that will make God love you any more,*
> *And there is nothing you can do that will make God love you any less."*

Now let's put religion to one side (I'll leave it to you to choose sides) and think about that. If we believe in the possibility of unconditional love, regardless of where, when, how or by whom, then our behavior, no matter how wonderfully "good" will not earn us brownie points in heaven, and no matter how "bad" cannot make whoever it is doing the unconditional loving love us any less.

The question is, if "good" and "bad" stop being the relevant criteria for our behavior, how do we decide what to do when faced with a difficult decision?

From theory to practice . . .

On Unconditional Love

Think about a difficult decision you're facing, then answer each of the following questions:

1. What is the "good" thing to do? What is the "bad" or "evil" thing?

2. If you believed in heaven and you knew that you would get in no matter what, what would you choose?

3. If you didn't believe in heaven and you knew that you didn't have to be unhappy no matter what the consequences of your choice, what would you choose?

4. What do you want to do?

5. What will you do?

Wouldn't it be interesting to know that whatever you choose, you'll be loved all the same?

Reason number two: Premature practicality

"The heart has its reasons that reason knows not of."
— Antoine de Saint-Exupéry

Having been brought up in a family of engineers and scientists, I learned to place a high value on scientific experimentation. But when it comes to the laboratory of their lives, I find that most people are unwilling to experiment, preferring to first figure out the "rules of the game" and then do their best to follow them.

In the real world, I have repeatedly found that there is a marked difference between the premature practicality of the mind and the inspired wisdom of the heart. When people follow the "reasonable" course of action, they get consistently moderate results; when they find the courage to follow through with what they really want to do, they either succeed gloriously or so enjoy their failure as to make it pale into insignificance.

And very often, what we *really* want just seems plain unreasonable in the context of how we've been living our lives.

It's not that your goals can't make sense in the big picture of your life—it's just that they don't have to. I find this to be a useful rule of thumb:

The number of reasons you have to do something is inversely proportional to how much you actually want to do it.

In other words, if you have too many reasons to do something, chances are you don't really want to do it. But if you can't think of a great reason to do something and you really do want to do it anyway, that's almost certainly an authentic heartfelt desire.

How to walk out on the drama of your life

One of the first questions anyone new to theater asks when they come to see the actors after a show is "How did you learn all those lines?" While every actor has their own tricks, the basic truth for all of us is repetition—speaking and hearing the same lines again and again until they're so much a part of your subconscious mind you could speak them in your sleep. (And to your wife's dismay, often do. Or is that just me?)

Our inner scripting is the result of repeating lines learned from a different source—the scripting we've received from our parents, peers, and media both implicit and explicit. If you hear yourself saying things like "I know I should," "I know I shouldn't," or even "Well, that's just wrong," you can rest assured it's your scripting speaking and you've learned your lines perfectly.

Here's a quick vocabulary list that can alert you to scripting-based decision-making:

Should/Shouldn't	Have to
Must/Mustn't	Supposed to
Can't/Couldn't	Ought to
Of course . . .	Need to . . .
Because . . .	It makes sense to . . .

If you hear yourself justifying your decisions or explaining your actions with these words, chances are you're listening to your scripting.

Of course, not all scripting is bad, and it is possible with enough therapy and self-analysis to make changes to your life scripts. But the purpose of this book isn't to replace your old scripting with some new and improved version; it's to help you in stepping outside the story of your life; turning up the volume on the still, small voice within; and allowing yourself to be guided to the life of your dreams.

Here's how to do it. . . .

1. Give yourself permission

I was sitting in a café with a friend I hadn't seen for years when he shared that he had recently had a successful operation to remove cancerous cells from his lungs. When I asked him how he was doing, he admitted with a little bit of sheepishness how wonderful his life had become since he became ill. He was far more intimate with both himself and his family, he'd learned that he loved gardening, and while he did continue to work part-time, it was no longer with a sense of "This is what I have to do" or even "This is what I should do," but simply "This is what I want to do."

"As we mused further about the situation, shared that many of the people I have spoken with who have contracted fatal or potentially fatal illnesses shared his experience

"Why is it," he asked, "that something I wouldn't wish on my worst enemy turned out to be the best thing that ever happened to me?"

My belief is that it is all to do with permission. Cancer or HIV or even a bad accident not only wakes us up to the reality of the finiteness of life, it also gives us a sort of permission to live outside the cultural norms. We feel that our more eccentric behavior, guided as it is by our authentic wanting instead of our conditioning, is suddenly excusable. "I know I'm not supposed to," we say to an imaginary audience, "but cut me some slack. I have cancer [insert illness/difficult life experience/etc. here]."

Of course, just because we have permission to do something does not necessarily mean that it is a worthwhile thing to do. Permission to treat yourself and others badly and do bad things does not mean that your life will improve by doing them.

But permission does open up new, wonderful possibilities for what we can do with our lives. And we don't have to wait until we are ill to make use of them.

When you stop doing what you "should" do and what you're "supposed" to do, the only way left to navigate is by what you want to do—and if you're not used to allowing yourself to do what you want, that can be a pretty scary prospect.

Here's a simple experiment to give yourself a taste for what it's like to be able to do whatever you want. . . .

From theory to practice . . .

Permission Granted

1. For the next 60 seconds, give yourself permission to go with your wanting and knowing. You can do *anything* you want. (That's a short enough time period that even the most mischievous among you can't get up to anything too crazy!) Notice if it feels familiar or strange. Notice if you find yourself behaving any differently than you habitually would.

2. As soon as you get comfortable granting yourself permission to want what you want and do what you do, extend the time period. Soon, you may find yourself going with your wanting and knowing for hours or even days at a time!

2. Practice radical self-honesty

One very good reason that many people don't trust themselves is that they are not really honest with themselves. When I've asked people about this, they often express a fear that if they acknowledge what they *really* think and feel about things, they won't like what they find. But without the willingness to be completely honest with yourself (regardless of what you choose to express to others), you will never (nor should ever) fully trust yourself, and your own "best guess" will invariably fall short of the mark.

Here are a few tips for increasing your self-honesty:

Make Sure That No One Overhears the Conversations in Your Head

One of the best cures for writer's block is to not show anyone your work until you're ready. This makes it okay to write utter drivel for as long as you need to until the ideas in your head start to take shape on paper.

While finding a coach, friend, therapist or mentor you can trust to be 100% accepting and discreet is a wonderful (if elusive) gift, in the meantime feel free to think utter, uncensored drivel— just be sure not to share your innermost thoughts with anyone you don't want to hear them until you're ready.

Choose Self-Honesty Over a "Positive Attitude"

One of my early teachers encouraged us to always answer the question "How are you?" with the exclamation, "Fantastic!" People are attracted to people with a great attitude, the teaching went, so if we wanted to score big in the world we needed to be the most positive people in the room.

I conditioned myself so well that you could call me at 2 A.M. and I would answer the phone in a voice so "up" and chipper you would swear I'd just been reading the comics or an exercise bike. Problem was, the more "up" I pretended to be, the more "down" I became. When I gave up my "positive attitude" for an accepting one, I got back in sync with myself. Oh, I may still tell the world I feel fantastic, but I tell myself the truth and feel a thousand times better for it. (In fact, I feel fantastic! Weird, huh?)

Realize That Your Opinion Is Still Only an Opinion

When my wife announced to me that she was pregnant for the first time, I was convinced that my life (and more important to me at the time, my acting career) was over. The only thing that kept me from giving up and running away was knowing that despite the strength and depth of my opinion that having children equaled poverty, misery, and pain, I was very often wrong.

Nine months and five minutes later, as I held my new son in my arms, I was relieved to discover that once again, I had been utterly, wonderfully wrong in my opinion. But by giving myself permission to be honest with myself about what I thought without attaching any undue importance to it, I was able to stay in tune with myself and remain "trustworthy" throughout the pregnancy even though what I thought wasn't remotely politically correct.

3. Learn which feelings to trust

"I write only when inspiration strikes.
Fortunately it strikes every morning at 9 o'clock sharp."
— W. Somerset Maugham

Another distinction that I have found to be absolutely critical in learning to trust yourself is the difference between something "feeling good" and "feeling right." While these feelings will inevitably overlap, using them as our guide will take us in two fundamentally different directions.

Following only what feels good in the moment can wreak havoc in our lives, causing us to blindly pursue immediate pleasure at the cost of future satisfaction. This doesn't mean we should avoid what feels good. As you probably realize by now, I believe quite the opposite. It's just that the pursuit of good feelings in and of themselves will rarely lead us all the way to success, happiness, or well-being.

True north, when we are using the compass of our inner senses as a guide, is a feeling of rightness—a knowing that what we are about to do is the best thing we know to do in the moment, regardless of what anyone else thinks, regardless of where the "evidence" points, and regardless of whether it feels good or bad, difficult or easy, familiar or foreign.

How do you consult with your own inner expert?

1. Ask yourself a question.

2. Answer it!

Here's a more in-depth version of this process that you can use to mine your own expertise on any of the most important issues in your life. It's based on the latest research into neurophysiology which reveals that the notions of "listening to your heart" and "trusting your gut" have a solid basis in science. . . .

From theory to practice . . .

Use Your Head, Listen to Your Heart, Trust Your Gut

1. **Use your head to design a really great question for yourself**
   Think about an area of your life in which you would like to make a breakthrough. If you were going to ask a very wise friend for advice but you were only allowed one question, what question would you most want to ask this person in this moment?

2. **Listen to your heart**
   Put your hands over your heart, take a nice deep breath, hold it for a moment and let go. Do this three or four times . . .

   Now think a happy thought. Think about something that you love or someone that you love, someone that loves you, something that loves you, a warm fuzzy. My daughter likes to imagine a little bunny rabbit in her heart. My son prefers to think about playing with his friends. I like to reflect on a really happy memory. Do whatever it takes to give yourself a nice warm, fuzzy feeling in your heart.

   According to research by the Institute of Heartmath, focusing on your heart in this way actually allows your body to align itself to the dominant rhythm of your heartbeat. When you've created this state of "heart coherence," you are in the ideal state to ask and answer any questions that you may have about your life.

As well as the question you have designed for yourself, play around with what you intuitively feel would make a positive difference in this area of your life. Use the following "sentence starters" until you find which one works best for you:

I've got a feeling . . .
I want . . .
I sense . .
I know . .

Example: How can I have more energy throughout the day?

I've got a feeling that eight glasses of water a day is too many for me. I want to eat less cheese and dairy. I sense that if I slept more, my skin would clear up. I know that the more often I tune in to my intuition, the better my life goes. I know that if I don't sleep, I feel tearful. I know that I feel best when I eat four or five times a day.

3. Trust your gut

When you've consulted your head and listened to your heart, be sure to trust your gut. Don't just assume that because your head or your heart said it, it must be right for you. Check in for a feeling of "rightness" in the very center of your tummy—a quite literal "no-brainer" yes or "no-brainer" no!

Remember that you are the expert on you—and be sure to put your inner wisdom to the test in some situations where making a mistake is no big deal before you use it in situations where your best guess will be mission-critical!

Time for a change

"Dismiss what insults your soul and your very flesh will become a great poem."
— Walt Whitman

When I used to do a lot of corporate work in the 1990s, I noticed an interesting trend. Within six months of my working with companies, nearly 40% of the people I had worked with had left their jobs. While I never listed that fact in my brochures, I believe it was significant in more ways than one.

To try to "make yourself" want something you don't or do something that feels intuitively wrong to you is somewhat akin to walking in whatever direction you are facing (or you are told to face) and manually pointing the needle in your compass toward north. While it may work for a while, as soon as you let up the pressure for even a moment, the compass will begin to self-correct and you'll see that you're off-track, maybe even headed 180 degrees away from your own best life.

Now if you've spent a lifetime ignoring your intuitive feelings and making the best of a bad job or a bad relationship, it may seem like it's too late (or too scary) to do anything about it.

But chances are that the changes you need to make to realign yourself with your inner knowing are nowhere near as dramatic as you think. So don't go leaving your family, quitting your job, selling your things, and joining the circus or nunnery or even a Fortune 500 company just yet. Because even if dramatic changes are called for, you don't have to make them in a dramatic way.

Life Math

A woman went to a success coach in the hopes of creating a better life.

"How can I be of assistance?" the coach asked.

"I'm stuck in a rut," the woman said. "I can do my job in my sleep, which is just as well because I'm tired all the time." She sighed. "They say everyone's life is either a warning or an example—I want mine to be an example."

"No problem," said the coach. "How much of your time do you spend doing what you love?"

The woman wanted to scream "None!" but she knew that wasn't quite true. She loved reading biographies, and she sometimes spent hours studying the lives of her heroes and heroines.

"I guess I spend about 10% of my time doing things that I love," she admitted. "Between my job and my other commitments, that's all I've got time for. And don't tell me to quit my job—I need the money!"

The coach smiled. "Don't worry about finding the time or doing anything dramatic. If you really want to experience more success, passion, and fulfilment in your life, all you have to do is to make the following commitment:

"Each month, stop doing at least one thing that drags you down and add at least two things to your life that you love."

While that seemed much too simple to really make a difference, the woman decided to go for it anyway. She stopped driving herself to work, which she hated, and arranged to share the commute with a colleague whose company she enjoyed. In addition, she began taking a yoga class on the weekends. Almost immediately, her energy levels increased and she felt better than she had in years.

The next month, she decided to subtract her morning sugar fix, which always left her feeling strung out by lunch time, and to add in a daily bottle of water and a weekly trip to the cinema. When one of her co-workers commented on how much happier she seemed and asked if she had found "someone special" in her life, she realized that she had—herself.

Each month, she added and subtracted until she could honestly say she was enjoying her life. Although she still didn't love her work, she had so many things to look forward to each day that it almost didn't matter anymore.

"That worked wonderfully," she reported to her coach. "Do you have any other things I can try?"

"Of course," the coach said. "Now that you've developed your 'math muscle,' make a list of the big ones.' What are the five biggest drains on your joy? What are the five most wonderful things you can imagine adding to your life?"

Some of the things she came up with were obvious to her—her job was still a big drain; finding a loving partner to share her life with and a job that was an expression of her highest values were pretty wonderful-sounding additions. Other things occurred to her later when she wasn't trying so hard to think—like how much easier her life would become if she stopped trying to impress her mother or be perfect all the time, and how wonderful it would be to actually meet some of her heroes and learn from them directly.

She decided to start with the easiest of "the big ones" first—creating a sacred hour at the beginning of her day to read, meditate, and do yoga. Then one day, she read something during her sacred hour that inspired her to make the biggest addition and subtraction of her life—to finally leave her job and start her own business doing work that made her come alive.

It was in a book by Joseph Campbell, and he was sharing a bit of advice given to a young Native American at the time of his initiation.

> "As you go the way of life,
> you will see a great chasm.
> Jump.
> It is not as wide as you think."

Some final thoughts on creating a life that makes you go "Wow!"

> "Desire marks the path."
> — Mandy Evans

I was driving to the store to buy some milk one day and was listening to a radio show on the importance of commitment and goals. "If you're not 100% committed to the achievement of your goals," the host was saying, "they're not really goals, they're wishes."

My inner rebel chafed at his strident tone, but I found myself exploring which (if any) of my goals I was truly 100% committed to, as in "I will get there or die trying." To my surprise (and slight disappointment), not one of the many things I wanted, including more money, nicer stuff, happiness, and spiritual enlightenment, fitted the "100% commitment" test.

"Surely," I said to myself, "I must be 100% committed to something."

I decided that perhaps the problem was the time-frame. Most of my "Wow!" goals would be a lifetime in the making. Perhaps I could commit 100% to reaching a certain target within the next five years? Three years? One year?

Finally, I negotiated myself down to the next five minutes. After all, I must be 100% committed to getting to the store, right?

But when I really thought about it, I realized that if I got a sudden inner prompting to go left instead of right, I would follow it. If I saw someone in need and was moved to be of service, the milk would have to wait.

It was in that moment I realized what my one true commitment was: to follow the voice of inspiration and the inner promptings of my highest self.

More than any other, this next exercise will help you to reset your compass to create a life filled with joy, inspiration, and desire. I call it "The Comfy Chair," both because it involves sitting in a comfy chair and because for some people, the first time they do it is a funny sort of torture. . . .

From theory to practice . . .

The Comfy Chair

1. Choose a comfy chair and a period of a few hours where you have no appointments or commitments. (You can do it for as little as five minutes at a time, but longer does seem to work better.)

2. Turn off the phone and go sit in your comfy chair. Your job is to stay in that chair unless and until you get in touch with an authentic heartfelt desire: something you're really inspired to do.

3. Each time you get an impulse to get up and do something, ask yourself if the impulse is coming from your scripting or your wanting the voice of the "should" or the voice of inspiration.

   - If you suddenly remember something urgent you have to do, it's probably just your emotions trying to reassert their authority. Kick their butts back into line by sitting on yours just a little bit longer.

   - If it's inspiration calling, get up and do it, then go back to your comfy chair and wait for the next authentic impulse. (It's important to always go back to the chair between each task.)

Here is the only commitment I will ask you to make in this book:

I, _____, commit to listening to the voice of inspiration and living an inspired life.

By making (and keeping) this one commitment, your life will change forever. Effortless success and all good things will begin to follow you, and it may seem at times as though the entire universe is conspiring to do you good.

Where will your inspiration take you? I have no idea. But tuning in each day and finding out will become the greatest joy in your life.

I'd like to finish this section of the book with the words of W. H. Murray, the author of *The Scottish Himalayan Expedition*:

"Until one is committed, there is hesitancy, the chance to draw back, always ineffectiveness. Concerning all acts of initiative and creation there is one elementary truth the ignorance of which kills countless ideas and splendid plans: that the moment one definitely commits oneself, then Providence moves too.

"All sorts of things occur to help one that would never otherwise have occurred. A whole stream of events issue from the decision, raising in one's favour all manner of unforeseen incidents and meetings and material assistance which no man could have dreamed would have come his way.

"I have learned a deep respect for one of Goethe's couplets:

> *'Whatever you can do or dream you can, begin it.*
> *Boldness has genius, power and magic in it'"*

PART II

An Obstacle Course
to Success

CHAPTER SEVEN

WHAT STOPS YOU?

Getting unstuck

"If the only tool you have is a hammer, you treat everything as a nail."
— Abraham Maslow

HAVE YOU EVER PLAYED the game Pooh Sticks, where as a child you placed a twig or small stick in a brook or river and watched it float downstream, often racing it against the twig or stick of a friend?

One thing that inevitably happens is that your stick will get stuck behind a rock or in a small eddy. In order to get it moving again, you must reach in and poke at it, usually with a bigger stick, until it unsticks itself and continues its journey downstream.

This is one of the fundamental differences between what I like to call "the coach approach" and more traditional therapeutic interventions. As a catalyst and coach, I'm not particularly interested in why someone is stuck. What I want to do is to get them unstuck as quickly as possible and back into the flow of their life.

In fact, here's my answer to pretty much any question about human psychology that begins with the word "Why":

Because!

Pick up a dozen psychology or self-help books and you'll find a dozen explanations for why you are the way you are. Which one is right? The one that works for you.

When you move past trying to figure out the "real" reason your life is the way it is, you can also move beyond excuses and on to solutions—and when you bring a solution orientation to your life, you tend to create fewer problems, better results, and an ever-increasing sense of hope, possibility, and wellbeing.

We can map the way most people think about life like this:

Cause → Effect

As a rule, we perceive other people or external events to be the causes in our life and our happiness, unhappiness, success, or failure as the effect. But if we slow the process down, we can see that there is at least one additional stage to the process—our reaction to what happens to us. An external event happens in the world and we experience a seemingly "automatic" reaction to it, leading to the ultimate effect in the world.

In short:

Cause → *Reaction* → *Effect*

For example, what would your automatic reaction be in each of the following situations? What would the ultimate effect most likely be?

- *You're driving a car and the driver in front of you does something stupid and dangerous.*
- *Someone in a position of authority (boss, parent, etc.) criticizes you in front of your peers.*

While your answers will be unique to you, they will probably be some variation of the following:

(Cause)   That other driver does something stupid and dangerous.

(Reaction)   You feel a surge of anger and honk your horn.

(Effect)   The other person expresses their displeasure with you in an X-rated manner.

Or in our other example:

(Cause)   Someone in a position of authority (boss, parent, etc.) criticizes you in front of your peers.

(Reaction) You feel embarrassed/humiliated/ashamed, then angry/fearful/sad. You either defend yourself, attack them, or make a joke to deflect the energy of the situation.

(Effect)   They fire you, send you to your room, or otherwise plot to take their revenge at a later time.

So what can we do if we want to change the effect and have a greater influence over the results we experience in our life?

Well, we could try to change the effect directly, but this is like trying to move a shadow without moving the object casting the shadow. We could try to change the cause, but generally speaking we have little direct control over what happens to us throughout the day. We could even try and not react to what happens—but even after years of meditation or therapy, most people concede that this is difficult at best and near impossible the rest of the time.

However, here's some good news. We can break our reactions down further into two parts—our seemingly automatic *emotional* reaction to what happens, and the *actions* we choose to take in response to that emotional reaction.

The process now looks like this:

Cause → Emotional reaction → Choice → Action response → Effect

Or even more simply:

Cause → Reaction → Choice → Response → Effect

This makes the difference between therapy and coaching clear.

Therapy deals primarily with the first half of the equation: the link between cause and reaction. Coaching deals with the second half: choosing your response and putting yourself "at cause" in relation to the effects you wish to experience in your life.

How do you find the moment of choice between your emotional reaction and your behavioral response?

Through the deliberate interruption, inhibition and/or restriction of your habitual, "automatic" emotional reaction.

In other words, the easiest place to interrupt our pattern is not before we feel, but before we act. We can do this most easily by "shutting down" our system: no thinking; no speaking; no doing. Instead, take a deep breath. Focus on your heart. Bite your lip. If you like, count to ten. Then, in what Holocaust survivor Viktor Frankl called "the space between cause and effect," you can ask yourself a simple question:

Do I want to nurture my reaction or choose my response?

The suicide thought

"Socrates said the unexamined life is not worth living.
But the over-examined life makes you wish you were dead.
Given the alternative, I'd rather be living."
— Saul Bellow

Perhaps the most dramatic example in my own life of the power of this kind of choice came during my adolescence. From around the age of 13, every time I was in a stressful situation (and daily from around 17 to 21), the thought would come to mind that life would be a whole lot easier if I stopped participating. Completely.

When I was 19, I had an experience where I felt as though my body was being sucked out of a dormitory window. Terrified, I phoned the Samaritans' suicide hotline, only to be answered by a busy signal. The irony of this amused me, even at the time, and I was able to phone a friend to come get me and take me somewhere where I would be safe for the night.

Although the suicide thought continued to pop up regularly for several more years, that night it lost all its power over me. The truth was, as I somewhat dramatically discovered, I didn't want to kill myself. I didn't even want to die. I just wanted some release from the stress and pain I was experiencing, and that was the only escape my unconscious mind could think of.

We can map it like this:

Cause (stressful situation) → *Reaction (suicide thought)*

From that day forward, rather than continuing to treat the "suicide thought" therapeutically as a problem to be solved, I recognized it for what it was: just a thought, no more significant than "chicken or beef," "plaid or stripes" or "I wonder what she's wearing under that?" (Hey, I was 19!)

We can map the new response like this:

Cause (stressful situation) →

Reaction (suicide thought) →

Choice (recognize that it's just a thought) →

Response (choose to address the stress or refocus on my desired end result) →

Effect (a more and more wonderful life)

After a few years, the "suicide thought" faded out of my daily routine, and now it comes to visit just occasionally. When it does, I greet it as an old friend, reminding myself of how far I've come and that I probably need to take a little bit better care of myself at that moment.

A few years into our marriage, I shared the story of the "suicide thought" with my wife, and she said, "Oh, I have one of those . . . I call it 'the divorce thought'!"

Apparently, there had been one or two occasions over those first few years where she experienced our relationship as "less than perfect," and in those moments the thought had come to her that maybe we'd be better off if we weren't together anymore. At some point, she realized that she did want us to stay together, but the thought came up whenever she needed some release from the pain or stress she was experiencing.

From that moment on, the "divorce thought" became just that—a thought—no more significant than "fruit or veg," "plaid or stripes," or I wonder if our kids are all right" (Hey, we're getting older!).

The obvious solution

"When you hear hoof beats, look for horses, not zebras."
— Medical school maxim

I was once hired to model the problem-solving strategies of a top Silicon Valley troubleshooter. When I asked him how he would begin to solve an extremely difficult problem, his surprising answer was, "I never solve extremely difficult problems. If I find a problem is too difficult, I know I've defined it wrong."

While I marveled at his reply, it reminded me of one of my favorite stories from the world of psychotherapy.

Jay Haley, one of the most prominent therapeutic innovators of his time, was reportedly asked at a conference where he was presenting how he would treat a patient diagnosed with schizophrenia.

Haley paused to reflect before answering.

"Schizophrenia," he mused aloud. "We still haven't come up with a cure for that, have we?"

On being reassured that the newly categorized disease was still without a cure, Haley replied:

"Then I would never diagnose one of my patients with it. Why would I diagnose a patient with a disease I didn't know how to cure?"

Defining our problems (or more accurately "explaining" their cause) in terms of an easily implementable solution works because the way we explain the cause of our problems predetermines the solutions we will attempt to implement.

Let's say I am struggling to meet a romantic partner. If I diagnose my problem as low self-esteem, what's the obvious solution? Anything I believe will raise my self-esteem, from making "downward comparisons" to people who are worse off than I am to repeating affirmations like "I like myself" into a mirror.

If I believe the reason I am not yet in a romantic relationship is that I don't know how to tell whether or not someone is interested in me, then the obvious solution would be to read books on body language, or perhaps to take a course in "How to Flirt."

If I decide that the problem is that I am not sufficiently attractive to draw a potential mate, the obvious solution might be to get a new haircut, a new wardrobe or even a new face. (I live in Hollywood—this is actually one of the first things people try out here!)

In short, the way we diagnose, define, or explain the problem (or its cause) determines where we go to look for a solution. Therefore, if we are stuck or unable to solve a problem, we need to come up with an alternative diagnosis, definition, or explanation.

From theory to practice . . .

Finding the Not-So-Obvious Solution

Here is a simple process I use with myself and my clients whenever we get stuck in the face of a seemingly insoluble problem:

1. What is the problem I would like to solve?
   Example:
   I want to feel less tired and have more energy.

2. Why do I believe I have this problem? (Bear with me; we're using the "Why?" question for a purpose here!)
   Example:
   I am tired all the time because I'm not inspired by my job and I dread going to work in the morning.

3. What are some "obvious" solutions to this problem?
   Example:
   Finding a new job; finding aspects of my current job I could get inspired about; looking for inspiration in my life outside my work.

4. What are at least three other possible explanations for this problem and their "obvious" solutions?
   Examples:
   a. I could be tired because I don't sleep enough. The obvious solution would then be to get more and better sleep by going to bed an hour

---

earlier every night, getting a more comfortable mattress and creating a "going to bed" ritual that I would really look forward to.

b. My tiredness might be the result of a physical problem. The obvious solution would then be to get checked out by my doctor and find out if there's anything that needs to be addressed and possibly to begin an exercise program.

c. I might be tired because I haven't been eating well. The obvious solution would then be to do some reading about nutrition and choose a healthier "high-energy" diet. Also, I might try some vitamin and mineral supplements designed to boost my energy and wellbeing.

5. Implement at least one of your alternative solutions. If it works, great! If not, move on to another alternative.

The Obstacle Analysis Grid™

About 15 years ago, a friend and I sat down and made a list of all the different things that could possibly stop us from being, doing, and having what we wanted in our lives—everything from insufficient talent to the outbreak of World War II. Eventually, we whittled our list down to nine things—nine categories of obstacles that might stand between us and living the life of our dreams.

Over the next few years, I tested and refined the model against the experience of hundreds of clients and trainees, and then began using and teaching it consistently as a formal model for obstacle analysis in goal setting.

The Obstacle Analysis Grid is a quick way of separating out the nine major categories of life obstacle and choosing appropriate responses and interventions. Most people find that while all the categories are somewhat relevant, their major life obstacles consistently fall into one or two of the "obstacle areas" on the grid.

People have reported using the model to help themselves overcome everything from difficult people at work to agoraphobia; from dealing with a messy divorce to starting a new career at the age of 50-something.

The grid looks like this:

Information	Skill	Belief
Well-being	Other people	Motivation
Time	Money	Fear

Here's a quick reference guide to each of the obstacles. To learn more about them (and how to move over, under, around, through, or beyond them), go to the specific chapter that addresses that obstacle area. I've designed the rest of this book so you can either read through from beginning to end or dip into the section that seems most relevant to your life right now.

Eventually, you'll want to read through all of them, as many of the strategies in one section are equally applicable in the others.

OBSTACLE AREA	INDICATORS
Information	"I don't know what to do, and I don't know where to go to find out."
Skill	"I don't yet have the skills I need to succeed in this area."
Belief	"This is impossible, or at best unlikely to ever work/happen." "Other people might be able to do this, but it's just not possible or likely for me."

Well-being	"I'm way too stressed/tired/unwell to deal with this."
Other people	"My boss/spouse/child/friend/etc., makes it difficult for me."
	"It's just not up to me."
Motivation	"I just don't care enough."
	"I can't seem to get started."
	"I can't seem to create or sustain any momentum."
Time	"There's not enough time in the day."
Money	"I'd love to, but I don't think I can afford to."
Fear	"I feel sick at the thought of pushing myself through this."

If you're still not sure which area is most relevant to your situation, feel free to guess. Remember that the idea is not to get it right or even to "understand" why you're stuck. It's simply to do whatever it takes to unstick yourself and get back into the flow of your life.

From theory to practice . . .

What Stops You?

1. Give yourself a score from 1 to 10 in each of the nine areas, where 1 means this is an area of total weakness for you and 10 means this is an area of total strength.

2. Think of a specific problem or challenge you are facing and identify which of the nine obstacle areas seem most relevant. The following nine questions will serve as a useful guide.

Are you experiencing a problem because:

- You don't know what to do? **(Information)**

- You know what to do, but you don't feel capable of doing it? **(Skill)**

- You don't believe it can be done? **(Belief)**

- You don't have the energy or are too stressed-out to do it? **(Well-being)**

- Other people stand in your way? **(Other people)**
- You just don't seem to care enough? **(Motivation)**
- You don't have the time? **(Time)**
- You don't have the money? **(Money)**
- You're scared? **(Fear)**

3. When you've identified the key area or areas for you, go to that section of the book to learn more about how to "unstick" yourself!

Of course, if you're not sure where to get started, you might not have enough information yet—in which case the very next chapter is the perfect place to begin. . . .

CHAPTER EIGHT

INFORMATION

Information	Skill	Belief
Wellbeing	Other people	Motivation
Time	Money	Fear

All about the black rhino

"Education is the key to unlock the golden door of freedom."
— George Washington Carver

IN OUR EAGERNESS TO BLAME OURSELVES for pretty much everything that goes wrong in our lives, it can be easy to assume that when we don't complete (or even begin) a project or goal, it's due to some sort of a character flaw, like laziness, sloth, or stupidity.

Yet often it is much simpler than that—we simply are missing some piece of information about how what we are doing needs to be done.

For example, when my son Oliver was six, he walked into my office in tears, insisting that the report he was supposed to do for his school and had been putting off until the last minute was "stupid, boring, and too hard" (words I'm sure those managers and leaders among you have never heard from your colleagues and subordinates!).

When I asked him what part of the assignment he was finding too hard, he said, "All of it." After a few more questions, it became clear that what was making it so difficult for Oliver to finish his report was neither a character flaw (like laziness) nor a physical problem (like dyslexia), but a simple lack of information—he'd never seen a report and he genuinely didn't know how to do it.

The next day, we went to his school and asked to look at a few "model" reports—examples of what his teacher felt were some of the best of what other people had done. Later that night Oliver proudly handed me his first report: *All About the Black Rhino*.

This sort of "information underload" is all too common in the business world and is made worse by the fear that admitting you don't know what you don't know will be cause for embarrassment, demotion, or worse.

That's why I believe one of the most powerful phrases in the world is this:

"I don't know . . . let's find out!"

Here are some of my favorite ways of "finding out":

Learn to succeed

> *"The only sustainable competitive advantage is the ability to learn faster than your competitors."*
> — Arie de Geus

If learning is one of the master keys to sustaining your competitive advantage, then accelerating your learning will accelerate your journey to personal and professional success. There are two main principles involved in learning how to learn more quickly:

1. All learning is state-dependent

> *"There are no stupid people, only stupid states."*
> — Anthony Robbins

Everyone knows that people behave differently when they are happy than when they are miserable. What you might not have known is that your emotional state has a powerful effect on your ability to recall and make use of what you already know.

Think of a subject that invariably makes you feel stupid, incompetent, or "less than optimally resourceful." Now notice how you feel. Do you think you are more or less likely to succeed if you continue to approach this subject in this particular state of mind?

Because your mood helps determine which bits of your brain you can access (and therefore how "smart" you are in any given moment) then learning to choose your mood is one of the most critical skills for effective learning.

To instantly increase your ability to learn, resolve that from now on you will only approach that subject when you are feeling resource-ful (happy, confident, loving, playful, laughing, etc.).

2. Failure is a prerequisite for success

*"If people learned to walk and talk the way they're
taught to read and write, everybody would limp and stutter."*
— Mark Twain

It's important to realize that "failure" is a requisite part of the learning process, not the end of it. In fact, people never fail—strategies, tactics, and plans fail. What do you do if your strategy, tactic, or plan fails to produce the desired result? Change your strategy, tactic, or plan until you find one that succeeds!

Once you realize that each "failure" is nothing more than an occasionally frustrating stepping-stone on your path to success, the whole idea of "failure" loses its negative charge and regains its rightful place as an essential companion on your journey.

From theory to practice . . .

Overcoming Fear of Failure

1. Choose a goal, project, or area of your life where you are feeling stuck.

2. Deliberately "fail" at least ten times in the next week. You'll have to define failure for yourself:
   - *If you're in sales this might mean collecting at least ten rejections.*
   - *If you're learning to ride a bike, make sure you fall off at least ten times.*
   - *If you're a writer, write at least ten horrible pages.*

   You will find that before you even finish this experiment, your fear has shifted and your energy will once again begin to flow.

Studying made fun

"If you have an apple and I have an apple and we exchange these apples then you and I will still each have one apple. But if you have an idea and I have an idea and we exchange these ideas, then each of us will have two ideas."
— George Bernard Shaw

My mother (who has a Ph.D. in organic chemistry) once confessed to me that she used to study for exams by putting her textbook under her pillow in hopes that the information would absorb into her brain while she slept.

While you're more than welcome to give her system a try, here are some slightly more practical ways to make studying fun. May they be of use to you in gaining knowledge, developing wisdom, and experiencing the delights of learning.

1. A dialogue between thinkers

In college, my friends and I devised a wonderful process for getting the most out of our assigned reading. We would take a book and based on the title and back-cover blurb, we would spew forth all our own personal thoughts on the topic. By the time we actually opened the book to begin reading, we had primed our minds. Instead of just listening to the "expert" author lecture us about his or her opinions on the subject, our reading took on the form of a dialogue between two thinkers, each with our own ideas to share.

Even now, I almost never read or listen to anything without a pen in hand and my books and notebooks are filled with underlines, side notes, commentary, and (if I really disagree with the author) the occasional obscenity. I may sketch out little doodles of what the author is talking about, either in the form of a mind-map or in mini-cartoons where stick-figure characters act out the key points of the author's theory. In short, I engage actively and viscerally with the material wherever possible.

You can use the same technique to get more out of any studying you may do, whether it's technical training at work, listening to lectures at school, personal development coursework, or even reading this book.

All you need to know is the title of the book, lecture, or talk you are about to engage with and, if available, a paragraph or so about the theme. Then take a bit of time before you get started to brainstorm your own ideas about the subject. Don't worry if it makes sense or if you think you don't know anything about it—you'll be amazed at what you come up with when you let yourself "make stuff up." Then, when you've got your ideas about the topic in mind, open the book, turn on the tape, or walk into the lecture and let the "dialogue between thinkers" begin!

2. If this wasn't stupid . . .

There is a story that legendary rock guitarist Jimi Hendrix once spent an entire evening in a New York City nightclub listening to a guitar player who was charitably referred to by Jimi's manager as "the worst guitar player in the history of the planet Earth." When the manager asked Jimi why he would possibly want to stay to listen to the noise, Hendrix said, "This guy is so bad, he just might play something that's never been played before—and if he does, I want to be here to learn from it."

In the introduction to their biblical commentary, *Five Cities of Refuge*, playwright David Mamet and Rabbi Lawrence Kushner highlight this secret to learning by pointing out that given a book as seemingly filled with contradictions as the Old Testament, you have two choices: You can presume that you are smarter than the book, or you can presume that the book is smarter than you. If the book were smarter than you, anything that doesn't seem to make sense would not be a mistake in the book, but rather a blind spot in your understanding.

By being willing to give equal time to both points of view, you can sometimes discover great wisdom in the strangest places. (Yes, it pains me to admit I've even learned a thing or two from *People* magazine . . .)

3. Teach to learn

The phrase "We teach what we most need to learn" is often used as a sort of covert put-down, as if to suggest that anyone who puts themselves forward as a teacher must in some way be covering up for their own inadequacies. Yet to this day, I know of no better way to master a subject than to teach it to others.

This is because nothing will reveal what information you are missing as quickly as attempting to share that information with other people.

By deliberately teaching and writing about what I most want and need to learn, I have not only become more knowledgeable and more effective, I've also had the opportunity to touch the lives of tens of thousands of people.

Even if you don't have the luxury of a classroom of willing students or a practice of patients or clients, give yourself the gift of sharing what you most want to learn with a friend or colleague. As you prepare yourself and your material for presentation, you will discover both how much you already know and perhaps more important, what you don't really understand yet and is still waiting to be learned and mastered.

From theory to practice . . .

Studying Made Fun

1. If you were going to write an essay on "Studying made fun," what would be your three key points? Take a few moments to jot down your answers, then go back and read through this section again. Notice how you engage with it differently the second time through.

2. Choose one of the following popular personal-development titles and resolve to read (or listen to) it in the next month. Before you do, take some time to make notes about what you would write if you were using that title for a book of your own.
   - *Feel the Fear and Do It Anyway* by Susan Jeffers
   - *Awaken the Giant Within* by Anthony Robbins
   - *There's a Spiritual Solution to Every Problem* by Wayne Dyer
   - *Change Your Life in Seven Days* by Paul McKenna

3. Pick an author you feel is somewhat "beneath you," but has somehow nonetheless gained the ear of others. Decide for the time being that this person is not completely nuts and spend some time exploring that author's material as if it's *you* who's missing something. Carry on until you've found at least three great ideas you've never thought of before.

4. Take one idea from this book (or anything else you are currently studying) and resolve to teach it to at least one other person before the end of the week. You will make countless distinctions as you prepare for your presentation and even more when you actually do it.

> If you really want to accelerate your learning, be sure to ask them to ask you lots and lots of questions. I find I learn more from being on the "A" side in Q&A sessions than in almost any other area of my studies.

The Marx Brothers' guide to increasing intelligence

"The left hemisphere of the brain controls the right side of the body and the right hemisphere of the brain controls the left—that's why left-handed people are the only ones in their right minds."
— If Groucho Marx did brain research

Dr. Roger Sperry's Nobel Prize–winning research into the differing functions of the left and right hemispheres of the brain identified the following functional distinctions between the hemispheres:

Left side
Verbal, analytical, literal, words,
logic, numbers, sequence

Right Side
Nonverbal, rhythm, metaphor, movement,
big picture, color, imagination

Sperry's initial research involved severing the corpus callosum (which joins the left and right hemispheres of the brain) as a means of limiting the negative effects of epileptic seizures. What has been done with his research, largely as a result of the work of one of his colleagues, Joseph Bogen, is a renaissance of scientific enquiry into the nature of creativity.

More recent research into intelligence and the physiology of the brain (most interestingly by the neuroanatomist Marian Diamond who studied Einstein's brain) has shown that the primary correspondence between measurable genius and brain physiology lies neither in the right or left hemisphere, but in the connectivity of synapses between the two halves. This connectivity is increased through frequent use.

In other words, the way to increase your intelligence and to function at the peak of your current level of brain power is to learn to use your left and right brain simultaneously.

In trying to explain the above research into integrated heterolateral brain functioning (phew!) to my now 11-year-old son, I came up with the following analogy, which should make the whole thing clear to anyone who's ever spent a night at the opera or a day at the races, but will no doubt be as confusing as animal crackers in a bowl of duck soup to the rest of you. . . .

Chico Marx represents the left brain: witty, clever, and highly verbal, but without a great degree of visual or imaginative flair.
Harpo Marx represents the right brain: imaginative, physical, and creative, but lacking in logic and verbal skill.

Groucho Marx represents an idealized synergy of both hemispheres, switched on and working together for maximum impact.

What follows are some of my favorite intelligence-building and creativity-unleashing techniques that use the Marx Brothers' secret to success: developing both right and left hemispheric skills to create a synergy of synapses that leap across the corpus callosum!

1. Mind mapping

I always found it funny that a mind map is meant to be, in the words of creator Tony Buzan, "the external expression of the natural way in which the brain functions." I've certainly never noticed my brain thinking in a series of many multicolored lines branching out from a central core with words and images on it, but mind maps are pretty, and often pretty useful.

To begin benefiting from mind mapping (a visual form of note taking), try the following simple exercise:

1. Write down a key word or phrase **(Chico)** that represents what you think to be at the core of what you are learning.
2. Draw a picture **(Harpo)** that represents that key word or phrase.

3. Repeat the above sequence until you have created a visual representation of all the important intellectual concepts in whatever it is you are studying **(Groucho)**.

Not only will you find yourself remembering more of the material than before, you will continue to make new distinctions (and brain connections) each time you work with your map.

2. Life mapping

A variation on mind mapping, which reverses the sequence, is what I call "life mapping." Feel free to adapt the format below to fit your individual needs:

1. Draw a picture that represents your career/relationships/life as it is now **(Harpo)**.
2. Draw another picture that represents how you would ideally like your career/relationships/life to be **(Harpo)**.
3. Describe aloud or in writing what the pictures mean to you and what you've learned from drawing them **(Chico)**.
4. Use what you've learned to create a verbal/pictorial plan to get you from where you are to where you want to be **(Groucho)**.

3. Image streaming

Dr. Win Wenger is the godfather of increasing intelligence, and image streaming is his core technology. I've taught image streaming in my workshops and seminars for years as a means of increasing your ability to visualize—that is to see visual images in your mind's eye. The added benefit? This is the only visualization technique I know of that has been scientifically proven to create a permanent, measurable increase in IQ (approximately $2/3$ of a point for every hour of practice).

Why not try it for yourself?

From theory to practice . . .

Image Streaming

1. Close your eyes and become aware of the stream of seemingly random images that continually run through your brain **(Harpo)**.

---

2. Begin describing aloud what you are seeing, no matter how vague it may be **(Chico)**. The simple guideline? Say what you see!

   Example:
   I see a gray blob, and it's getting bigger, and now it's turning blue, etc.

3. Have someone ask you questions about your image stream—allow it to affect your imagery and describe what you see. If you're working alone, you can tape record your initial stream, then play it back and allow it to influence your new image stream **(Groucho)**.

Creating your own techniques

Why not use the Marx Brothers to help you create your own intelligence-expanding methodologies? Here's how: take one item from the Chico list and one from Harpo and force a Groucho-like connection!

Sample Chico (left-brain) activities:	Sample Harpo (right-brain) activities:	Sample Groucho (integrated heterolateral) activities:
Describing	Drawing	Dancing to poetry
Writing	Daydreaming	Coloring numbers
Speaking aloud	Coloring	Analyzing metaphors
Focusing on details	Listening to music	Image streaming
Finding the logic	Dancing	Life mapping
Analyzing	Dreaming	Mind mapping
Rationalizing	Making metaphors	Goal sensing
Calculating	Doodling	Crawling
Moving the right side of your body	Moving the left side of your body	?????????????

You might just find that you invent a few techniques of your own. And if you want to master them, what better way to begin than by teaching them to others?

Here's one last tool you can use to incorporate learning as an intrinsic part of your approach to happy success.

The success cycle

The three essential elements of any successful project are preparation, action, and learning. By consciously examining and "cycling" through each of these stages, you will find it easier to gather and maintain momentum on your projects, goals and dreams.

Part I: P.R.E.P.

"If you fail to prepare, prepare to fail."
— Coach John Wooden

You can use this simple four-step model to help you prepare for anything

1. Plan your strategy

Take some time to work out how you are going to go for what you want.

2. Rehearse your plan

In France, actors rehearsing a play are participating in *la répétition*. By repeatedly moving through the steps and stages of your plan over and over in your mind and in the world, you will be able to relax and trust your body when it comes time for real action.

3. Establish your intentions

Make a mini-checklist of things you want to do during the upcoming event or project. These can be both outcome-focused (e.g., get the job, have fun, learn heaps, etc.) and action-oriented (e.g., relax my body, choose my state, make a connection with each person in the room, etc.).

4. Play with possibilities

Now that you know what you want to do and how you want things to go, take some time to consider other options. What might go wrong? What might go more right than you expected? How else could you get where you want to go? How can you have more fun, do less and get further?

Part II: A.C.T.

After you've done your P.R.E.P., you're ready to get into action. Here are three quick steps to success. . . .

1. Aim for the specific target or intentions you created in your P.R.E.P.

As we discussed throughout the first part of this book, it is easier to get what you really want than what you think you can get. Put that principle into action by making sure you're aiming yourself in the direction you really want to go.

2. Choose your state

What is your ideal performance state for this project, meeting, or call? Summon up your favorite memories of being in that state until you can begin to feel those feelings in your body now.

3. Take the first step

People often get obsessed with planning seven steps ahead, as if life was a chess game and we were all in training to be grand masters. While advance planning is certainly a useful skill, life has a funny way of making moves we couldn't have predicted. As Ken Roberts says in *The Rich Man's Secret*:

"Take the first step—no more, no less—and the next will be revealed."

Part III: L.E.A.R.N.

"Wisdom comes from experience, but experience alone is not enough. Experience anticipated and experience revisited is the true source of wisdom."
— John Grinder

Regardless of which actions you take, your ability to learn from everything that happens to you is the only competitive advantage you will ever need. Here's a simple way to make sure you are learning what will be most useful to you as you move forward:

1. Look back over what happened

Take a few moments to review the highs and lows of your actions and the results you created through them.

2. Evaluate against specific criteria

If you haven't decided on specific criteria by which to measure your performance, you'll wind up judging yourself according to how you "feel" about what happened, which is a notoriously fickle barometer. Remember those intentions you set when you did your P.R.E.P.? Now you get to use them to evaluate your performance!

3. Acknowledge your mistakes

Let me guess . . . did everything not go according to plan? That's because it's not supposed to, at least not when you're dealing with something as unpredictable as living creatures. It's like my physics teacher used to say: "If you kick a football, you can predict exactly where it's going to land by calculating mass, wind speed, velocity, friction, and a host of other variables. If you kick a dog, there's no telling where he'll wind up." (He wasn't a very nice man, but it's a good point!)

4. Reinforce what you did well

When Vince Lombardi took over as coach of the Green Bay Packers, he insisted that the game highlight films be edited so that only the successful, well-run plays were shown. He wanted the players to reinforce what worked by watching themselves successful, game after game. The result? Two Super Bowl championships, an American footballing dynasty and a coaching legend.

5. Next time, I will . . .

Everyone always talks about "the benefit of hindsight" as if it's a bad thing. Knowing what you know now, having learned what you've learned, what do you want to do differently next time?

Let's put it all together into a simple experiment . . .

From theory to practice . . .

The Success Cycle in Action

1. Choose a meeting, phone call, or project that you can work on tomorrow. This can be anything from a sales call with a major account to a negotiation with your

three-year-old over how many vegetables she'll eat with dinner in order to get dessert.

2. Take at least one minute with each step of your preparation. **P**lan, **R**ehearse, **E**stablish your intentions and **P**lay!

3. When it's time to take action, **A**im at your desired result, **C**hoose your state and **T**ake the first step.

4. Notice the results your action(s) have created. Make a mental or physical note of both what happened and how you felt.

5. Look back and **E**valuate against the criteria you created in your prep. **A**cknowledge your mistakes, **R**einforce what worked and **N**ext time, decide what you're going to work on doing even better.

Of course, like anything else, successful learning and learning to succeed are skills to be mastered, not inherent gifts that some people have and others lack. In the next chapter, I'll take you through some of the most useful strategies for accelerating your mastery of any skill you choose. . . .

CHAPTER NINE

SKILL

Information	**Skill**	Belief
Wellbeing	Other people	Motivation
Time	Money	Fear

Doing your life

"You are creating your next moment. That is what's real."
— Sarah Paddison

ONE OF THE BIG DEBATES among spiritual philosophers, religious fundamentalists, and traditional psychologists is to what extent people create their own reality.

At one end of the debate are those people who believe that we create 100% of our reality, from the horrors of 9/11 to the thrill of winning the lottery, and everything in between. Since we are creating our reality through our thoughts, words, and actions, the most important thing for us to do is to be vigilant in choosing what we think, say, and do.

At the other end are people who believe in absolute karma, fate, or destiny. Since everything is preordained and predestined, there's no point in trying to change anything (but if you do succeed in changing anything, that was predestined, too). According to these philosophies, it doesn't particularly matter what we think, say, or do. Our job is simply to be who we are, do what we do, and enjoy the ride.

Having spent the past 18 years or so exploring spiritual philosophy while practicing and teaching practical psychology, I have settled on a useful distinction somewhere between the two extremes:

We are creating 100% of our experience of reality, moment by moment by moment.

In other words, whether or not we are the creators of our reality, we are absolutely the creators of our experience of that reality. Regardless of what is going on with you right now, you can enhance the quality of your experience (and therefore the quality of your life) by making different choices in this very moment.

If you are experiencing an area of your life as easy, joyful, meaningful, and productive, that's because you're "doing" ease, joy, meaning, and productivity.

If you are experiencing an area of your life as hard, problematic and filled with suffering, it's because in that moment you are "doing" hard, "doing" problems and "doing" suffering.

How do we "do" a problem, state, or condition?

Well, here's how I might talk it through with one of my NLP or coaching clients:

Client: (*standing with her head down, speaking softly*) I'm really depressed at the moment.

Me: How do you do that?

C: What do you mean?

Me: Well, let's say I was going to take over your problems for a day. After all, everyone deserves a day off now and then, don't you agree?

C: Um . . . okay . . .

Me: I'm an actor, so I'll get hair and makeup and wardrobe, and I'll look just like you. And I'll work on the voice and the walk as well, so nobody will even notice you're taking the day off.

C: I'm a woman.

Me: Not a problem. I went to drama school for three years.

C: Ouch! Okay, so you're me for the day.

Me: Right. Now how do I do "depressed" the way you do it?

C: I don't know. It just happens.

Me: Well, I know it seems that way, but would it "just happen" if I stood on tiptoe and started barking like a dog? *(I then stand on tiptoe and begin barking like a dog. Really.)*

C: *(laughing)* No. You'd probably need to stand like this. *(She demonstrates an exaggeration of her previous posture: shoulders drooped, head down, eyes down and to the right. She sighs heavily.)*

Me: Okay, so I can do that. *(I copy her posture.)* Now, how do I know when to do that? Do I jump out of bed and begin drooping? *(Again, I exaggerate her posture until I'm moving around the room like Quasimodo in* The Hunchback of Notre Dame.*)*

C: Nooo! *(laughing and speaking to me as if I'm an idiot, which is entirely possible at this point)* You lie in bed, open your eyes, and begin to think about all the things you've got to do today and how hard it's going to be.

Me: *(trying it on in my mind)* Do I do it like a movie or a series of still photographs, like in a slideshow?

C: Oh, it's definitely a movie, and I'm sitting in the front row, looking up at it. And for a soundtrack, you replay your mother's voice telling you how worthless you are and that you'll never amount to anything on an endless tape loop.

Me: *(still trying it on in my mind)* Wow—that really works—I feel horrible!

C: *(laughing)* No kidding!

Me: So, are you going to do it again tomorrow morning?

C: Hmm . . . *(actually considering it)*. No, I think I'll try beginning the day by thinking about the people I'm looking forward to being with and listening to my favorite music. I might even experiment with sitting up straighter than normal throughout the day and "keeping my chin up," literally and figuratively.

Me: Let me know how it goes!

In other words, whatever you're doing is a skill, and while every person is different, I have never yet met anyone who is not "doing" their life. Because we are (mostly) unconscious of how we do things, it often feels like they just happen to us. But as we slow the process down and add some nonjudgmental awareness to the process, we can begin to "do life" differently, make different choices, and create a completely different experience of being alive.

From theory to practice . . .

Doing Your Life

1. Think about a situation in your life that has felt as if it's just happening to you—a problem, feeling, or condition that you "have."

2. Imagine I'm there with you. If you had to teach me to do that problem, feeling, or condition in exactly the way that you do it, what would I need to know?

   Think about:

   - *When do I do it? When do I not do it? How do I know it's time to start or stop?*

   - *How do I use my body to do it? Does it matter how I sit or stand? What's my tempo? How quickly or deeply do I breathe?*

   - *What kinds of pictures do I need to make in my head? What kinds of things do I need to say to myself? What mental movies do I play? What do I use for soundtracks?*

3. When you have a real sense that you are "doing" the situation, ask yourself if you want to continue doing it or if you are ready to stop.

4. What would you like to do instead?

   Say to yourself, *"I've been doing _____; now I'm going to experiment with doing _____ instead."*

The enjoyment cycle

When I lead skill development trainings, one of the core models I share is what I call "the enjoyment cycle." Here's an easy way to think about it:

If you do more and more of something, do you tend to get better at it or worse?

Most people recognize that the more they do something, the better at it they get. So let me ask you another question:

If you are getting better and better at something, do you tend to get better result or worse?

No real mystery here. Higher levels of skill lead to better results pretty much every time. Next question:

If you are getting better and better results, do you tend to enjoy something more or less?

For most people, the answer is that the better results you create, the more you enjoy the process of creating them. Here's one final question:

If you enjoy doing something, do you tend to do more of it or less?

Unless you're just being contrary, the answer is that we invariably do more of what we enjoy doing and less of what we don't.

So, to review, the enjoyment cycle for skill development goes something like this:

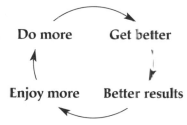

And of course the opposite is equally true:

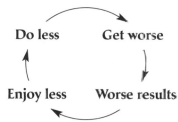

But since we can jump into the loop at any point, where's the easiest and most impactful place for us to place our attention? What's the best way to develop any skill?

Let's check out the options. . . .

1. Do more

I used to believe the secret of successfully developing any skill was simple: do the thing you want to learn every single day. Do it every day, do it every day, do it every day. The only problem is, how often have you set out on a new training regimen only to give up long before achieving any significant progress? This is why it is in the early days of learning a new skill, long before the motivation of noticeable improvement begins to kick in, that most people give up.

2. Get better

Bizarre as it may seem, this is not uncommon motivational wisdom. Well-meaning though it may be to encourage someone to "do it better next time," it is a piece of advice that ranks alongside "just try harder" as difficult to act on and even more difficult to quantify.

3. Get better results

In school, were you ever encouraged to "get better grades?" If so, you may have attempted to work even harder in order to meet the wonderfully high expectations that were held of you. Trouble is, if at first you don't succeed, the tendency is to give up. "After all, what's the point?" we may say. "I'm not getting any better."

4. Enjoy it more

Is it possible to enjoy learning more in any moment? Let's find out . . .

Give yourself a rating from 1 to 10 as to how much you are enjoying reading this section of the book, where 1 is "*Oh my God . . . I've never been so bored in my entire life*" and 10 is "*Wow! This is way better than sex!*"

If you had to increase your score by one point right now, how could you do it?

For example, if you scored yourself at 4, you could probably get your enjoyment up to 5 by shifting in your seat to make yourself more comfortable, taking a nice deep breath, and thinking a happy thought. You might be able to move from 7 to 8 by taking a moment to think of a time where you were feeling really relaxed, perhaps on a beach or just hanging out with your friends. You might even be able to take yourself all the way up to 10 just by putting a smile on your face and deciding to have fun playing around with these ideas instead of taking them all so seriously.

The point is, however much you are enjoying what you are doing, you can almost always find a way to enjoy doing it more. The more you enjoy it, the more you'll tend to do it. The more you do it, the better you'll get. The better you get, the better results you'll begin to create. And the better and better your results, the more you'll enjoy engaging in the skill that creates them.

From theory to practice . . .

Have Fun and Learn Heaps

1. Pick a skill where you would like to take your ability to the next level.

2. Give yourself a rating for how much you currently enjoy practicing the skill on a scale from one to ten.

3. If you knew that the more fun you have doing something (i.e., the more you enjoy doing it), the faster and better you will learn, what might you do differently than you are doing now?
   Example: *Learning to sing*
   Currently about a 5. If I knew that the more fun I had learning how to sing the faster and better I would learn, I might:
   - *get myself a collection of only songs I like to sing*
   - *ignore the "experts" and practice singing songs at least as often as I practiced singing scales*
   - *get a karaoke machine and throw a party*

The five stages of mastery

At some point in your education, you may have come across a learning model that breaks the development of any skill into four stages:

Unconscious Incompetence
↓
Conscious Incompetence
↓
Conscious Competence
↓
Unconscious Competence

To illustrate the model, let's take the analogy of learning to drive a car. In the *unconscious incompetence* stage, we have watched others drive, but have no real awareness of how difficult or complex a task it really is.

As we begin to learn the skill of driving, we become *conscious* of our own *incompetence*, overwhelmed by the sudden awareness of how much we have to learn.

Next comes the *conscious competence* stage, where we silently talk ourselves through the process of shifting gears and three-point turns.

Finally, the day comes where we suddenly "wake up" at the wheel and realize we've been driving down the freeway at 65 mph without even noticing. Our *competence* has become *unconscious*, which is to say we no longer need to pay conscious attention to our task in order to be effective.

Is unconscious competence the ultimate goal of learning and skill development?

Certainly there are numerous actors, athletes, artists, musicians and craftspeople who take a strange sort of pride in not knowing how they do what they do and avoid analyzing their process so as not to "disturb the magic."

There is, however, a fifth stage in the skill development process—a stage where we can both act without thinking and analyze, understand, explain, and improve on what we do. It is only in this fifth stage, which I call *Conscious Unconscious Competence*, that we can truly express our mastery.

From theory to practice . . .

Skill Mastery

1. Choose a skill that you would like to master.

2. Assess yourself from 1 to 5 to indicate where you are in the learning cycle. (1 = Unconscious Incompetence; 5 = Conscious Unconscious Competence)

3. Once you've assessed where you are, here's how to get to the next level:

If you are in Stage One:
Spend at least an hour this weekend practicing the skill, no matter how horrifying the results. If you would like to paint, but never

have, grab a brush and give it a go. Always fancied yourself as a novelist? Write Chapter 1. Ever wondered what it would be like to drive a racing car? Be safe, get professional training and see what you can do.

If you are in Stage 2:
Many people find conscious incompetence so frustrating and ego-damaging they give up rather than persist. My prescription is simple: have fun! Focus on enjoyment over results and allow your natural drive for pleasure to carry you through this necessary part of your journey to mastery.

If you are in Stage 3:
Repetition is the mother of skill, but you can enhance your repetition by practicing in a physiology of mastery. In order to do this simply practice now with all the casual ease and focused relaxation you'll bring to the task once you've mastered it!

If you are in Stage 4:
Now is the time for you go out and teach what you have learned in order to cement your own understanding. Be sure your student asks you lots of "what," "why," and "how" questions. Don't let yourself get away with "You'll just get a feel for it after a while." (Read the following section on "Training your replacement" for more on this.)

If you are in Stage 5:
Celebrate!

Training your replacement

When I was trying to earn the money to go to drama school in London, I took a job in the shipping department of an engineering firm. My responsibilities included building oversized wooden boxes for the odd-shaped parts we sent out, inventorying and packing the parts, loading them onto trucks for delivery, and inventorying and unpacking any new stock that came in. My colleagues were mostly World War II veterans approaching retirement age who delighted in telling me stories of when they went to London for the first time some forty years earlier (and in teasing me for reading Victor Hugo instead of the sports pages).

The only time I truly enjoyed my job was in the time between giving notice and leaving; a two-week stretch during which my number one responsibility was to train my replacement. Rick actually *wanted* to work there, a concept that shocked me at the time but which I now realize is precisely why he was so much better than me at the job.

During this time, I would walk Rick through a typical day, answering his continual questions as to what exactly I was doing, why I was doing it, and how specifically it needed to be done. The funny thing was that in the process of explaining to him the "what," "why," and "how" of the job, what had become automatic was once again brought into my consciousness and I began to have fun, quickly discovering that there were far more efficient and effective ways of doing the job than I had previously thought of.

I have since learned that this process of "training your replacement" is a great way to develop your skill in any activity. And what's more, it works whether you are teaching a real person or an imagined one . . .

From theory to practice . . .

The Imaginary Employee

1. Choose an activity to experiment with. In my experience, it is usually best to start with an extreme—either extremely mundane (washing dishes, preparing dinner, watching TV, etc.) or extremely important (playing an instrument, making a sale, coaching a client, etc.).

2. The next time you are engaged in the activity, begin to train an imaginary employee in how to do whatever it is. You can do this either in your mind or out loud. Be sure to tell them what you are doing, why you are doing it and how specifically it is done. You can go into as much or as little detail as you like. Work from the assumption that they know absolutely nothing about how you do what you do.

Here's an example of how I might train my imaginary employee to open a locked door:

"Take the key in your hand between your thumb and forefinger. Look at the shape of the lock to give yourself a clue as to which way up to hold the key. When you're ready, press the key firmly into the lock. If it fits easily, you will hear or feel it slot into place. If not, remove the key, turn it the other way and try again. Turn the key about half a turn to the right until you hear a solid click and/or the door handle begins to turn. The door is now unlocked."

Here's one last model you can use that can save you massive amounts of time in the development of your new skills. . . .

Borrowing excellence

"Human beings, who are almost unique in having the ability to learn from the experience of others, are also remarkable for their disinclination to do so."
— Douglas Adams

In order to achieve pretty much anything we want in life, we must have at least four things:

1. A Goal or set of goals (direction)
2. A clear Evidence procedure for how we will know we are on- or off-track toward reaching that goal.
3. A list of Action steps toward achieving that goal
4. A Recovery strategy for what we will do when we find we are off-track

These four elements, which make up what I call the G.E.A.R. model, allow us to benefit quickly from the skill of someone else and to learn the difference between what we are doing to get something that we want and what someone who is more successful might be doing in the same context.

They also allow us to learn from our own best practices: what we do in those areas of our life where we are extremely effective as opposed to those in which we are generally pretty ineffective.

For example, I used to wonder why I was so much more successful as a trainer than I was in marketing my trainings. I did a quick G.E.A.R. analysis on what was different between how I operated in the two contexts. Here's what came out:

Effective Context: Training

• Goals:
  – *to assist people in making shifts and getting what they want*
  – *to share the best information I have available*
  – *to love them unconditionally*
  – *to believe in their ability to make new choices in every moment*

• Evidence:
  – *verbal feedback (success stories, etc.)*
  – *nonverbal feedback (nodding heads, smiling faces, etc.)*
  – *the "click" (an internal sense of being "in the flow" of things)*

- **Actions:**
  - *tell stories*
  - *make jokes*
  - *set up and run exercises*
  - *give information*
  - *ask and answer questions*
  - *review and test learning, comprehension, and mastery of material*

- **Recovery:**
  - *keep going, keep going, keep going*
  - *get specific*
  - *work one-on-one (coach)*
  - *refer to assistants*
  - *do something completely different, usually physical to break the "stuck" state*
  - *pick out the most difficult example in the room and work with that (once that works, everyone else will follow)*

Notice the "subtle" difference in what was at that point my ineffective strategy:

Ineffective Context: Marketing Trainings

- **Goals:**
  - *to sell that training*

- **Evidence:**
  - *people show up and pay money*

- **Actions:**
  - *print and post brochures*
  - *answer questions and give info in person and on the phone*

- **Recovery:**
  - *give away free places*
  - *cancel the training*

Of course, the real magic didn't come just from noticing the differences, but from "shifting G.E.A.R.s"—transferring my own best practices from my effective context to my ineffective context.

For example, I immediately expanded my marketing Goals to include sharing information more freely. I also decided to love the people I was marketing to. (In the past they needed to pay me before I started loving them, which I came to realize was an entirely different profession!)

I expanded my Evidence procedure to begin noticing how people were responding to my pitch nonverbally, and I began tuning into my inner world to see if I was "in the flow" of the marketing river or struggling my way along the river-bank.

I took new Actions and began both telling jokes and stories as part of the marketing process and asking questions as well as answering them.

And when things weren't going according to plan, I implemented the radical Recovery strategy of getting specific, deliberately rising to the most difficult challenge and "keep going, keep going, keep going!"

What was the difference that made the difference?

For me it turned out to be remembering to love people whether they bought from me or not and to keep going toward my goals even when it seemed as though I wasn't going to reach them.

Not only did I sell out my very next training. I began enjoying the process of marketing the trainings almost as much as delivering them, something that seemed an impossible dream before engaging in this process.

From theory to practice . . .

Shifting G.E.A.R.s

1. Think of an area of your life where you would like to be more effective.
   Examples:
   Making money, getting along with family or co-workers, making presentations, etc.

2. Now, think of an area of your life where you already excel; something you do extremely well and/or effectively.
   Examples:
   Your profession, your hobby, getting along with your friends, telling jokes, etc.

3. Create a G.E.A.R. analysis for each context.

   Goals
   What are your goals in this context? What is it that you are setting out to achieve? What results are you intending to create?

Evidence
How do you know that you have reached your goals? How do you know when you are on- or off-track? What do you see, hear, and feel?

Actions
What do you do to achieve your goals? What actions do you take?

Recovery
What do you do when you are off-track or not achieving your desired results? How do you respond to the situation, internally and externally?

4. Finally, shift G.E.A.R.s: take as many of the things you do when you are being effective and incorporate them in the context where you used to struggle. In some cases you may completely replace your old strategy; in others you will simply expand and add to it.

5. Repeat steps 1–4 with a model of excellence in the area you want to improve. Elicit your own G.E.A.R. strategy, then ask them the above questions to elicit theirs. You may be surprised and delighted by how much you learn!

When you are willing to shift G.E.A.R.s, you can get where you want to go faster than you may have believed possible. Which brings us to our very next obstacle . . .

CHAPTER 10

BELIEF

Information	Skill	**Belief**
Wellbeing	Other people	Motivation
Time	Money	Fear

A story about nuns

"The word 'belief' is a somewhat vague concept to most people, even when they'll gladly go out and kill for one."
— Richard Bandler

Our beliefs are our stories and explanations about why our lives unfold the way they do. Shifts in our belief systems can happen gradually and incrementally over time or in a dramatic "flash" of new insight. They can also make the difference between staying stuck or breaking free of limited ideas and perspectives.

One of my most powerful lessons in the power of a belief to hold someone back came when I was teaching an NLP Foundation Skills seminar for a group of educators in Bristol. After four days of intensive training in managing their emotional states, the final exam was for each person to get up on stage in front of the whole group and tell a joke with confidence and ease.

Now, that might sound like a rather simple final exam for those of you who went to a university, but you'd be amazed at what happens to people's nervous systems when they stand up in front of a room full of people and try to be funny. (If you're not amazed yet, why don't you stand up right now and tell a joke to whoever's in the room with you. You can carry on reading when you're done. . . .)

Well, there was one woman in the room who wouldn't do it— she was absolutely adamant. She said, "I am not getting up there on that stage. I will not get up there under any circumstances."

What seemed odd to me is that she didn't appear to be scared—she just refused to get up and tell a joke. So I started to talk to her about it, and I asked her why it was that she didn't want to complete the assignment. Her answer was, "Because if I go up there and tell a joke, the nuns will have won."

I have to say that this was one answer that I really hadn't expected, so I asked her to explain. And it turned out that as a girl, she had gone to a Catholic school and she felt that she had been made to do many things that she didn't want to do by the nuns. On the day of the final exams for her year, she summoned up her courage, walked out of the school, and never went back. She said that for her, that decision to leave was a defining moment in her life. She had finally overcome the nuns and established her independence as a woman.

In order to understand how such a seemingly positive experience (establishing her independence) had become one of the bars in her mental prison, let's take a quick look at how the process of "make-believing" actually works. . . .

The self-fulfilling prophecy

"A map is not the territory it represents,
but if correct, it has a similar structure to the territory,
which accounts for its usefulness."
— Count Alfred Korzybski

Dr. Leonard Orr, the founder of the American rebirthing movement, says that within every one of us there are two people— one is a thinker, the other a prover.

The thinker, who roughly corresponds to your conscious mind, is that part of you that thinks up ideas and generates possibilities.

The prover, who approximates to your unconscious mind, has the job of collecting just the right facts to support whatever it is that the thinker thinks.

"Orr's Law," as described by author Robert Anton Wilson, is this:

Whatever the thinker thinks, the prover proves.

In other words, although we all know "the map is not the territory" (and the menu is not the meal), instead of trying to align our map with the reality of the world, most of us wind up trying to fit reality into the world of our map. We do this by focusing in on whatever reinforces our preexisting notions and judgements about how the world works and filtering out anything that seems to contradict them.

So as soon as we have a thought that hooks our attention or get an idea that captures our imagination, another part of us immediately begins searching for any evidence that supports the idea and filtering out any evidence that doesn't. Because we are continually interpreting our experiences to fit our mental maps, over time our map *becomes* the territory.

This is why unless we carefully examine the ideas before our minds, we are liable to interpret the events of our lives through some rather odd filters. And the more emotionally charged an experience, the more apt we are to generalize our interpretation of it into a new belief or "rule for living."

This is what happened to our ex-Catholic school girl. After her highly emotional experience of breaking free, her "prover" kicked in and she began unconsciously collecting evidence that supported the generalization that completing anything meant compliance with an unjust authority.

Sure enough, when I asked her about her history, she had left her last job when she was due for a promotion and she had ended her most significant relationship less than a month before her wedding day. Rather than causing her to change or even question her belief, those disappointing experiences had instead become more links in a chain of evidence "proving" that the only way to assert her independence was to walk away from anything that challenged or threatened it.

In the end, by using some of the same techniques I will be sharing with you in this chapter, she was able to step out beyond her limiting belief and see that there were many ways of being free without running away from life's inevitable challenges. She then stood up on stage and told what I still think is a great (if somewhat politically incorrect) joke:

After a long, hard day at the convent, a nun was relaxing in a warm, soothing bath when a knock came at the bathroom door.

"Who is it?" asked the nun.

"It's John the blind man," replied a gruff, masculine voice.

Too weary to get out of the bath, the nun decided it would be okay if she let him come in.

"It's unlocked," she called out, closing her eyes and returning to her reverie.

The man walked through the door.

"Great tits, sister," he said. "Now where do you want me to put these blinds?"

From theory to practice . . .

Putting the Thinker and Prover to Work for You

1. Choose an outcome, intention or goal to focus on.
   Example:
   To live with passion and thrive regardless of how much sleep I get each night.

2. Begin the process of "proving" to yourself that you can have what you want. To do this, complete the following sentence as many times as you want in relation to your goal:

   **I know I can have this in my life because . . . ;
   for example, . . .**

   Example:
   My intention is to live with energy and thrive regardless of how much sleep I get.

   – *I know I can create this in my life because I see other people thriving on far less than the "official" eight hours a night; for example, most U.S. presidents and world leaders, successaholics like Donald Trump, people in the caring professions like Mother Teresa, etc.*

   – *I know I can create this in my life because I'm willing to make changes in my schedule to accommodate naps and other restful activities and to take really good care of myself in other ways (diet, exercise, etc.). For example, I scheduled and took a 20-minute nap into my afternoon today, I ate a light lunch, I'm drinking eight glasses of fresh water a day, etc.*

   – *I know I can create this in my life because I can change my energy levels simply by deciding to be energized. For example, when I woke up this morning, I felt really awake until I saw the that it was only 5:30 A.M., then I started to get sleepy. As soon as I realized my eyes were still blurry and saw that it was actually 6:30 A.M., I perked back up. I know the clock didn't make me tired or wake me up, so I know that I can make that difference for myself on purpose.*

Please note that it is not necessary for you to believe what you write in step two. This is a process of "make believe" that will ultimately culminate in your making new beliefs about what is possible for you.

Three schools for learning helplessness

"The secret of success—fall down seven times; stand up eight."
— Chinese proverb

Of all the beliefs and stories we make up about how the world "really" works, the most limiting ones are those that take several isolated incidences of failure and generalize them to mean that we will be unsuccessful in all areas of our lives for all time. This phenomenon is known in psychology as "learned helplessness"— the self-fulfilling belief that nothing we do will make any difference to the quality and circumstances of our lives.

In my experience, there are three primary ways in which people learn that there's nothing they can do and no point in even trying. I like to think of these as the Elephant School, the Piranha School, and the School of Common Knowledge.

1. The Elephant School

"How is it," I wondered as a child looking at a picture book of a circus, "that the great big elephant is tied to a tiny wooden stake, yet doesn't run away?" The answer comes in careful training. From the moment an elephant can stand, she is tethered to a wooden stake, which at that time is sufficient to hold her. Early on, she learns that it's not worth the effort to try and pull away and that learning lasts for life. When she's older, even though she could now break free without breaking a sweat, she has never even tried.

When I was a boy, my father seemed to know everything about how to fix things. Anything that went wrong with our house was quickly and effortlessly taken care of. In my 20s, when my wife and I bought our first home, I felt incompetent to change a lightbulb let alone fix a leaky roof. I decided there was no point in my even attempting to fix things—the DIY gene had clearly skipped a generation. Twenty years, several houses, and hundreds of repairs later, I now realize that my father's abilities were skills to learn, not gifts to inherit, and that I must now appear to my son to be the "fix-it" genius that my father was to me.

The fact is, when we are young, we are genuinely physically, mentally, and emotionally incompetent to perform many of the tasks we observe as second nature to the "grown-ups" around us. Without proper context and explanation, the Elephant School teaches us to believe that our early limitations are permanent parts of our identity, not temporary challenges to be overcome and outgrown through training, time, and experience.

2. The Piranha School

While I rarely see animal-rights activists protesting the mistreatment of piranha fish (not cuddly enough, I guess), there was an interesting experiment done on them. These cute little fish (who only rarely eat their own young) were placed in a large tank, separated from their "food" by a see-through glass divider. After several days of ramming their adorable little heads against the glass, the piranha gave up. The glass wall was then removed and the piranha starved to death while swimming freely in a world filled with food.

In essence, the Piranha School teaches us that if at first, second and third we don't succeed, we may as well give up. "After all," we may say to ourselves, "repeating the same actions but expecting different results is practically the definition of insanity."

The flaw in this line of thinking is that the nature of the universe is change, and an enterprise that at one time felt like banging our head against a brick (or glass) wall might now yield instant and marvellous rewards.

3. The School of Common Knowledge

The curriculum of the School of Common Knowledge is made up of our cultural mythology. Now, most people think about mythology as little more than ancient stories about forgotten gods. But included in the dictionary definition of a myth is "a popular belief or tradition that has grown up around something or someone, especially one embodying the ideals and institutions of a society—an unfounded or false notion."

So when I talk about cultural mythology, I'm not talking about winged horses, green knights, or hammer-throwing gods. I'm talking about the implicit and explicit beliefs, ideals, and rules for behavior that exist in any given culture.

Cultural mythology is spread in two primary ways:

a. Explicitly, through the explicit and often conflicting teachings of our parents, teachers and peers.

"Sex between a man and a woman can be absolutely wonderful—provided you get between the right man and the right woman."
— Woody Allen

Sex, drugs, and money are either good or bad depending on whether you chose to listen to your parents or your friends (and depending on which version of the myths of sex, drugs, and money they took on for themselves). What is important is not which side of the debate you tend to come down on, but the scope of your generalization.

Let's face it—the abuse or misuse of anything, including sex, drugs, and money, leads to bad things happening. The proper, judicious use can lead to good things. Where would the world be without procreation, penicillin and the money to promote continued learning and discovery? For that matter, what would your life be like without sex, money for food and the occasional aspirin?

b. Implicitly, through the heroes and villains of our culture and cultural stories, music and art.

"Give me the child until he is seven and I will give you the man."
— Jesuit maxim

Like evangelists preaching poverty and humility while living like rock stars, there is for me something comical about watching a group of rock stars like the Rolling Stones, who by all accounts have done pretty much what they love and want to do for the past 40 years, telling millions of adoring fans that they "can't always get what they want." But as with most of our cultural mythology, unless we are consciously examining the messages that are continually bombarding us in advertising, music, movies, and TV, we tend to take them in unquestioningly.

And that's the real danger of an implicit myth. Because nobody ever formalized it or put it into words for us, we've never had a chance to question it. It just went straight into your unconscious mind without getting filtered; something you just picked up subliminally from reading a book or watching a movie that came out of somebody's warped imagination. (And living and working in Hollywood, I've seen just how warped some of those imaginations can be!)

While both the Elephant and Piranha schools rely on your learning helplessness through experience, the School of Common Knowledge is staffed with teachers who pass the limitations of their own skills and experience on to their unwitting students.

Typical statement: This can't be done (is impossible, etc.).

Translation: I couldn't do this (if, in fact, I ever even tried).

Result: *A new generation of people who never try it, perpetuating the myth it can't be done.*

While it can be useful to learn from the experience of others, even the most well-intentioned failure can only teach you so much about what it takes to succeed.

Here is a story that I like to believe is true about how simple overcoming learned helplessness can really be, regardless of which school of thought you learned it in. . . .

The Room of 1,000 Demons

Every hundred years, members of an ancient order of monks gather in a secret location high in the Himalayas for a sacred ritual. For one day only, every monk is given the opportunity for instantaneous enlightenment. All they have to do is to walk through a room known only as "The Room of 1,000 Demons"—and come out alive!

Rumor has it that The Room of 1,000 Demons is pitch-black and filled, as you might expect, with 1,000 of the nastiest demons from the netherworlds of hell. These demons appear to you in the guise of your biggest and worst fears—giant spiders, poisonous snakes, sheer precipices, or whatever they sense would fill your heart with terror.

There are only two rules to the challenge: first, once you enter, no one can come in and rescue you; second, it is impossible to leave by the door you entered. For those few brave souls who dare to face their fears in pursuit of happiness, success, and enlightenment, there are also two bits of advice:

1. *Remember that whatever you think is going on around you, it is just a projection of your own mind.*

2. *No matter what you think you see, hear, think, or feel, keep your feet moving. If you keep your feet moving, you will eventually come out the other side.*

How to spot a limiting belief

Think about one of the things you really want. Do you believe you can have it yet? If not, your reasons for believing that are the very beliefs that are holding you back from really going after whatever it is.

From theory to practice . . .

Why You Can't Have What You Want

1. Choose something you really want but don't think you can have, either because it's "impossible" or it feels out of your reach.

2. Ask yourself, "Why can't I have this?"

   Write at least a paragraph explaining why you believe you don't yet have what it is you really want in your life.

   You can also ask yourself:
   • Why shouldn't I have this?
   • Why don't I already have this?
   • What stops me from having this?

3. Look through what you've written and highlight any beliefs, assumptions or statements of fact that make your current lack of success seem "reasonable."
   Example:
   What do I want?
   To write and publish a best-selling book.

   Why can't I have it?
   I've never written a book before, <u>first books are nearly impossible to sell</u>, there are so many books out there already, <u>do I really have anything worthwhile to say?</u> I'm not desperate enough. I don't want it bad enough, I don't know anything about the publishing world and <u>if things don't come easily for me I tend to give up</u>

4. Identify whether your statements are of the Elephant, Piranha, or Common Knowledge school of learned helplessness.

Examples:
- *First books are nearly impossible to sell—Common Knowledge.*
- *Do I really have anything worthwhile to say?—Elephant.*
- *If things don't come easily for me I tend to give up—Piranha.*

5. Finally, for each statement, make a plausible case for the opposition. The easiest way to do this is to enrol your "prover" to seize on any piece of evidence that would support the opposite assumption.

Examples:

Limiting assumption—*First books are nearly impossible to sell.*

Opposite assumption—*First books are the easiest to sell.*

Evidence—Everyone who's ever been published has sold their "first book," even if it wasn't the first book they ever wrote. When you

don't have a "reputation," you have absolute freedom for the only time in your career to establish your style and your voice. Some authors" first books have sold nearly a million copies when they were still relative unknowns.

Once you've identified the beliefs and assumptions that are most holding you back, you can use this next tool to propel yourself even further forward on the path to your "Wow!" goals and inspired dreams. . . .

The incisive question

> *"A question works because, unlike a statement which requires you to obey, a question requires you to think. The mind seems to prefer to think, not to obey."*
> — Nancy Kline

In her excellent book *Time to Think: Listening to Ignite the Human Mind*, management consultant Nancy Kline introduces a tool she calls "the incisive question."

Rather than challenge an assumption or belief head-on, the incisive question makes the assumption temporarily irrelevant, allowing you to step beyond your old way of thinking into a whole new world of possibilities.

You can use the incisive question as a way to reactivate the mental and emotional resources that believing we can't have what we want switches off. As you explore what life would be like out

beyond the edges of your limiting assumptions, you will often
receive a rush of inspired ideas and proactive actions.

From theory to practice . . .

The Incisive Question

1. Think about something that you want but are having difficulty
   getting
   Example:
   A fantastic new relationship.

2. What might you be assuming that's holding you back from
   getting it?
   Examples.
   I'm not good enough, I'm too old, nobody would want me, etc.

3. Choose the assumption that feels the most "bedrock"—the one
   that you sense is at the heart of the problem. What for you
   would be the positive opposite of that assumption?
   Examples:
   Limiting assumption—*I'm too old.*
   Possible positive opposites—*I'm the perfect age; it's not about age, it's
   about experience.*
   Limiting assumption—*I'm not good enough.*
   Possible positive opposites—*I am exactly what my perfect partner is
   looking for; I am worthy of having a great relationship.*

4. Frame an incisive question using one of the following forms:
   'If I absolutely knew for a fact that [positive opposite of your
   limiting assumption], what ideas would I have about [your goal,
   situation or challenge]?"
   Example:
   "*If I absolutely knew for a fact that it's not about age, it's about
   experience, what ideas would I have about creating a fantastic
   relationship?*"
   or
   "If I absolutely knew for a fact that [positive opposite of your
   limiting assumption], what would I do to create or bring about
   [your goal, situation or challenge]?"
   Example:
   "*If I absolutely knew for a fact that I am exactly what my perfect
   partner is looking for, what would I do to bring about a fantastic
   relationship?*"

The "right" question is the one that feels right to you. Play around with different positive opposites until you find the one that fits well and unleashes your creativity and inspiration.

5. Follow through on your most inspired ideas and actions.

Of course, even when you believe that you *can* have what you want, you won't get very far if you're spending the majority of your time trying desperately to cope with the stresses and strains of your everyday life. That's why dealing with this next obstacle is crucial in keeping your feet moving and your eyes on the prize. . . .

CHAPTER 11

WELL-BEING

Information	Skill	Belief
Well-being	Other people	Motivation
Time	Money	Fear

Stress relief for busy people

*"Many men go fishing their entire lives
without knowing that it is not fish
that they are after."*
— Henry David Thoreau

WHEN EMPEROR SAGA OF JAPAN traveled, his every day was planned down to the minute. One day, he was scheduled to meet a delegation of monks and tour a local Buddhist temple for exactly ten minutes. The emperor and his entourage entered the temple precisely on time, but the building was empty and the monks were nowhere to be found.

The aide responsible for setting the emperor's schedule alternated between desperately searching for the missing delegation and making panicked excuses for their absence, but the emperor simply stood in the center of the room and said nothing. Exactly ten minutes later, the emperor indicated that it was now time to leave. On their way out of the temple, Saga turned to his aide and said, "I enjoyed that appointment very much—please schedule me another one tomorrow."

For myself, there are numerous times where I get so caught up in the busy-ness of my life that I feel I'm stuck on a treadmill going at ever faster speeds.

Fortunately, I have learned a number of ways to "step off the treadmill" and stop running, at least long enough to catch up with myself. Once I'm back in my body and the present moment, I can refocus on what really matters to me and remember the best of what I already know.

1. Take a day out

Taking a day out to overview your life direction, meaning, and purpose is one of the most powerfully productive things you can do, so even we confirmed busyholics can often justify it to ourselves.

For maximum impact, remove yourself completely from your home and work environment to minimize the siren call of busy distractions. Let's face it, it's easier to not answer e-mail or take phone calls when you're nowhere near a computer or telephone!

2. Slow down and smell the cheese

When my daughter Clara was two, her favorite song was called "Slow Down and Smell the Cheese." In the song, a frantic mouse named Tutter is running everywhere, pushing his cheese around the mouse hole, when he finally calls out in exhaustion, *"So little time, so much cheese to push around!"*

Just for today, spend time in the slow lane, literally and metaphorically. Leave yourself some extra time this morning and drive to work in the slow lane. If you travel by train or bus, make a deal with yourself that you will not rush to catch the next one, no matter what.

As the mouse's friend, a bear named, appropriately enough, Bear, sings, *"Life is so much better when you smell the feta!"*

By taking the time to slow down and catch up, what kind of day you have today is wonderfully up and down to you.

3. Recognize situational fatigue

There is a story told by the late hypnotherapist Dr. Milton Erickson of a housewife in the 1950s who suffered from a mysterious paralysis of the lower body that defied all traditional medical diagnosis. After working with her for a time, she appeared to have made a full recovery. Yet only a few hours after going home she had to be rushed back to the hospital.

When they asked her husband what had happened, he replied, "I don't know. One minute I was welcoming her home and telling her how glad I was that she would be able to take over the cooking and cleaning and looking after the children again, and the next minute she collapsed!"

It was my wife who first accused me of exhibiting similar behavior, pointing out that I consistently and mysteriously fell ill shortly before participating in what were to me objectionable tasks. Any time there was a job to be done that I didn't want to do, I would suddenly become exhausted, develop a headache, or worse. On one occasion, I nearly knocked myself unconscious at the outset of a major spring clean!

While at first I dismissed the notion out of hard (I am, after all, perfect), a quick trip down memory lane revealed to my horror that she was right. The problem was, I didn't do it on purpose—it was as though my body would shut itself down to prevent me from having to do what my personality could not find the courage to say "no" to.

In exploring this phenomenon in myself, I began to consistently come across it in others. A woman I know gets unbearable migraines before every family gathering, canceling her visits at the last minute so often it's become a family joke. A client with CFS (chronic fatigue syndrome, sometimes known as ME or more disparagingly "yuppie flu") discovered that her level of energy rose and fell according to the amount of permission she was willing to give herself to do only those aspects of her job she liked. And almost everyone I talked to shared the experience of looking at a huge stack of unfinished paperwork (like their taxes!) and suddenly feeling exhausted, regardless of the time of day or how much sleep they'd been getting.

Here are my three favorite theories for why what I call "situational fatigue" happens . . .

a. "Loser's limp"

The next time you are watching a competitive sporting event, keep an eye out for a phenomenon athletes, coaches, and sports psychologists refer to as loser's limp. If someone misses an easy catch or makes a mistake that enables their opponents to score a goal, you will notice they suddenly "come up lame," clearly exhibiting a previously unseen injury to their arms, legs, or head that obviously explains why they made such a bad mistake.

The theory behind loser's limp is that in our society, failure must always be accompanied by blame. In order to avoid being blamed, we "create" (usually unconsciously) an illness or injury on which we can blame our failure. The more comfortable we are with ourselves and the idea that no matter how well prepared we try to be, "stuff happens," the less need we have to blame ourselves when things go wrong.

b. Testosterone

Testosterone is an energy-enhancing drug naturally produced in the bodies of both men and women. High levels of testosterone are linked with aggression, strength, high sex drive, and euphoria; low levels of testosterone are linked with depression, impotence, and fatigue. What is interesting is that levels of testosterone in the body do not remain consistent over time, but vary from day to day, hour, to hour and situation to situation.

Studies measuring the levels of testosterone in athletes before and after competitive sporting events show that the victorious athletes nearly always exhibit significantly higher levels of testosterone than the losers, to the degree that without knowing anything about the event or the athletes involved you can accurately "pick the winner" by comparing their post-competitive testosterone levels.

One theory explaining this uses the example of the animal kingdom. In traditional "pack animal" cultures, the alpha males fight for leadership of the pack. After losing a battle, lowered testosterone levels in the defeated animal literally take away the will to fight, preventing further defeats and allowing time for wounds to heal. Similarly, the increased testosterone levels in the victor give it the renewed strength, confidence, and vigor to face any additional challengers.

In business, most of us have experienced both the "thrill of victory" (e.g., sales made, jobs won, deals completed) and the "agony of defeat" (e.g., clients lost, contracts broken). Think back to your energy levels the last time you "won" or "lost" at work and you may become aware of how these same forces are at work inside you.

c. Assertiveness and boundaries

When Milton Erickson began treating the paralyzed housewife after her sudden "relapse," he coached her on how to set up personal boundaries and on how to assert her right to say no when she didn't want to do something, even if it was part of her family's expectations of her as a wife and mother. He also taught her to recognize the numbness in her ankles as an early-warning signal that she was about to follow her social programming and not her heart.

For many of the people I've talked to, situational fatigue arises when saying no feels either too frightening or too embarrassing. Often, these feelings are tied in with the desire to be loved or to be seen as "a good person." As with Dr. Erickson's housewife, setting clear boundaries and learning how and when to say no can have a remarkably positive effect on people's health and energy.

But there is something else that is even more important than assertiveness and boundaries in consistently allowing us to perform at our best when it matters most . . .

Unleashing your natural energy

"Life begets life, energy begets energy.
It is by spending oneself that one becomes rich."
— Sarah Bernhardt

We are all continually engaged in the process of taking care of ourselves. But because society frowns on the idea of putting ourselves first (except in airplanes, where we're always reminded to put our own oxygen masks on before attending to the needs of our children), we tend to find subtle and not so subtle ways of manipulating the people around us in an attempt to meet our needs.

The trick is that when we begin to take better and better care of ourselves consciously, we stop needing to manipulate the world into doing it for us. The more cared for we are, the better we feel, the better we feel, the more energy we have, the more energy we have, the more capable we feel, the more capable we feel, the more capable we become, the more capable we become, the more we accomplish the more we accomplish, the better we feel. (Phew!)

I first came across the idea of creating a daily program for spiritual and inspirational self-care when I participated in an extraordinarily powerful 12-week program called "What One Person Can Do." The program leader asked a question that scared the living daylights out of me. I had joined the workshop seeking more of a sense of meaning and value in my work, and everything had been going along swimmingly until he asked:

> *"What activities do you (or could you) participate in*
> *on a regular basis which would come under*
> *the heading of 'spiritual self-care'?"*

For ten years or so, "spiritual" had become a bit of a dirty word in my mental house, a sort of backlash against a mid-1980s infatuation with New Age spirituality that nearly cost me my relationship and my sanity. When the question came up, I realized I was finally going to have to face up to the fact that my life had no spiritual component and possibly even do something about it. "*Oh God,*" I remember thinking. "*Not God again!*"

Dreading my turn to speak, I listened carefully to the other participants, hoping to be able to "borrow" someone else's answers as my own. One by one, people shared their practices—morning meditations on the beach (appealing, but rejected by me as too long a drive, even in Los Angeles); baths by candlelight (too girly); and various rituals involving altars and chanting (too weird).

When it was my turn, I racked my brains in a desperate attempt to come up with something I did that sounded vaguely spiritual. "Could you repeat the question?" I asked, stalling for time.

This time the question came out differently.

> *"What do you do (or could you do) on a regular basis that*
> *makes you feel inspired about yourself and your life?*
> *When in your life do you feel most content?*
> *Where in the world do you feel most at peace?"*

It was in considering the last question that I had my first epiphany—my equivalent to candles, incense, and the Pacific Ocean was the peace and contentment I felt sipping a cappuccino and dipping into a new release at my local bookstore.

While I was tempted to reject this as too "earthly" a practice to qualify for an ideal as noble as "spiritual self-care," it was then I had my second epiphany:

Spiritual self-care is no more or less
than the care and feeding of your spirit.

We all have the experience at times of being in "high spirits"; in the arts, a "spirited" performance is one filled with life. In fact, the word "spirit" comes from the Latin word for breath, so your spirit is quite literally your life force—that part of you that makes you feel alive. Spiritual self-care then is the deliberate in-spiring of ourselves—the daily focus on what it is that makes us come alive.

In that instant, I went from being someone who avoided anything that even smacked of God or spirituality to someone who designed his life around the care and feeding of his spirit. I begin most days with a spiritual self-care routine. I make time for inspirational input throughout the day and I finish my day with quiet reflection and contemplation. In return, I've become happier, healthier, more energetic, and my original longing for a sense of meaning and value in my life seems by and large a distant memory.

I have learned that for me, spiritual self-care is not just a good idea—it's the mother of all good ideas. I've also learned that whenever my clients or friends report that they are having a difficult week, there is only one question I need to ask—what are they doing for spiritual self-care at the moment? How much time are they taking for the care and feeding of their spirit?

Inevitably they tell me that they've "been too busy this week." Whenever I hear this I am reminded of the story of Mahatma Gandhi, who on reviewing a particularly full day reportedly said, "I have so much to do today, I will have to meditate twice as long."

Why is it so hard for so many of us to make time for breakfast, let alone prioritize taking the time to take really good care of our bodies, minds, and spirit?

Well, as I mentioned before, one reason is that we are taught from an early age to put others, needs before our own. Throughout childhood, most of us unconsciously absorbed the idea that our own wants and needs are secondary to those of our parents, siblings, friends, or neighbors. We are taught names for people around us who put themselves first, like "selfish" and "spoiled."

If we dared to insist that following our dreams and living our truth really was more important than the hopes and wishes of those around us, we were called different names, like "egotistical" and "self-centered."

And as adults, our conditioning now completed, we shame ourselves into feelings of worthlessness by comparing ourselves with a spiritual all-star team of "selfless saints" and finding the contribution we make with our lives sorely wanting.

But do you not take wonderful, extraordinary care of yourself because "you're no Gandhi, Mother Teresa, or Dalai Lama" or are you not a Gandhi, Mother Teresa, or Dalai Lama because you don't prioritize taking extraordinary care of yourself?

As Marianne Williamson famously said:

"We ask ourselves, 'Who am I to be brilliant, gorgeous, talented, fabulous?' Actually, who are you not to be? You are a child of God. Your playing small does not serve the world."

By taking time each day to recharge your batteries and revitalize your spirit, you can ensure that you happen to life as often as life happens to you.

While at times I still feel guilty about taking so much time for myself when there is work to be done and a family to care for, whenever I'm feeling at my most unworthy I've learned to live by a variation on a popular self-help dictum.

When it comes to the care and feeding of your spirit:

Feel the unworthiness and do it anyway.

Spiritual self-care in action

*"The central method for achieving a happier life
is to train your mind in a daily practice
that weakens negative attitudes
and strengthens positive ones."*
— The Dalai Lama

I began working with Franklin at a time in his life when he was feeling particularly low. He had just broken up with his supermodel girlfriend, his most recent film had flopped, and he was wondering what to do next with his life.

While I knew that a lot of people aspired to have problems like his, I also knew that as long as he was out of touch with his spirit, he was unlikely to be able to turn things around. I asked him to make a list of things that inspired him—things that he knew from experience made him feel more alive.

*What are those things that make you feel alive—
things that on the days when you do them,
you feel better and things go better
than on the days when you don't?*

Franklin stared at me somewhat angrily and insisted that there was nothing that made him feel alive. Knowing that he was somewhat religious, I asked him if prayer or reading the Bible made a difference to him. He grudgingly conceded that when he used to read the Bible as a child, he had found great comfort in it, but that he hadn't done it in years.

"Not a problem," I said. "Put it on your list. It's not about what you're doing now or even what you think you should be doing—it's about what works or has worked in the past to bring you into a state of inspiration, equanimity and well-being."

After another stand-off of a few minutes or so, Franklin found a second item for his list.

"I like to box," he said. "Twice a week I go to a gym and I hit people—I hit them really hard. And I know it doesn't make a lot of sense, but when I leave the gym I'm a lot more patient with everyone, including me. I just feel better in myself."

"Perfect," I said. "What else?"

Eventually he got his list up to six things, including trips to museums, watching great movies, and driving in the countryside. I encouraged him to keep experimenting over the next few weeks and aim to get his list up to around ten things—few enough that he could theoretically do all of them in a day, but also "many" enough that he wouldn't have to.

I also suggested that he pay special attention to see if there were one or two things that made a particularly profound difference—that way he could make a point of doing those things every day, no matter what.

Here is the same experiment I gave to Franklin . . .

From theory to practice . . .

The Spiritual Self-Care Chart

1. Create a chart with a list of those activities that nurture your spirit, make you come alive, remind you of your true self or purpose, and enrich your waking experience.

Here's an example of how it might look:

Things that nurture my spirit:	Su	Mo	Tu	We	Th	Fr	Sa
Inspirational input							
Meditation/prayer							
Keeping a journal							
Drinking cappuccino							
Exercise							
Random act of kindness							
Go for a walk in nature							
Go to religious meeting							
Connecting with family							

2. Each day, check off as many of those activities as you participate in. You can either set yourself a goal (say, "five a day") or simply track what you do naturally and notice your results over time.

About six weeks after beginning to use the spiritual self-care chart, Franklin phoned me. Without even saying hello, he lit into me.

"I want you to know," he began angrily, "that I'm a very complex person. Which is why it pisses me off," he continued, his voice softening, "that on the days where I have more things checked off, I'm happier and my life works better than the days when I have less."

Franklin has kept all his charts for the past four years and the steady rise in his film career mirrors the increased number of check marks on his chart, month in and month out.

The true purpose of self-care

"If I had to live my life over again, I would have made a rule to read some poetry and listen to some music at least once a week; for perhaps the parts of my brain now atrophied would have thus been kept active through use. The loss of these tastes is a loss of happiness and may possibly be injurious to the intellect and more probably to the moral character, by enfeebling the emotional part of our nature."
— Charles Darwin

I no longer remember the day when I first realized that meditation, diet, and exercise were not self-inflicted punishments for stress, overeating and sloth, but rather ways of experiencing more love, peace, and joy in my body and my life. As I have said to my clients on more than one occasion, "When you would no sooner miss your daily self-care routine than a chance to have great sex with someone you really love, you've probably got it about right."

One of the most profound evolutions in my own self-care has come from shifting my primary focus off the *process* of self-care (i.e., what I do to take care of myself) and on to the *outcome* of self-care (i.e., the state of peace, presence and well-being from which I like to live my life).

Rather than focusing on "whether I meditated long enough" or if I wrote enough pages in my journal, I now focus on the state of body, mind, and spirit that meditation and journal writing has enabled me to access.

In recovery, there is an acronym called H.A.L.T., which stands for Hungry, Angry, Lonely, and Tired. The idea is that when you notice yourself experiencing hunger, anger, loneliness, or fatigue, you should "halt" what you're doing and focus on taking care of yourself. Otherwise, you will tend to give in to temptation and make poor choices in an unconscious attempt to meet your needs in the moment instead of making those choices that support living the life of your dreams. Once you've taken the time to take care of yourself (i.e., you've eaten, rested, connected with others, and gotten yourself back to some semblance of equanimity), you can move forward confident that your inner guidance system can once again be trusted.

One of the benefits of spiritual, inspirational self-care as a daily priority is that we avoid getting ourselves into situations where we need to H.A.L.T. Consequently, we find ourselves living from strength to strength, confident in our hearts, free in our minds, and secure in our ability to trust ourselves moment by moment.

How do you know if you've done enough self-care today?

Because you feel totally cared for in your self.

Going to the garden

> *"One truth stands firm.*
> *All that happens in world history rests on something spiritual.*
> *If the spiritual is strong, it creates world history.*
> *If it is weak, it suffers world history."*
> — Albert Schweitzer

One of my favorite exercises, which I use with many of my clients to both check in with how things are going in their lives and as a part of their ongoing self-care routines, is based on a Hawaiian system of healing and self-care.

Feel free to adapt it in whatever way works for you. Some people like to read all the way through the exercise before doing it; some have someone read it to them the first time they go through it, while others prefer to simply follow along, taking a few moments to close their eyes and imagine what is being described before opening their eyes again and reading further. . . .

From theory to practice . . .

The Garden of Your Life

Take a few moments to relax. "Inspire" yourself by taking a few deep breaths and really enjoy the sensation of your body filling and emptying itself of air. If you like, you can close your eyes, counting backwards from 10 to 1. . . .

Now, imagine yourself stepping into a shower of light. Let all the cares and stresses of the day be washed away until you are feeling clean and clear and refreshed. Continue to enjoy the shower and notice that the light outside awakens the light inside and your body begins to fill with light. . . . As your body becomes lighter and lighter, you are becoming more and more relaxed. Soon, every cell in your body will be infused with the most beautiful light you can imagine. Enjoy the experience of clarity, lightness, and ease. . . .

Now, as the being of light that you are, float up out of your body and into a garden. This is the garden of your life. In it you will find every aspect of yourself and your light reflected. . . .

When you are ready, wander around your garden and notice what you notice:

- *Is your garden large or small?*
- *Is it neat and tidy or rambling and overgrown?*
- *Are there any particular features that draw your eye toward them?*

Here are some of the things to check out while you are exploring your garden. You may find any or all of them already waiting for you, or if there is a feature I describe that you are particularly attracted to, you can always add it in yourself. Remember, it's your garden!

The areas of your life

In every garden, you will find (or can create) areas that represent the areas of your life. At the very least, I recommend you find parts of the garden to represent health, wealth, and relationships, but many people also enjoy planting things to do with their career, social causes, and spirituality.

The fountain of inspiration

I used to find my own garden a bit bland until I added a fountain of inspiration. Whenever I need to recharge, I sit by the fountain and enjoy being refreshed by the cool splash of inspiration!

The flame

Your inner flame can be representative of your current levels of health, energy, inspiration, and well-being. One of my clients has a sacred shrine in her garden where she sees her inner flame like an eternal candle; another has his in an outdoor fireplace that burns brighter or more dimly depending on what he has been doing in his life. There is a saying often attributed to Mother Teresa that "if everyone would sweep their own doorstep, the city would soon be clean." I would put it like this:

> **As each of us tends to our own flame,
> the world will be able to bask in
> our collective warmth and light.**

Animals

Many people like to have animals in their inner garden. But unlike in the outer world, the animals (and pretty much anything else) in your inner garden can talk back to you. If you ever come across something in your garden you don't understand, ask it what it's doing there and what its message is for you. If it feels like you're just making it up, it's working perfectly!

The master gardener

For many of my clients, their favorite thing about visiting their gardens is the time they spend in conversation with their "master gardener." The master gardener is a wise aspect of yourself (or if you prefer "beyond yourself") you can turn to for inspiration, counsel, and assistance in tending your garden.

For some people, the master gardener appears as a historic or religious figure; for some he or she is someone that they know, love, and respect; for still others it appears more as an energy or symbolic rather than human form. (One of my clients has Chauncy Gardener, the Peter Sellers character from the movie *Being There!*)

You will know you have found the perfect master gardener for you when you feel peaceful and at ease in their presence.

What to do in your garden

There are no limits to what you can do in your garden, but here are a few things I recommend:

1. *Weed your garden regularly.* Anything in the garden you don't like can go. If you're not sure why something is there or if you keep removing something and every time you return to the garden it's grown back, ask the master gardener (or the thing itself) what its importance is and why it keeps returning.

2. *Nurture what you love.* Taking time to water and even talk with the plants and animals can be extremely rewarding. In the garden, a useful guideline is that if it feels good to do it, it is good to do it.

3. *Plant new things, particularly in areas of your life where you would like to see changes.* It never ceases to amaze me how changes I make in the garden are reflected in my life (though I wouldn't necessarily talk about it with some of my more scientifically minded or mentally conservative friends!)

4. *If you pray or meditate, going to the garden is an excellent way to begin.* Many people tell me their experience of prayer or meditation is greatly enhanced by this simple practice.

5. *Enjoy it!* As you cultivate your garden, you will find it a more and more peacefully invigorating place to be. Especially in your garden, resist the temptation to overwhelm being with doing.

> When you have explored and enjoyed your garden fully, leave any final instructions w ta your master gardener for changes you would like made before your next visit.
>
> When you are ready to leave, say a silent "Thank you" to your garden and float back down into your body. Imagine stepping onto an energizing beam of light until your body is filled with energy—open your eyes, wiggle your fingers and toes, and ease your way back into the world. . . .

For many people, visiting the garden becomes a regular part of their inspirational self-care routine. For others, it is a place to visit in times of great change or upheaval. Once you have gone through this exercise a couple of times, you will find it easy to return to your garden any time you choose.

In our next chapter together, we'll take on one of the central obstacles that most people face in their lives. . . .

—————◦◊◦—————

CHAPTER 12

OTHER PEOPLE

Information	Skill	Belief
Wellbeing	**Other people**	Motivation
Time	Money	Fear

The Ferryman and the Travelers

Once upon a time, many years ago from now, there were two travelers riding on a ferry across a great river that flows between two distant lands. As much to pass the time as anything, the first traveler decided to strike up a conversation with the ferryman.

"What are the people like on the far side of the river?"

The ferryman looked at him curiously.

"What are the people like where you come from?"

The traveler grunted in disgust.

"Horrible, selfish, greedy, and mean-spirited. That's why I'm leaving!"

The ferryman shook his head sadly.

"I'm afraid you'll find the people on this side of the river are much the same."

A bit later in the journey, a second traveler approached the ferryman and once again asked, "What are the people like on the far side of the river?"

The ferryman looked at her curiously.

"What are the people like where you come from?"

The traveler sighed.

"Wonderful, kind, supportive, and generous. I hate to leave them behind."

The ferryman smiled.

"I wouldn't worry about it. I think you'll find the people on this side of the river are much the same."

A question of perspective

> *"Hell is other people."*
> — Jean-Paul Sartre

The secret to overcoming seeing other people as an obstacle in our lives is simple:

The problem is in the seeing.

Any problem you will ever have with another person will be the result of some combination of these two things:

- You're attempting to control them (often as a reaction against them trying to control you)
- You're taking their actions or reactions personally, blaming yourself for their choices (or blaming your choices on them)

In the first part of this chapter, I'll highlight some simple perspectives to help you recognize what is within your control and what isn't when it comes to your interactions with others.

During the rest of the chapter, we'll explore ways of taking responsibility for your communication, and I'll share several highly effective ways to heal toxic relationships without resorting to blame, fault, or shame.

For now, all you need to remember is this:

The only reason someone will ever behave in a mean, cruel, or fiercely unreasonable way is they are unhappy or unwell in themselves and doing the best they can to take care of themselves, usually by blaming you for their unhappiness or lack of well-being.

The only reason you would ever respond in a mean, cruel, or fiercely unreasonable way is that you are unhappy or unwell in yourself and doing the best you can to take care of yourself, usually by blaming your unhappiness or lack of well-being on them.

In other words, when you're unhappy in yourself, "hell" may indeed be other people—but when two happy people get together, heaven is never more than a heartbeat away.

Minding your own business for a change

"I can find only three kinds of business in the universe: mine, yours, and God's.
(For me, the word 'God' means 'reality.' Reality is God because it rules.
Anything that's out of my control, your control, and
everyone else's control —I call that God's business.)"
— Byron Katie

Imagine a row of stores, each owned by one of the significant people in your life. How much of your time do you spend in their stores, trying to get them to change their store policy, their inventory, or even the way they stock their display shelves?

What if they came into your shop all the time and told you that you needed to change all your policies to make them more like theirs. Would you be grateful for all their helpful advice and go along with whatever they said?

Does this start to sound a little bit like your life?

For example, have you ever noticed that no matter how much time you spend trying to fix everyone else's life and put the world to rights, nothing much changes and nobody's suitably grateful for your efforts?

Worse still, when we spend too much of our time "out to lunch," cobwebs start to form in the corners of our minds—the machinery of our bodies becomes rusty, and the delicate inspirations of the still, small voice within disappear into the cacophony of everyone else's problems. Days weeks, months, and even years vanish from our primary inventory—the amount of time allotted for our lives. (And in this analogy, it's God's business just how much of that time you're going to get!)

Let's take a closer look at the three kinds of business:

1. My business

I was talking to one of my mentors a few years back, trying to work out exactly why I had got certain acting jobs and not others, when he said, "I'll tell you exactly why, if you really want to know."

Expecting some great words of wisdom, I got this instead:

"The ones who hired you did it because they did,
and the other ones didn't because they didn't."

Seriously underwhelmed, I replied, "But if that were true, then all I could do to advance my career is be prepared, show up, and do my best!"

In his silence (don't you just hate it when they use silence?), I had a chance to reflect on and realize the truth in what I'd just said. . . .

All I can do to advance my career; win the man or woman of my heart; raise happy, healthy children; and bring about world peace is to:

• Be prepared
• Show up
• Do my best

2. Other people's business

My mother used to always say to me, "Le goût et le couleur ne dispute pas." While it took me years to learn enough French to figure out what she meant, I finally realized that it roughly translated to "There's no point in arguing about matters of personal taste."

What it's taken me even more years to figure out is that EVERYTHING is a matter of personal taste—that is, people will choose to believe what they want to believe, say what they want to say, and do what they want to do no matter how obvious it is to me that they're wrong and I'm right!

If someone does choose to think, speak, or act differently after an encounter with me, it was still their choice—I just provided a context and an opportunity for them to reconsider what they were doing and choose differently.

3. God's business

Whether it's praying for our favorite sports team to win, negotiating for a new car, willing our bowling balls out of the gutter, or working out our karma with God ("Please, just get me out of this mess and I promise I'll be good!"), we all have little and not-so-little ways of trying to make the world do our bidding.

But why are we so concerned with controlling the universe?

According to Dr. Phil McGraw, it's because we fear we won't be able to cope if things don't turn out the way we want. Yet the more we focus on our business (developing the strength, flexibility, and wisdom to deal with whatever life has to offer us), the less we need to try to control the uncontrollable—the outcomes of our life.

From Theory to Practice . . .

Three Kinds of Business

1. Make two lists on a piece of paper. On the left, list as many things you can think of that are under your direct control. On the right, list as many things as you can think of that are NOT under your direct control.

2. Choose a situation in your life you are finding stressful. Break it down into which elements are your business, which are other people's business, and which are God's business.
   - Do the same with one of your significant life or career goals.
   - Do the same with a dream for the well-being of the planet (e.g , world peace, better education, putting an end to hunger and homelessness, etc.)

3. Experiment by spending one full day minding your own business—focusing entirely on those things that are under your direct control. If you notice yourself getting caught up in "helping others" or "playing God," smile, acknowledge yourself for noticing, and get back to your business.

The relationship triangle

"Nobody is smart enough to be wrong all the time."
— Ken Wilber

When I was eight years old, I was blown away when a friend folded a piece of blank paper into about ten lengthwise sections, pinched it in the middle, and enacted an epic version of this classic dramatic scene:

Villain (with folded paper as mustache):
You must pay the rent!

Damsel in Distress (with folded paper as bow in hair):
But I can't pay the rent!

Villain:
You must pay the rent!

Damsel in Distress:
But I can't pay the rent!

Hero (with folded paper as bow tie):
I'll pay the rent!

Damsel in Distress:
My hero!

Villain:
Curses—foiled again!

Little did I know at the time that what I was witnessing in that little scene was not just great theater, but also a wonderful insight into the dynamics of human relationships—what relationship experts Gay and Kathlyn Hendricks describe as "the relationship triangle."

According to R. Buckminster Fuller, a triangle is not only one of the most stable structures in architecture, it is the basic structural unit of the universe. And the relationship triangle is no different.

If you explore your relationships with other people and the world around you, you will notice that at times you fall into each of the roles in the above melodrama. These three roles—the victim, the villain, and the hero—form the three corners of the relationship triangle.

- Victims create a need for Villains, Villains create a need for Heroes, Heroes create a need for Victims.
- Villains create a need for Victims, Victims create a need for Heroes, Heroes create a need for Villains.

The fundamental problem with living on the triangle is that even if you switch roles (i.e., "stop being such a victim"),the triangle dynamic is so stable your relationship melodrama will continue on unabated.

The trick to stepping off the triangle is simple but not always easy:

Take full responsibility for your own thoughts, feelings, and actions and let go of trying to blame, control, or change the other person or the relationship.

The cleanest analogy I have come up with for the difference between taking responsibility and distributing blame is the difference between the questions "Who is responsible for spilling the milk?" and "Who is responsible for the spilt milk?"

The first question seeks to distribute fault, liability, and blame; the second invites us to acknowledge the reality of things as they are and make an active contribution toward making them the way we want them to be.

Any one of us could be held accountable for our part in spilling the milk, from the child who actually knocked it over to the older sibling who left it close to the edge to the parent who chose to make reading his paper more important than pouring out his children's milk. (Not that I'm speaking from experience, obviously . . .)

But all of us have the opportunity to take complete responsibility for the spilt milk—to choose to focus our energies on our own unique contribution to the positive resolution of the situation, whatever it may be.

In this sense, the distinction between distributing blame and taking responsibility becomes clear:

Blame is a way of disowning the past; responsibility is a way to take ownership of the present and create a more positive future.

From Theory to Practice . . .

Stepping Off the Triangle

(Please use some common sense here—if this is your first time experimenting with this concept, it's probably NOT the time to explore deeply seated therapeutic issues!)

1. Choose a significant relationship from your life to explore.
   Example:
   I'm having difficulty parenting my daughter.

2. Write or tell the story of this incident as if you were completely the victim.
   If you like, go ahead and tell it in a "damsel in distress" voice, even if (or perhaps especially if) you are male.
   Example:
   "I work so hard all day long and then just when I'm finally going to get a chance to sit down and relax, my daughter comes in and asks me to do a million things for her. Honestly, I don't know how other people do it—it's all too much!"

3. Next, tell the story as if you were the evil villain. Do your best "Dastardly Dan" impression and go for it!

Example:
"My daughter is a nightmare—she takes no responsibility for her behavior and if I didn't rule the house with an iron fist, she'd run roughshod over everything. Give her an inch and she'd take a mile! She's lucky to have me in her life—if it wasn't for the discipline I give her, she'd grow up to be a complete loser!"

4. Now, tell the story as if you were the hero who saved the day!

Example:
"My wife and daughter were really arguing, so I stepped in. The problem is, my daughter's too young to deal with all the homework they give her at school and my wife's too emotional to deal with it. In the end, I spent a few hours finishing off my daughter's school project for her while I set her up with milk and cookies in front of the television, then I went and gave my wife a massage, brought her a cup of tea and ran her a hot bath. Honestly, it's a good thing I was here today—otherwise I think they would have killed each other."

5. Notice which of these roles is the most familiar. Which version of the story is closest to the one you've been telling yourself and others?

6. Tell the story one last time, taking 100% responsibility for your part and 0% responsibility for the thoughts, words, and actions of any other people involved in the incident.

Example:
"I've been working a lot of extra hours lately, at least partly to avoid having to deal with my wife and daughter. It's become clear to me that we're not getting on as well as I'd like, and I feel scared that if I actually spent more time at home, I'd have to acknowledge it to them and I wouldn't be able to continue to project my image of us as "the perfect family" to my colleagues. Much as I wish it wasn't so, I really like being admired for being a great 'family man.'"

s"I know that I want to give both relationships more time and attention and find out how much better I can make things. My first action is going to be to come home early from work today. I don't know how they'll react, but I feel good about taking a concrete action towards my goal."

Healing Toxic Relationships

"I recently read that love is entirely a matter of chemistry.
That must be why my wife treats me like toxic waste."
— Dave Bissonette

A healthy relationship is one in which the energy between you and the other person or people flows freely. An unhealthy, or "toxic" relationship is one in which the energy between you and the other person or people is blocked or restricted.

Therefore, in order to heal a toxic relationship (or strengthen a healthy one), you can either do things that increase the energy flow or that help release the energy blockages.

The single most potent guideline for keeping the energy flowing in your most important relationships is this:

Don't fake your orgasms!

In other words, if you want to get on well with others, a great place to start is by giving and inviting open, honest feedback.

I first recognized this principle while talking with a client who told me the following story:

He was in bed with his wife of eight years engaging in a bit of foreplay when he nibbled on her ear, an act that traditionally elicited moans of approval and delight. However, on this particular occasion, she went quiet, sat bolt upright in the bed, and very hesitantly said, "You know, honey, I really hate it when you do that. . . ."

The man was duly confused, and asked her why she had made pleasurable sounds for the past eight years.

She replied, "I didn't want to hurt your feelings!"

Now let's pretend that you and I want to have great sex. If I don't tell you what you do that I like, you may or may not "accidentally" do more of it. If I don't tell you what you do that I don't like, you may or may not unwittingly do more of it. But if I pretend to like what you do that I don't like, you will almost certainly do more and more and more of what I don't want, and chances are I'll get fed up and either yell at you, break up with you, or feed you to my dog without your ever having the slightest idea of what went wrong in our relationship!

So how do we encourage people to give us the kind of feedback that will be of genuine use to us?

Here are a few suggestions . . .

1. Make a distinction between criticism, feedback, and encouragement, and ask for the one you really want.

- Criticism is filled with judgments based on right and wrong, good and evil.
- Encouragement is the intentional act of supporting someone in pursuing their objectives, regardless of how it's going at the moment.
- Feedback is open, honest communication about how we or our actions are being perceived by other people.

2. Say what you mean without saying it mean.

Setting the standard for the quality of feedback can be a powerful tool.

3. Be willing to smile, nod, and say "Thank you"

The number one reason most people don't automatically offer you open, honest feedback is because they know you don't take it very well. You either defend your position, attack them in return, or ignore them completely and give them the cold shoulder until they are either forgiven or ostracized forever. An appropriate response to any sort of feedback is to smile, nod, and say "Thank you."

When Harry Left Sally

A man named Harry went to his neighbor Sally's house to borrow her lawnmower. On the way to her house, he began to imagine how the conversation would go. He could hear her in his mind berating him for all the times he had been late in returning things, complaining about things he'd returned broken or with missing pieces, and generally berating him as unworthy of the loan of her lawnmower.

He began to argue with the Sally in his head, pointing out all the things he'd loaned her (including the time she lost his biggest ladder and he didn't even complain about it) but all to no avail—the Sally in his head wouldn't let up.

Finally, he arrived at Sally's house and rang the doorbell.

"What can I do for you?" a delighted Sally said as she welcomed her friend and neighbor.

"You can keep your damn lawnmower!" Harry screamed, slamming the door in the now stunned Sally's face as he stormed away.

Some things aren't better left unsaid

A sure sign that there are unresolved issues and unspoken conflicts interfering with a relationship is when you have regular, frequent, or continued arguments and unpleasant conversations with the other person in your head. Sometimes these will be "instant replays" of real conversations and other times they will be completely made up, but in either case they reveal "bricks of silence" that are forming part of a wall that is either gradually building up between you or already firmly established.

The following experiment is an excellent way of taking the first step in removing the "bricks" and reopening the flow of communication in your relationships . . .

From Theory to Practice . . .

The Letter

1. Choose a relationship in which you would like to improve the quality of your communication and the depth of your connection.

2. Write a letter to that person in which you express EVERYTHING you are thinking and feeling but not saying about them and about your relationship. Be sure to include the good, the bad, and even the ugly. Express yourself in whatever language comes to mind. Don't worry about offending them—they're never going to see this!

3. When you've completed the letter, go back and see if there is still anything left unsaid. You can add it as a P.S. or include it in the body of the letter.

4. Put the letter away for at least 24 hours. At that point, you may tear it into pieces, save it for your future amusement (I love coming across my "Dear A#$%hole" letters from years gone by!) or if you think it's appropriate, send it and/or use it as a guide for a future conversation.

If you're like most people, you'll notice at least one of three things happen almost immediately:

a. Your own level of tension and discomfort about the relationship will ease, sometimes disappearing altogether.

b. Some things that you thought you could "never say" for fear of blowing the relationship will now flow easily and naturally in future conversations

c. Any conflicts you had with the other person will mysteriously disappear. It is not uncommon for the person to whom you have written to "spontaneously" phone or write you to bring up the very subjects you wrote about in your letter.

Three keys to effective communication

If you do decide you really want to communicate some or all of what you've written in your letter to the other person, there are three core elements that influence whether or not the message you intend to send is the message that will be received.

One is the clarity of your outcome—as the Cheshire cat said to Alice, if you don't know where you're headed, it doesn't matter which way you go to get there!

Another is the current strength of your relationship. You can test in your own experience whether you're more or less likely to listen carefully to someone you care fully about than someone you either don't know or are continually irritated with.

The third is your emotional state and the emotional state of the person listening. When our emotions take over our logical brain switches off, and it doesn't matter how sensible your message, it will either never get said or never be heard.

So what is the most effective sequencing of these three elements for effective communication?

1. Emotional state

It doesn't matter how much you like somebody or how clear you are in your outcome, if they're lost in their heads thinking about something else, they're unlikely to hear you. Get in the habit of beginning every phone call, face-to-face meeting, and even e-mail with a quick "state check" to make sure that they're in a resourceful enough state to understand you and you're in a resourceful enough state to be understood.

2. Relationship

If there's tension in your relationship today and what you want to communicate isn't about that, consider holding off on your other message until you've addressed what's taking up space in both of your minds. As a friend from Texas's father used to say, "Don't talk sense to a barking dog!"

3. Outcome

One of the great killers of effective communication is the hidden agenda. The clearer you are about what you really want out of the communication, the easier it will be for you to notice the response you're getting and adjust your communication accordingly.

Here's a good rule of thumb:

What you want to say is generally less important than what you want the other person to hear, think, feel, and do as a result.

From Theory to Practice . . .

Designer Communication

1. Think of a meaningful conversation or meeting you will be having later on today or tomorrow. (If you're planning to have 24 hours of mindless chit-chat, use the experiment to write someone a meaningful letter and adapt it accordingly.)

2. What is your outcome for that conversation? That is, what do you want the other person to think, feel, and do as a result of your having communicated? Take a few moments to think about how you'll know that your communication is having the desired effect (i.e., seeing their head nod, seeing them smile, hearing them make "agreeing" noises, or looking thoughtful, or relaxing their body, etc.).

3. Take one more minute right now to imagine that you are about to have that conversation . . .

   You check your body to make sure that you're all right, and take a moment to make sure that they're all right. If they look upset or otherwise distracted, clear that up first! (Let's face it, they're going to be less receptive to you if their pet goldfish just died.)

Now do a quick mental relationship check—is there anything you need to clear up between you before you can both focus cleanly on the matter at hand?

Finally, imagine yourself communicating, noticing their response and adjusting your behavior accordingly, all the way up until the happy ending. (After all, it's your fantasy!)

4. When it comes time to have the actual conversation, repeat the sequence you imagined in reality.

How to not get divorced or fired

Think about a significant relationship in your life—it can be with your spouse, your child, your boss, your colleague—anyone who is by necessity, happenstance, or choice a major player in the adventure of your life.

Have you made the decision to do what it takes to make that relationship successful, or are you still "waiting to see how things turn out?"

At first glance, the "wait and see" approach to relationships seems to make sense—after all, we don't control other people (damn it!) and even our best efforts to make things work may fail.

The problem with the wait-and-see approach to relationships is that if you wait long enough, you're bound to see things you don't like!

Of course, making the decision to make a relationship successful is not a guarantee that it will last forever. What it does guarantee is that the myriad of molehills that inevitably arise from spending time with people who aren't you won't turn into mountain ranges of trouble that separate you from the people you have chosen to share your life with.

While some relationships may well be worth giving up on, the only thing you really need to give up is trying to control the other person by taking responsibility for their (or God's) business. And once you've let go of that, you will find the relationship will either begin to flow or it will let go of you.

Here are four of the simplest strategies I know for immediately re-opening the flow of energy in your most important relationships . . .

1. Listen to them

Just for today, take at least five minutes to pay attention to the other person in a relationship you would like to heal. The simplest way to do this is to take five minutes to really listen to them. Orient yourself towards them physically and mentally. Allow them to be the most important person in the world for five minutes (you can take the job back after that!)

If you can't or won't make five minutes to listen to them, it may be time to let go of that relationship from your life.

2. Laugh (or cry) with them

The old saying that a problem shared is a problem halved and a joy shared is a joy multiplied is particularly true when it comes to your relationships. Even something as simple as watching a funny movie and laughing together (or sharing a cry at a weepy one) can be incredibly healing.

Plus, both laughter and tears release endorphins, and are two of nature's ways of easing pain and releasing toxins from the body. Not a bad reward for watching a great movie!

3. Have an argument

Frank Farrely, the developer of the field of "Provocative Therapy," tells the story of his work with a catatonic patient. One by one, he began pulling the hairs off the man's leg. With each hair, he went higher and higher until he was past the upper thigh and still climbing. Just before he could pull the last hair, the catatonic "woke up" and punched him in the face—his first sign of life in over 20 years.

The most common thing I hear from people who are on the verge of breaking up with their partners is, "I want us to stay friends." Unfortunately, in many cases this can only be accomplished by continuing to repress the many unspoken "bricks of silence" that can ultimately dam up the flow of communication, and in most cases led to the problems in the relationship in the first place.

Not expressing what is really going on for you in a relationship can create ever increasing amounts of tension as the internal pressure builds up on both sides of the "dam." If you are a person who avoids confrontation at all costs, allow yourself to speak your truth in your relationships today and watch the energy begin to flow. (Of course, you might have to be prepared to duck . . .)

4. Reach out and touch someone

Let me be honest here—I am not one of the world's great huggers. Oh, you may see me put my arms around my fellow man from time to time in an awkward replica of a loving embrace, but my social conditioning runs deep, and I'm far more comfortable with a hearty handshake or a gentle (but manly) punch on the arm.

But because I am aware that one of the most healing things in any relationship is a loving touch, I am working to overcome my conditioning and I touch when I feel comfortable touching. My wife gets hugs. My kids get hugs. And if and when we meet, feel free to greet me with a hug. Oh, I may tense up a bit, pat you on the back, and turn a bit red in the face . . . but it's a start!

Some closing thoughts

I was teaching this material in a workshop once when a participant said to me, "If I really take responsibility for my business—I stop trying to fix other people's problems and just focus in on living an inspired life—won't they think I'm being selfish?"

"What they think of you is their business," I replied. "But you can care just as deeply, experience less stress, and be far more effective with the people, goals, and causes that matter most to you by learning to mind your own business while being fully involved in the lives of the people you care about."

In fact, if you really want to make a difference in someone's life, the most powerful way to do it is to focus on what is completely within your control—your ability to express your love for them and to believe in their ability to make different choices and have what they want—a life that makes them go "Wow!" As the saying goes, "It is not up to someone else whether or not you love them."

Our final experiment in this chapter is one of my favourites, and comes directly from my work with Bill Cumming, creator of the wonderful "What One Person Can Do" program, which is used in boardrooms, schools and prisons across America:

From Theory to Practice . . .

The Case Study

1. Choose a person to work with who you would like to see make positive changes in their life—to experience themselves as more capable and able to make a difference in their lives and in the world. This can be a child, spouse, parent, co-worker, or friend.

2. Let them know that you love them unconditionally—that nothing they can do will make you love them any less, and nothing they can do will make them love you any more.

3. If they choose to discuss any of their problems, difficulties, goals, or opportunities with you, resist "helping" by offering them any advice, assistance, motivation, or empowerment. Instead, choose to see them as powerful, capable, and able. If you like, highlight the choices they are making and affirm their capacity to transform their experience by exercising their power to choose differently.

   While this may feel awkward at first, particularly if you are used to playing the hero or clucking sympathetically while they play the victim, you will be amazed at how quickly they change, "all by themselves."

Of course if you're having trouble getting round to actually doing any of these experiments, the trouble may not be what you think it is. We'll explore that in more depth as we go head to head with our next obstacle. . . .

—⚬〰⚬—

CHAPTER 13

MOTIVATION

Information	Skill	Belief
Well-being	Other people	**Motivation**
Time	Money	Fear

Are you a procrastinator?

ONE OF THE MAIN REASONS I hear from my clients as to why they don't yet have what they want in their lives is that they procrastinate—they don't do what it is they think they should do to make their dreams come true.

But in my experience, procrastination isn't so much a character flaw as a blanket label for five separate obstacles:

1. Inertia
2. Learned helplessness
3. Resistance
3. Forcing the flow
5. Chasing the wrong goal

In this chapter, I will describe each obstacle and share the same strategies I use with myself and my clients to get up and get going on the things that really matter to us. . . .

1. Overcoming inertia: Understanding the law of motion

"An object at rest tends to stay at rest; an object in motion tends to stay in motion."
— Sir Isaac Newton

So often in life, when we find ourselves unable to get started on a new exercise program or stick to a New Year's resolution, we label ourselves as bad or wrong or lazy. We then go on seminars and listen to tapes designed to increase our willpower, develop our discipline, and master our "self."

The problem with using willpower and discipline to overcome and master ourselves is that once again, we are not the enemy. The real reason you can't get started on your goals, stay focused on your dreams, or change your habits isn't you—it's physics.

The Oxford English Dictionary defines "inertia" as follows:

---

inertia

noun [MASS NOUN]

1. a tendency to do nothing or to remain unchanged
2. a property of matter by which it continues in its existing state of rest or uniform motion in a straight line, unless that state is changed by an external force.

Sound familiar? Do you know anyone who has "a tendency to do nothing or to remain unchanged unless changed by an external force?"

Fortunately, once we do get into action, inertia becomes momentum, and momentum is the force of nature that can help turn us into forces of nature in pursuit of our goals and dreams.

How do you overcome inertia and get into action?

Here are my some of my favorite strategies. . . .

Starting Small

The advice I most often give to my clients who want to make major life changes is to start small. If you want to lose weight, start by subtracting one aspect of one unhealthy eating habit from your life and adding one healthy one. If you want to save money, begin by putting aside $10 a month. If you want to exercise, begin by walking around the block, or jogging for one minute a day.

There are two reasons the "starting small" approach often works. The first is the "Hey, inertia, your shoelaces are untied!" phenomenon. By baby-stepping your way into action, your brain doesn't notice that you are sneaking out of the zone of the familiar and into action until you've already begun to benefit from the momentum of change.

The second reason is what I call the "silly factor"—at some point, it just seems silly to only walk one block—may as well walk two, or three, or even more.

Save $10 a month? Well, that's just silly—I may as well put away $50, or $100, or more.

Only cut out second helpings on dessert but keep everything else the same? That's plain old silly—it will be just as easy to cut out second helpings on everything as on one thing.

Many of my client success stories began with such simple steps, and I use the "little and often" approach myself nearly every day.

Starting Big

No matter how much fun it is to take the gentle approach, there are some chasms you just can't cross in three simple steps. In fact for years, I was unable to get myself to do any of the three things I've been using as examples. I would exercise, but only sporadically. I would eat healthier for a few weeks, but then slip back into old habits. And as for my savings account, let's just say it spent quite a few years suffering from attention deficit disorder.

So how have I overcome my "failure" to profit from my own best advice? By learning that sometimes, it pays to start big!

My regular exercise routine began when I stopped trying to fit a little bit of exercise into my already busy life and instead forced my life to fit in around a six-day-a-week program of intense weights and aerobics. I lost 22 pounds (and have kept them off) not by eating a bit less cheesecake but by radically overhauling my diet and being so diligent about eliminating carbohydrates from my diet that I even went so far as to have tea without milk for two weeks. (Those of you who looked away from that last sentence with horror have some idea of how sacrilegious that was in my household.) My savings account finally got the consistent attention it deserved when I upped my sporadic $50 contributions to the at the time seemingly insane to me sum of $2,000 a month.

Here's another example of the power of starting big. Many people on my trainings complain that they "just can't find the time" to take 15 minutes for themselves in the middle of a busy day. And I agree with them. It's too easy to find 15 minutes in a 1,440-minute day to take it seriously. But what if you decided to take an hour a day for yourself? Or two? Or three? At that point, you would no longer even try to "find the time"—you would know that you need to make it.

How about earning more money? In my experience, it's considerably harder to increase your income by 10% than it is to double it. The reason is the same—you KNOW you have to make substantive changes to how you do things to double your income, but it's easy to believe you can increase your income by 10% without changing much of anything.

The secret to "starting big" is to look for ways to make what it is you want to take on inconvenient, unwieldy, more difficult, and more time-consuming. What this does is shatter the illusion that you'll never need to disrupt your life in order to transform it. It forces you to redesign your day around what you really want to do instead of trying to change without changing and cram "a few" more things into an already overstuffed schedule.

From theory to practice . . .

Starting Big, Starting Small

1. Choose something you've been wanting to do for a long time but just haven't been able to get yourself to do consistently.
   Examples:
   Learn Italian, pay off your credit card debt, keep a journal.

2. What would you do if you were going to "start small?"
   Examples:
   Learn Italian—memorize one new word a day. Credit cards— pay off $3 over the minimum on each card this month. Keep a journal—commit to writing one sentence each day for a week.

3. Now, brainstorm some ways to "start big."
   Examples:
   Learn Italian—book a trip to Rome in a month and decide you will speak no English the entire time you're there.

> *Credit cards—pay more money than you can afford to into reducing your debt. (Lest you bombard me with cries of "but that would be irresponsible," recognize you most likely have credit card debt because you paid more money than you could afford into creating it!)*
>
> *Keep a journal—commit to writing for at least an hour every day this week.*

4. Put at least one of your strategies into action in the next 24 hours!

Time Boxes

Sometimes what freezes us into inaction is the idea that if and when we overcome inertia and start, we won't be able to stop!

A time box is a period of time you put around a project or a goal with a definite beginning and a definite end, regardless of whether or not the project or goal is complete.

I use time boxes of around 15 minutes continually throughout my day as a way of overcoming inertia in areas like filing papers, going through my e-mail, and doing my taxes; time boxes of a month seem to work well for me in the creation of a new habit, be it an exercise program, a diet, or even experimenting with a new attitude.

Remember, the key here is to commit to the time box, not the result.

Accountability

When you're working for somebody else, your boss, manager, or supervisor is usually the person who "helps" you to overcome inertia, generally by threatening you with loss of life, limb, or revenue, but occasionally by being genuinely loving and supportive. In fact, one of the often overlooked great things about working for somebody else is that it sets up a kind of an accountability for your actions that's extremely difficult to maintain on your own.

For those of us who are our own boss (and everyone is their own boss in at least some areas of their life), it can be useful to deliberately create relationships with people to whom we choose to become accountable.

Here are my three favorite variations on the above theme—a veritable ABC to overcoming inertia and creating momentum:

a. Action buddies

A weekly phone call or meeting where you and your buddy take turns running through what you did and accomplished last week and what you plan on doing and accomplishing this week.

b. Barn raisings

Remember that scene in *Witness* where Harrison Ford and his neighbors in the Amish community gather together to build the foundations of a barn in a day? Throwing a "work party" can be a fun way of blasting through inertia, hanging out with friends, and eating some really good food!

c. Call a coach

Personally, I like using a coach—my weekly sessions become like a time box within which I organize my thinking and actions, and it's amazing how much I get done on the Monday before my Tuesday morning sessions.

2. Overcoming learned helplessness: Where there's a way, there's a will

"We will either find a way or make one."
—Hannibal (shortly before he and his elephants lost the Punic Wars)

So often we are exhorted to motivate ourselves by increasing our motive—by finding more and more reasons to get what we want. (In fact, some direct selling organizations encourage their sales people to go into debt so they'll have to work twice as hard just to maintain their lifestyle!)

The idea here is that our willpower is increased by increasing our desire—that if we just want it bad enough, we'll push ourselves hard enough. This approach is summed up by motivational guru Tony Robbins who says, "If you can find enough reasons to do something, you can get yourself to do anything."

So why aren't you living the life of your dreams yet? Do you not want it badly enough? Are you not desperate enough to succeed? Do you lack "the will to succeed?"

Let me suggest an alternative explanation . . .

While conventional wisdom suggests that "will" precedes "way," my experience is that in most cases the opposite is true—where there's a way (i.e., a plan—a clear path from where you are to what you want), there's a will.

We can find that way (and therein develop our will to succeed) in three steps:

A. Open to the possibility

One of my favorite games when working on a new goal is to brainstorm all the different ways success could "just happen." While these brainstorming sessions do not always yield practical results (no matter how many different ways I come up with for my favorite movie stars to meet and fall in love with me without my wife minding, it doesn't seem to happen), each time you participate in one of these "possibility sessions" your sense that what you want is possible will increase—as will your will to do what it takes to make it happen.

B. Enhance the plausibility

How do you take your ideas from possible to plausible?

• Make plans

> "In preparing for battle I have always found that plans are useless, but planning is indispensable."
> — General Dwight D. Eisenhower

Many people avoid making plans because they think they've got to get them just right in order to succeed. Think of a plan instead as a plausibility trainer—a way of convincing yourself that there is a way to get from here to there. I like to create two plans for every goal—one that goes forward from where I am, and another that goes backward from where I want to wind up. When the two plans meet in the middle, I know I'm on to something good!

• Gather evidence

When I was 12, I gambled a stamp and sent off for the Charles Atlas "Don't let that bully kick sand in your face!" isometric bodybuilding course. When the precious pages arrived, I instantly leapt into action and, within a week, I'd completely . . . well, the truth is, I'd completely given up. Every time I saw my pudgy little pre-pubescent tummy in the mirror and compared it to the rippling abs of Mr. Universe, I would head for the nearest refrigerator and comfort myself with a microwaveable cheeseburger, fries, and a milkshake.

Then one day, I caught my reflection in the mirror and for some reason, I thought I looked pretty good. Maybe I ought to give those Charles Atlas exercises another try. . . .

The more I did them, the better I looked. The better I looked, the more often I looked. The more often I looked and liked what I saw, the more I exercised. And before I knew what hit me, I had become the manly 13-year-old of the girl-next-door's dreams.

In the field of solution-oriented brief therapy, therapists are trained to begin the very first session with variations on the following question:

"How has your problem or situation improved since you booked your appointment to see me?"

Not only are people invariably able to answer the question, it enables the therapist to begin highlighting successes and focusing on what works, thereby reinforcing the idea that not only is success possible, but it's already happening—that there is indeed a way to get from where you are to where you want to go.

C. Increase the probability

"Confidence is preparation in action."
— Ron Howard

You increase your probability of success any time you choose attitudes and actions that are both within your control and increase the likelihood of getting what you want either now or in the future. Things like preparation, daily action, and inviting others to participate in our goals and dreams not only make our success more likely in reality, they make it more believable in our minds and hearts, increasing our will to succeed by making the way more and more apparent.

From theory to practice . . .

A Simple Key to Motivating Yourself

1. Pick a dream or goal you are in the process of bringing into being.
   Example:
   Creating my ultimate relationship.

2. On a scale from 1–10, where 10 is living the dream/reaching the goal and 1 is just starting out, where are you now?
   Example:
   Currently, I'm at a 4.

3. Working backwards, think about milestones you achieved in the past that let you know you've progressed past 1.
   Example:
   1 was deciding I wanted to be in a great relationship, 2 was realising the one I was in wasn't it, 3 was actually ending the relationship I was in, and 4 was making a list of the characteristics of my ideal partner.

4. Now go ahead and choose milestones to represent each number between where you are and a perfect 10.
   Example:
   5 will be working on myself to become the kind of a person who might attract my dream partner, 6 will be the first time I proactively ask "a likely suspect" on a date, 7 will be when we've gotten past the initial "whoosh" and still like each other, 8 will be when I am willing to acknowledge to others that this one is special, 9 will be when I feel sufficiently secure to stop trying to change them into being more like me, and 10 will be when I feel sufficiently secure to stop trying to change myself to get them to like me.

5. For those of you who want to stretch your imaginations (or just really, really liked *This is Spinal Tap*), what would be at 11?
   Example:
   All of the above with really great sex!

The more you play with increasing the plausibility (through planning and gathering evidence) and increasing the probability (through taking action) of reaching your goals, the less "motivation" will seem to be an obstacle and the more and more action you'll find yourself taking towards what you want to create in the world.

3. Overcoming resistance: Allowing yourself to succeed

> *"Do not conquer the world with force,*
> *for force only causes resistance."*
> — Tao Te Ching

Would you like to double your levels of motivation and productivity in the next month?

Try this little four-step experiment:

1. Gently push against a nearby wall.

2. If it doesn't fall over, push harder.

3. Continue pushing until either:
   a. the wall falls over, or
   b. you decide "This is stupid" and give up

4. Just when you're beginning to relax into not pushing against the wall, convince yourself that you need to get back up and try again.

Now, I'm guessing you didn't actually try this experiment. One of the reasons you didn't do it is that you could immediately see the futility of it—it was extremely unlikely to produce any useful results.

Yet every time you try to "make yourself do something" you've been resisting or putting off, you are engaging in precisely the same process.

Let's take another look at the four steps, but this time as we normally experience them . . .

1. Tell yourself that you should do something you are not doing.

2. If you don't do it, push yourself harder. Threaten yourself with dire consequences for not doing it, or yell at yourself loudly inside your mind.

3. Continue pushing until either:
   a. you do what you think you should do; or

b. you get tired of the inner struggle and resign yourself to the "fact" that you're just not motivated, you're a procrastinator, you're a bad person, etc.

4. As soon as you're starting to accept that you're not going to do it, start to beat yourself up about it again so that you can at least stay in conflict in hopes that one day, the state of inner tension will drive you to take action and the wall of resistance will finally fall over.

The truth about resistance is shockingly simple:

**You are almost never resisting performing a task;
rather you are resisting being "forced" to perform the task.**

The irony is that it is generally you doing the forcing!

Here's how it usually works:

Let's say I'm putting off making some calls for work. Since making the calls is clearly in my best interests, I assume that the only reason I'm not making them is that there must be something wrong with me—self-hate, fear of success, laziness, or some other major character flaw.

I then either beat myself up for being such a horrible person and try to goad myself into action, "sneak up" on my resistance using my favourite time management trick from Chapter 14, or give up on completing the task altogether.

But what if I'm not resisting making the calls? What if I'm actually just resisting being told what to do?

Then the obvious solution would be to get off my own back and trust that left to my own devices, I actually will do the things that matter.

The reason so few of us ever even consider this possibility is that at heart, we do not believe we will act in our own best interests. We've been taught from the time that we were little children that there's something wrong with us, and we carry on the self-hypnosis initiated by our parents, peers, and role-models by telling ourselves repeatedly;

"But if I don't force myself to do it, it will never get done!"

Hmm . . . can you really know that that's true? Have you ever left it long enough WITHOUT PUSHING to find out?

Early on in our marriage, my wife used to complain that I never picked up around the house. And she was quite right—the house just never seemed to get messy enough for me to want to tidy it up. I quickly convinced myself that there was something wrong with me (too lazy, too chauvinistic, etc.) and resolved to try harder.

At first, my "I suck" motivational strategy seemed to work—I was more conscious of tidying and my wife felt that her complaining had worked. Unfortunately, my resolve would invariably fade after a few weeks and the cycle would repeat itself.

It wasn't until the first time my wife went away for a few days that I discovered that once again, I was not the enemy. The reason I never seemed moved to take care of the house was that my natural inclination to live in a clean, ordered environment just kicked in later than hers, so our house almost never got to the point where I wanted to clean it (as opposed to feeling I should, ought to, or must). A couple of days after she left, I started spontaneously and without resistance picking stuff up.

All the while I thought I was resisting doing what I didn't want to do, I was in fact simply exhibiting a basic human trait:

When we are pushed, we tend to push back.

To see how intense your own resistance to being pushed is, take the "Rebel Test":

From theory to practice . . .

The Rebel Test

In each of the four following situations, rate the strength of your reaction on a scale from 1 to 5, where 1 is "couldn't care less," and 5 is "frothing at the mouth in a murderous rage":

1. Imagine you are about to do something at work when your boss orders you to do it "or else"! (You can substitute a parent or spouse if you don't work or if you're the boss!)

2. Imagine you have been standing in the "ten items or less" line in a supermarket for 20 minutes when you finally get to the front. The clerk refuses to serve you because you have 11 items.

3. Due to a postal strike, your check for the electricity bill arrives one day late. They cut off your service and insist you pay a $200 reconnection fee.

4. After driving around for half an hour, looking for a parking space, you finally pull into a loading zone and run into the drugstore to pick up an important prescription. When you come out two minutes later, the parking attendant is writing you out a ticket. Despite your explanations, all they can say is, "I'm just doing my job."

5. You'll need someone to help you with this one . . .
Ask a friend or colleague to push you in the chest, repeatedly. Score 5 points if you want to push back on the first go, 4 points for the second push, 3 points for the 3rd, and so on.

SCORING:

20–25 points:

You're a rebel with no need of a cause. Take a look at those things you are denying yourself because it would mean giving in to "them!"

15–19 points:

You're pretty normal, but you would probably benefit from imagining the "petty tyrants" in your life as drill instructors, training you in the development of emotional mastery and peace of mind!

10–15 points:

You're abnormally healthy—write me and tell me your secrets!

Less than 10 points:

Three possibilities:
a. You have a poor imagination!
b. You're an enlightened master living among us mere mortals.
c. You're a walking doormat—visit my website and ask for some tips on assertiveness!

4. Overcoming forcing the flow: Perfectly timing the universe

"Don't push the river."
— Barrie Stevens

Sometimes, in our desperation to make things happen NOW, we ignore the fact that despite our most positive intentions, life continues to unfold at its own pace. While most people think of that as an obstacle to be overcome, I've come to realize that there is a strange sort of perfection to following the rhythm of life instead of trying to force things to happen on your schedule.

For example, have you ever put off phoning someone and then when you do finally get round to phoning them, it turns out they only just got in and wouldn't have been around to answer your call if you had tried earlier?

Every time I think I'm procrastinating and begin to come down on myself for it, life reminds me of the fine line between procrastination and perfectly timing the universe.

When I first moved to Hollywood as an actor. I needed to run off some extra résumés at the local photocopy shop. It had been on my list for a few days, and I was beginning to think this was a classic case of self-sabotage. After all, without the résumés, I wouldn't be able to send off my pictures to agents and managers, without whom the likelihood of my acting career going anywhere was pretty much nil. However, after exploring my deeply held subconscious beliefs around success for a few hours, I noticed that I still wasn't at the photocopy shop, so I gave up and played a few rounds of Donkey Kong on the Nintendo with my son.

Two days later, I finally got round to going to the photocopy shop. I copied my résumés, cut them down to size, and proceeded to the checkout. The guy behind the till looked at the pile, and somewhat bemusedly asked, "Do you have a headshot?" Having already been in LA for a few weeks, I realized the correct answer was, "Yes—they're in the bag next to my screenplay."

The man checked out my picture, read through my résumé in more detail, and asked me, "Are you looking for a manager?" Within the hour, I was on the phone to a top management company, having had a personal introduction from a guy who only works at Kinko's on the one day of the week I finally got around to going in.

Coincidence? You decide!

From theory to practice . . .

Timing Is Everything

1. Choose something that you're working on that you are willing to experiment on and take some chances with. It can be anything from a project at work to a piece of art you are creating to a

report you have to write. (Don't choose anything with life or death consequences, literally or figuratively!)

2. Decide that for the duration of this project, and this project only, you are going to allow your body to be smarter than you. If you don't feel like doing it, DON'T!

Example:

If you think you should be doing some research related to the project and you notice that you're watching reruns of Star Trek: The Next Generation *instead, remind yourself that this is exactly what you're supposed to be doing to perfectly time the universe, sit back, and enjoy trying to spot the joins in the Klingon's makeup!*

3. Wherever you feel like it, do some work on the project, trusting that your timing is inevitably perfect. Keep note of any coincidences, serendipities, and other "happy accidents" that happen along the way.

Remember, there's no way to screw this experiment up. Whatever you find yourself doing, it is exactly what you are supposed to be doing in order to perfectly time the universe. Enjoy!

5. Overcoming chasing the wrong goal: What's your motivation?

"I think the big mistake in schools is trying to teach children by using fear as the basic motivation. . . . Interest can produce learning on a scale compared to fear as a nuclear explosion to a firecracker."
— Stanley Kubrick

There are numerous anecdotes peppered throughout Hollywood folklore about overly earnest young actors who want to know, "What's my motivation?" before filming every scene.

One of my favorites came from a friend of mine who was working with Marlon Brando toward the end of the great actor's career. A young actress playing Brando's daughter objected to the direction of a scene that called for her to mix a drink in the midst of receiving terrible news.

"But what's my motivation?" she asked.

Brando smiled at her and took her to one side.

"Imagine a hat the size of the state of Montana," Brando said. "And imagine that hat is filled to overflowing with one-dollar bills. Can you imagine that hat?"

The actress nodded, a bit confused but following along.

"That's how much money you're being paid to be in this movie," Brando continued, "and that's your (expletive deleted) motivation!"

When we take the same question outside the world of acting and into the somewhat more real world of our daily lives, it becomes far more useful.

There are essentially only three motivations for any action you take or goal you find yourself pursuing in the world:

1. Desperation, or "Because I have to"
2. Rationalization, or "Because I should"
3. Inspiration, or "Because I want to"

I recently came across the amazing story of Sabriye Tenberken, the founder of *Braille without Borders*.

At the age of 26, Sabriye (who lost her sight at the age of 12) left her native Germany and headed out to Tibet to teach blind children to read, use computers, and most important, to develop confidence in their value and worth in the world.

In talking about her own blindness, she said:

"Maybe it's good that I'm blind, because people who can see, see all the reasons why they can't do something. I don't see the obstacles. I only see the one reason I can do it . . . and that is because I want to!"

As we have discussed throughout this book, the more in tune you are willing to be with your wanting, the more naturally your life will flow—and the more effortless your success will seem to be.

From theory to practice . . .

Desperation, Rationalization, or Inspiration?

1. Review some of your current goals and ask yourself, "What's my motivation?" for each item on your list.

   Your answer will fall into desperation, rationalization or inspiration—in other words, because you have to, should, or want to.

2. If you're motivating yourself from a sense of desperation ("I *have* to do/be/have this, because . . ."), consider the external "real

world" consequences of doing or not doing whatever it is. If you were already happy, would you still "have to" be/do/have it?

3. If your goal is coming from a sense of rationalization ("I *should* be/do/have this, because . . ."), once again explore the real consequences of your impending action.

These questions may prove useful:
– *What would happen if I did?*
– *What would happen if I didn't?*
– *What wouldn't happen if I did?*
– *What wouldn't happen if I didn't?*
– *If nobody noticed and nobody cared about it, would I still want it?*

4. If it seems as though you are about to follow your inspiration ("I *want* to do/be/have this, because . . ."), notice what happens if you allow yourself to finish the sentence "I want to be/do/have this because . . . I want to!"

This is the benchmark of a truly inspired goal or course of action—one which will not only tend to meet with success but will also begin bringing about coincidences and synchronicities "undreamed of in the common hour."

Of course, even when you're motivated to go for what you really want, you may well feel like you don't have the time to do whatever it is you think you have to do to get it. We'll deal with that obstacle right in this moment now. . . .

———⊂⊃⊃⊃———

CHAPTER 14

TIME

Information	Skill	Belief
Well-being	Other people	Motivation
Time	Money	Fear

The Yoda principle

"There is no try—there is only do or not do."
—Yoda, in *The Empire Strikes Back*

MOST PEOPLE ARE SURPRISED to hear that not one of my clients has weight problems, relationship issues, or career challenges. Is this because my clients are so cool? (Well, they are, but no!) It's because 99 out of a 100 times, the challenges we all face in our lives are actually about prioritization.

Why isn't your diet working?
Because you're not really sticking to it.

Why isn't your relationship working?
Because you've not really made it the most important thing in your life.

Why aren't you where you want to be in your career?
Because you allow other things to take precedence over it on a daily basis.

"Not me," I hear you cry. "I try my best, but money (traffic/my partner/my kids/my boss/insert excuse here) won't let me do what I want to do!"

For most of us, when we say we will "try" and do something, we mean one of two things:

1. We have no real intention of doing it and want to get our excuses in early ("Well, I did say I'd *try* . . .")

2. We don't feel the project/task/outcome is worthy of our full effort and commitment. However, if we can accomplish it without too much focus or effort, we will.

In fact, every time someone tells me that their biggest obstacle is not having enough time, I know their real problem is one of prioritization—how they're choosing to spend their 1,440 minutes a day, 168 hours a week, and 365 days of the year.

Here's the secret to overcoming time as an obstacle in your life:

**The most important choice you make
is what you choose to make important.**

For the rest of this chapter, we'll take a look at some of the different choices you can make that will make a tangible difference in both the results you produce and the quality of your life. (You know, if it isn't too much trouble and if stuff doesn't come up . . .)

The million-dollar question

Years ago, I was understudying the role of Jennifer Saunders' husband in a play called *Me and Mamie O'Rourke*. The actor who actually played the part was unfortunately talented, reliable, and as healthy as an ox, so I spent a lot of time sitting in my dressing room during the run of the show.

As much to pass the time as anything, I made a list of everything I wanted to have in my life and kept it up on the dressing-room wall. The list was vast and indiscriminate, covering everything from starring in my own TV show (which happened three years later) to flying to the moon (still waiting for that one) to getting a dog (we now have two, and they're wonderful!).

One item on my list puzzled me—it was "five new pairs of socks." What was puzzling was not why I wanted it—there are only so many days you can play "Concentration" with your sock drawer before re-stocking becomes the only viable option. What puzzled me was why I didn't just go down to the store and spend the ten bucks or so it would've cost me to buy them.

I finally gained new insight into the whole "sock mystery" when I discussed it with a friend who pointed out that it sounded as though I had no intention of getting new socks.

Now, brilliantly insightful though he clearly thought this was, I didn't give it much thought until I realized he had meant it literally. I didn't manifest the socks because I had no *intention* of manifesting socks—that is, I hadn't chosen to make bringing more socks into my life sufficiently important to get it done.

Think about that for a moment. How many things are there on your goal or to-do list do you have no real *intention* of doing, being, or having, ever if you really do want them in your life?

I have found the simplest way to discover and subsequently raise our level of commitment and intention in relation to whatever we are doing is to ask ourselves the "million dollar question":

If I were going to offer you a million dollars for the successful achievement of whatever it is you say you want in your life, what would you do differently to go about getting it?

For example, I remember seeing a poster for the movie *White Men Can't Jump* featuring the actor Wesley Snipes, t-shirt off and six-pack abs on full display. When I compared my rather more rounded abdomen to his, I justified the disparity to myself by thinking, *When I get paid six million dollars to get that fit, I'll find the time and put in the work to do it.* Then it dawned on me—I was getting paid six million dollars to put in the work—I just wasn't being paid in advance!

What if you decided to apply the million-dollar question to your most important relationships?

If you knew that you were going to be paid a million dollars (or whatever would be exciting and inspirational for you) for finding time to create a fantastic relationship with the people who matter most in your life, what would you do differently to make it fantastic?

Would you be more loving? More patient? More present? More honest? Then love, patience, presence, and honesty will be the benefits you reap when you approach your relationships with million-dollar intention.

How about work—do you currently approach your work with million-dollar intention?

If I were going to give you a million dollars for showing up for work each day on time and inspired, how would you do it? What preparation would you do each morning? How would you make sure you maintained that level of inspiration throughout the day?

What asking ourselves (and others) the million-dollar question and then living our lives with million-dollar intention does is remind us that how we spend our time and how we show up for our lives each day is largely a matter of choice—and the choice is always ours.

Why Not Just Put a Gun to Your Head?

> *"Knowing you are going to be hanged in the morning focuses the mind wonderfully."*
> — Samuel Johnson

If you knew that anyone who arrived late to a meeting would be killed, would you prioritize leaving earlier and arriving on time? If you knew that the difference between your loved ones living and dying was your ability to not lose your temper with them, would you prioritize mastering the skills of emotional control?

Unpleasant though these images might be, a lot of things that we call "impossible" suddenly become extremely possible if someone had a real or metaphorical gun to our heads.

Indeed, some people have learned to live like this, keeping themselves under the constant threat of poverty, abandonment, and self-hatred if they don't perform up to whatever standard they have decided upon. The problem with this motivational strategy is simple:

**If you keep putting a gun to your head,
at some point you're going to want to pull the trigger.**

While such an aggressive approach can certainly reap results in the short term, my preference for the inspiration of the million-dollar question over the motivation of what NLP creator Richard Bandler calls "Smith and Wesson therapy" is less to do with sustainability than it is to do with enjoyment. The fact is, life is never more fun than when you live it like it matters.

From theory to practice...

A Question of Priorities

1. Take some time this week to prioritize noticing what you're prioritizing in your life. When do you choose TV over conversation? When do you choose the newspaper over work? When do you choose what you're supposed to be doing over what you really want to be doing?

2. Listen to your language when you make promises or excuses. Are you blaming (or preparing to blame) circumstances for your actions and results? If you're not sure, run your situation through the million-dollar question or offer yourself a bit of hypothetical Smith and Wesson Therapy!

3. Choose a relationship in your life you would like to enhance. The next time you are with this person, act as if he or she's the most important person in the world and notice how it affects your time together.

4. Make at least one commitment to yourself this week that you will definitely keep (as opposed to "try to keep"). This can be to be on time for your appointments, to exercise daily, to spend time with your partner or family, etc. If you find yourself "forgetting" or "failing" to keep your commitment, notice how you would behave differently if you'd really made it a top priority.

"Big rocks" time management

There is a story about a seminar leader who placed a large jar on a table. By the side of the jar he placed a bucket of gravel, a bucket of sand, a bucket of water, and three big rocks. He then challenged his participants to find a way to fit everything on the table into the jar.

After numerous attempts, it became clear that the only way to successfully fit everything in was to start with the big rocks first.

The gravel filled the gaps between the big rocks, the sand filled the gaps in the gravel, and the water filled the gaps in the sand.

When it comes to what we choose to make important, it's pretty easy to get caught up in the daily gravel, ground down by the sand, and swept away by the water. What can be tricky is finding ways to prioritize the "big rocks"—those things in our life that matter most.

There are essentially four types of "big rock"—that is, four priorities that we can choose to focus on in any given moment, allowing the ever-present minutiae of life to fill in the gaps as we go.

Big Rock One—Activities

Sometimes, the most important thing about a day is an activity or set of activities. If you're an athlete, you may prioritize exercise; if you're a salesperson, you may prioritize making calls. In either case, you are prioritizing the activity over the desired end result.

Big Rock Two—Goals

One of the most potent things you can prioritize is your goals. What's the difference between making something a goal and making it a priority? Goals are rarely within our direct control—our priorities always are.

Big Rock Three—Intentions

Sometimes, the most useful thing for us to prioritize is neither an activity nor a goal, but a way of being. These intentions carry on in the background as we engage in activities and pursue our goals. Some useful intentions include "staying present," "enjoying whatever it is that I am doing," and "listening and speaking from my heart."

Big Rock Four—People

As oxygen is to the body, attention is to the spirit. When we make a person our priority, we are committing to give them the greatest yet simplest gift we possess—the gift of our full, undivided attention. And of course it's a good idea if at least once a day you make sure the person you prioritize is yourself.

How, specifically, do you prioritize something?

1. Do it first

One of the simplest ways to prioritize something is to begin with it—to put it right at the top of the agenda and stick with it until it's done. This approach works particularly well with activities and "mini-goals"—i.e., goals that can be completed within the course of a few minutes to a few hours.

2. Do it now

I have yet to meet the person who isn't blown off course during the course of a day. In fact, no matter how many Post-It note reminders you stick on your computer, fridge, and dashboard, I guarantee you'll forget about your chosen priorities again and again. The solution? When you remember, shift your focus and do it now! This approach is particularly useful when you are prioritizing intentions, and people.

3. Do it often

How do you eat an elephant? One bite at a time. How do you prioritize a goal? By coming back to it again and again and again. This approach is equally useful with activities, goals, intentions, and people.

From theory to practice . . .

Billable Hours

1. Choose a life role, project, or goal which you would like to take to the next level.

2. Just for fun, guesstimate the number of billable hours you put into that area in the last week. This is the number of hours that you would feel comfortable billing a client for if they were paying you to work on it.

3. Starting today, and for the rest of the week if you're up for it, log all your billable time working in this area.

4. If you think the number of billable hours you are spending on the project "should" be enough, it's probably time to reexamine your strategy. However, in many cases you will realize that you simply need to make this area more of a "big rock," and spend a bit more time and attention on it.

Let's spend a bit more time on procrastination . . .

While I have already talked about procrastination at some length in the chapter on motivation, I also like to explore the theme from a different angle in my time management-oriented workshops. The fundamental philosophy behind these courses is that procrastination is not a mental or physical ailment, but simply the label we hang on any situation in which we disapprove of the way we've chosen to prioritize our time.

For example, if I watch a rerun of *Friends* on TV and I think I should have been working on my novel, I call it procrastination; if I don't disapprove of watching *Friends* (or don't have a novel), I call it a choice.

Early on in the workshop, I share Roger and Rebecca Merrill's distinction about the four quadrants of time management:

Quadrant One: Urgent and Important	Quadrant Two: Important but not Urgent
Quadrant Three: Urgent but not Important	Quadrant Four: Not Urgent or Important

The Merrills' thesis, made famous by best-selling author Stephen R. Covey, is that effective time management involves spending the bulk of your time in quadrant two, working on those tasks that are important but not urgent. While this is a wonderful theory, the problem is that most of us have developed the habit of trying to trick ourselves into getting things done by creating imaginary or self-inflicted consequences for not completing a not urgent and/or not important task. In other words, we take something we either want to do or think we should do and tell ourselves we *have* to do it.

Here's the test:

Are there any real world consequences to not getting this done today?

If the answer is yes, and it's a consequence you want to avoid (losing your job, paying a fine, going to jail, etc.), then by all means leave the task cn your urgent list. If the answer is yes, but the consequences are psychological or emotional ("I'll feel bad," "It'll mean I'm lazy," "It'll prove that I'm not motivated enough to succeed," etc.), pat yourself on the back for trying to motivate yourself through self-inflicted pain, but know that you will almost certainly continue to "procrastinate" on this task until it becomes genuinely urgent or you genuinely want to do it and/or get it done.

While being honest with yourself about what really needs to be done each day will not necessarily help you get through your daily to-do list any quicker it will go a long way toward making you feel better about what you do accomplish. In addition, you will find that when you allow yourself to spend as much time each day on what you want to do (as opposed to what you want to get done), you will find yourself taking the right action at the right time in the right place with the right people.

And if you need an affirmation for dealing with procrastination, feel free to borrow mine:

I cut myself infinite slack.

The juggler's guide to effective time management

"Everything should be made as simple as possible—but not simpler."
— Albert Einstein

Several years ago, my children were watching me practise juggling. They giggled as I tossed one ball into the air, were excited by two, thought it was magic as a third ball entered into the fray, but were absolutely befuddled by my inability to add a fourth, fifth, or sixth ball to the mix.

In trying to explain the difference between juggling three things and juggling more, I realized that one key to the process is that when you're only juggling three things, you can always keep a firm grasp on two of them. The more things you add to the mix, the more things have to be up in the air and out of your control.

How much simpler would your life be if you never had more than three things on your to-do list?

I first developed the following time-management system for a particularly scattered client. I liked it so much I began employing it myself, and it is now in regular use by hundreds of people around the world.

The system takes most people no more than ten minutes a month to use and is compatible with almost any other system I've come across. It combines the idea of no more than three priorities at a time with the power of consistent daily focus.

Here's how it works . . .

Once a Month

1. Choose up to three priorities for the month—if you have more than three, rework them!
   Example:
   Spend time with family, complete the first draft of book, lose 5–10 pounds.

2. Next, set up to three priorities for the next two weeks
   Example:
   Hire virtual assistant, complete tax returns, prepare for my vacation.

3. Into the home stretch—up to three priorities for the week ahead.
   Example:
   Collect tax data, read new exercise book, sort out kennel for dog.

Once a Week

1. Reset your top three priorities for the next two weeks. Remember to refer to your priorities for the month!

2. Reset your top three priorities for the next week.

3. Fill in your spiritual self-care items for the week (see the "well-being" chapter for more on how to do this!).

Daily

1. Choose your top three priorities for the day

2. Tick off your spiritual self-care items as you complete them.

   In setting your priorities, some useful questions to ask yourself include:
   a. *What's the most important thing for me to focus on?*
   b. *What's the most useful thing for me to focus on?*
   c. *What would I love to focus on?*

Your answers to the above questions can take the form of an activity, a goal, an intention, or a person.

Here's an example of the tracking sheet I give my clients as a part of their welcome package. If you would like to receive a full-size copy of this tracking sheet for your own use, send us an e-mail at **bigrocks@geniuscatalyst.com** and we'll e-mail one out to you within the day!

Weekly Planner for the week of _____

Priorities for the month

1. _____

2. _____

3. _____

Priorities—the next two weeks

1. _____

2. _____

3. _____

Priorities—this week

1. _____

2. _____

3. _____

Spiritual Self-Care	Mon	Tues	Wed	Thurs	Fri	Sat	Sun
1.							
2.							
3.							
4.							
5.							
6.							
7.							
8.							
9.							
10.							

Experiment with this system for a few weeks and adapt it until it works well for you, keeping as much or as little of it as feels useful, practical, and fun.

Of course, if you use this or any other time-management system purely to fit more activity into your day, you will find a lack of time continuing to seem like an obstacle between you and your wonderful life. That's why there's one more distinction I'd like to share with you before we move on. . . .

Being done for the day

Many years ago, before I developed the system I have just shared with you, I triple-booked an audition, a coaching client, and a business meeting into one half-hour slot in my schedule. Based on my inability to keep all three of those balls in the air at the same time, I decided it might be worth upgrading my time-management skills and booked myself onto a one-day training course for use with one of the more traditional time-management systems.

Once I got past the idea that my entire life was going to be managed out of a little black book (and dear God, was I terrified of losing that book!), I began to get into the daily and weekly planning sessions of ABC priorities and putting checks in the boxes next to my daily tasks.

Then one day, I had an extraordinary experience that I couldn't quite believe. It was around 4 P.M. and I looked into my book to see what was next. To my amazement, there wasn't anything left on my list. I was done with my work for the day.

Now while this might not mean as much to you if you begin work at nine and finish each day at five, if you are self-employed, own a business, or even try and maintain a home with a house full of children, you can imagine how bizarre it felt to me to actually be done for the day.

Of course, if I'd wanted to, I could've found things to do—my projects hadn't all magically completed themselves. But I had done enough—I had done what I set out to do.

So enticing was this magical state that I rode it to its limits. Formerly mythical notions like "getting eight hours' sleep" and "relaxing at home with my family" became commonplace occurrences, and I even found myself with time for (gasp!) reading novels and (gosh!) playing with my children.

While I have by no means mastered this art (as witnessed by the fact that my wife and three children recently fe : the need to remind me that I have a wife and three children), here are a couple of the key distinctions I've made that make it easier to experience the daily peace that comes with being done for the day:

1. *Take the time to get complete with your life*

In a number of personal-development, recovery and coaching courses, there is a notion of "being complete" with your life. These programs encourage you to tie up every loose end, make amends for every wrongdoing, even phone or otherwise contact every person with whom you have any unfinished business.

This is, in fact, doable (with a bit of creativity in how you finish off with Uncle Ned who's been dead for ten years) and can be a worthwhile project to take on, though I recommend making sure you are working with a coach or support network and that you allow yourself anywhere from a month to a year to get it done.

As you are working toward completing your life (and even if you're not!), an excellent practice is to begin dealing with potential incompletions and distractions as they arise. Simply making the tying-up of loose ends a daily, weekly, or even monthly priority will go a long way toward bringing you a sense of ongoing peace in your life.

2. *Learn to be complete FOR NOW*

A less daunting and more immediately practical version of this exercise is to learn to be complete FOR NOW.

Sometimes, the things you are carrying with you can't be resolved in a matter of minutes, but you can get to a place of peace with them anyway. There are essentially three ways to do this:

a. Take a step in the right direction

This could involve making a plan, doing a bit of research, making a preliminary phone call, or completing one part of a larger project.

b. Repeat a simple daily action

With large goals or projects, knowing that you are doing something every single day to move yourself toward your desired end result can often be enough to give you a sense of peace in relation to that larger goal.

c. Choose to put things down for the time being

In the theater, actors are encouraged to "leave their problems in the wings" when they go on stage so they can commit themselves completely to the world of the play. (Sir John Gielgud was actually known to leave the contents of his stomach in the wings, vomiting into an off-stage bucket before going out and delivering breathtaking performances of Hamlet or Mercutio).

We can use this same facility in ourselves by choosing to put down our mental baggage outside the meeting room, classroom, or work place, and redirecting our attention to being where we are. This then allows us to be completely present with whatever it is we are doing.

If our mental baggage is truly important, it will be there waiting for us when we're done with whatever it is we are choosing to deal with instead.

From theory to practice . . .

Being Done

1. Make a list of any people with whom you have unfinished business. (One way of identifying them is to think of anyone you would dread hearing from when you answer the phone.) Choose one of these people each day or week and write, phone, or otherwise contact them to resolve the situation. Continue until the list is complete.

2. Throughout the day, notice what (if anything) is between you and a sense of peace. Make a note of what it is and take at least one action toward resolution. Experiment to discover how much you need to do to feel complete FOR NOW.

3. Practice declaring yourself "done" by putting down your mental baggage before any personal interactions you have scheduled today. If you find this difficult, decide whether to postpone the interaction (and go take care of whatever is on your mind!) or to continue practising until this is second nature for you.

And with that, I officially declare this discussion of time to be done!

In our next chapter, we'll take on an obstacle that can prove more costly than any other. . . .

CHAPTER 15

MONEY

Information	Skill	Belief
Well-being	Other people	Motivation
Time	**Money**	Fear

An expensive obstacle

> 'If a man is after money, he's money mad;
> if he keeps it, he's a capitalist;
> if he spends it, he's a playboy;
> if he doesn't get it, he's a never-do-well;
> if he doesn't try to get it, he lacks ambition.
> If he gets it without working for it, he's a parasite;
> and if he accumulates it after a lifetime of hard work,
> people call him a fool who never got anything out of life."
> — Vic Oliver

WHEN I ASK PEOPLE what holds them back from living the life of their dreams, the number one answer they give me is money, or more specifically, the lack of it in their lives. And given that on average, we spend at least a third of our time each day in an attempt to collect money, money's place in our overall vision for our lives would seem pretty crucial.

Yet most people still think of money as at best a "necessary evil" or at worst, something that "those that have" use to keep down those that haven't. And as with any other area of our lives, it's our unexamined and unquestioned assumptions about money that have the most significant impact on how we relate to it.

I personally believe a large part of why my clients and I are consistently able to increase not only our income but also the pleasure, satisfaction, and meaning we get from money comes about as a result of consistently challenging those assumptions. We do this by asking and answering questions that reveal not only what we are believing about money but also why we are believing it.

Here are seven fun and powerful questions designed to give you a sense of how money and your ultimate life vision are interconnected.

Let's start with some biggies:

1. *What would you do if you won the lottery?*

2. *If all jobs paid the same, what would you choose to do?*

3. *If you were given a million dollars and you had to use it all up in a month, how would you spend it?*

I like questions like these; they inspire powerful fantasies and can help clarify your fondest desires. The trouble is, they're a bit impractical—you haven't won the lottery, all jobs don't pay the same, and statistically speaking, you're more likely to be kicked to death by a goat than given a million dollars.

So now, let's ask ourselves some questions a bit "closer to home" . . .

4. *What role does money currently play in your life? What role would you like it to play?*

5. *If wanting more money was a way to compensate for something you feel is lacking in yourself, what would it be compensating for?*

6. *What have you made more important than having money in your life? What have you made less important?*

7. *On a scale from 1–10, how much do you enjoy the whole subject of money? What is at least one thing you could do right now to up your enjoyment?*

While each of these questions will assist you in making powerful shifts in the area of money, perhaps the most fundamental shift in my own thinking came about as the result of asking myself an eighth question:

Is making money a worthy goal?

The reason this question seemed so fundamental to me was that if making money was a worthy goal, I wasn't putting nearly enough time, focus, and energy into it; if making money wasn't a worthy goal, I was spending far too much time, focus, and energy on it.

In NLP, we make a distinction between sensory-based language (about what you can see, hear, taste, touch, or smell) and vague language, affectionately referred to as "fluff." While good fluff has its place (most summer beach reading comes easily to mind), it is decidedly un-useful in making useful decisions. The simple truth of the matter is, vague questions lead to vague answers.

The way to de-fluff language is by seeking to recover any key bits of information that have been left out, distorted, or generalized. When I applied this idea to my original question, the "real" question was revealed:

Is making (how much money? In what time frame? For what purpose?) a worthy goal?

Initially, I filled in the blanks like this:

Is doing whatever it takes to make as much money as possible in order to guarantee I never need to worry about money again a worthy goal?

For me the answer to this question was a firm "no." While never needing to worry about money again seemed a worthy enough goal to me, I also realized from my work coaching millionaires that it is rarely achieved by attaining a certain quantity of money, no matter how large.

Similarly, while "Do whatever it takes!" sounds great coming out of the mouth of a motivational speaker or underneath a framed photo of a spectacular athletic achievement, it loses much of its magic if you imagine it coming out of the mouth of your least favorite dictator or under a picture of a village destroyed by war, famine, or poverty.

Next, I filled in the blanks like this:

Is making enough money this year from work I love and want to do in order to cover all our expenses, save 10%, give away 10%, make some home improvements and cover our tax bill a worthy goal?

This time, the answer was equally obvious—an unquestionable yes.

Just for fun, I filled in the blanks a third time:

Is making enough money over the next 10 to 15 years from work I love and want to do in order to look after my family, put my kids through university, create financial independence, and give away over a million dollars to charities and related causes a worthy goal?

Now, my answer was not only a resounding yes, but my brain began overflowing with creative ideas for creating and exchanging value in the world. Once again I had found my "Wow!"—my uniquely personal blueprint for success. And as money began to flow into my life at unprecedented levels, I realized once again that there is something almost magical that happens when you give yourself permission to really want what you want—even money!

From theory to practice . . .

A Worthy Goal

1. Do you consider making money a worthy goal for you? If you're not 100% clear on your answer, fill in the blanks for yourself until you get an unmistakable yes:

   "Is making (how much money in what time frame for what purpose?) a worthy goal?"

2. When you have found the amount of money, time frame, and purpose that makes making money an undeniably worthy goal for you, go for it!

The simplest secret

"Annual income twenty pounds, annual expenditure nineteen nineteen six, result happiness. Annual income twenty pounds, annual expenditure twenty pound ought and six, result misery."
— Charles Dickens, from *David Copperfield*

When I teach the obstacle course to success on seminars, I often lump time and money together because they have so much in common. Both are generally viewed as limited resources, controlled by others. And most problems that are associated with both time and money can be solved by consistently taking one frightfully simple action:

Write It Down!

- Not sure how much you're spending? *Write it down!*
- Worried about missing an appointment? *Write it down!*
- Wondering whether the money you're earning is worth the time you're spending? *Write it down!*

Why is writing things down so important when it comes to time and money? It's because neither time nor money really exist! Both are man-made, abstract constructs originally designed to make our lives easier but often resulting in making our lives far more complex. And as anyone who's ever slept through a philosophy class can testify, trying to hold abstract concepts in our minds can be exhausting.

Writing things down relating to time and money helps take them out of the realm of the abstract and bring them down into the realm of the concrete, where math replaces myth and the simple secret of lifelong wealth turns out to be so boring (*spend less than you earn and invest the rest*) that no one ever believes it could be that simple.

If you still believe money really exists, spend a few days studying the futures markets or basic economics. As my stockbroker housemate once explained to me, "If you pretend all those zeroes don't mean anything, losing a billion dollars is really quite easy to do!"

Which brings me to my next point . . .

Relax, relax, relax, relax, relax

> *"Don't worry—make money!"*
> — Richard Carlson

I was eavesdropping on a conversation in my head one day when I heard myself say, "*I'll relax when the check has cleared!*"

Now, this almost slipped past me, but I suddenly realized it was an expression that had some interesting implications. Apparently, I had decided to be tense until the check cleared and the money went into my account. Knowing what I know about the ill effects of excessive tension on health and well-being, and not sure of what mystical powers my physical tension might hold over the check-clearing systems at the bank, I thought it was probably time to examine those thoughts in a little more detail. The conversation went a little something like this . . .

Me (as Coach): Why do you believe that you need to stay tense until the check has cleared?

Me (as Me): Because when I relax, I don't pay attention to my finances.

MC: Can you give me an example?

MM: When we were struggling financially, I kept on top of my account balances. As soon as I had a reliable income source, I stopped tracking my expenses. If I had stayed uptight about money, I wouldn't have overspent.

MC: Why do you believe staying uptight would've kept you from overspending?

MM: Because when I feel comfortable financially, I get lazy— I overspend and I don't track expenses.

MC: Why do you overspend and not track expenses when you feel comfortable?

MM: I guess because I think it's okay to—I give myself a large enough buffer and then try and stick vaguely to a budget. Thing is, it doesn't work! I guess I've always believed that one of the perks of having money is that you get to not think about money.

MC: Why do you believe that?

MM: Now that I actually hear myself say it, I don't.

MC: What do you believe?

MM: I believe that one of the perks of thinking about money is that you get to have some!

MC: So what are you going to do?

MM: It's pretty simple for me to maintain the same spending habits no matter how much money I've got in the bank. All I have to do is go back onto a cash budget for me and set up a separate bill-paying account for the household.

MC: How do you feel about that?

MM: Relaxed! What's interesting is that I've always thought that financial ease came from having money; in my case, it actually comes from having a system in place that I can rely on.

While the specifics of that conversation were unique to me, I have found the ramifications to be universal. As in so many areas of our lives, when we realize we have been using tension, stress, and unhappiness to motivate ourselves, we can make new choices and begin to reap completely different rewards.

❖ ❖ ❖

From theory to practice . . .

Getting Relaxed about Money

1. How do you currently feel about money?

2. What are you afraid would happen if you didn't feel that way any more? (These are the hidden "benefits" of staying stuck.)

3. How would you like to feel about money?

4. What would you have to change in order to feel the way you want to feel and ensure you didn't lose out on the "benefits" you discovered in question two?

How to make more money

"A lack of money is the root of all evil."
— George Bernard Shaw

Of course, once you get comfortable with the idea of wanting more money (and relax more and more about having it), it's useful to understand a little bit more about how to get it.

Most people seem to approach the idea of making more money like a person arguing with an empty fireplace. "Give me more heat," they demand, "and then I'll consider giving you more wood!" But just as a fire cannot grow without fuel, your income tends not to grow without your first increasing the perceived value of what you are contributing to the world.

There are four main ways to increase the perceived value of your product or service. Let's take a quick look at each of these strategies in turn:

1. Focus on the benefits

How much of a difference is what you're doing making in the world, or at least in the part of the world you're trying to sell to? If you want to make more money, a great place to start is to make sure that what you're offering is of genuine value to the people you are offering it to.

For example, if you are currently unemployed, think in terms of what you have to offer a prospective employer. If you work for a company, you can think in terms of the product or service your company provides, but you can also think in terms of the product or service you provide to your company. If you work in a creative field (music, art, film, etc.), think in terms of what you have to offer to an audience, gallery, or producer.

2. Find out what's so special about you

Of course if benefit were the only key to creating wealth, teachers and nurses would all be millionaires. One reason that they're not is that there is another factor to consider—how unique is the product or service you are offering? This is where the law of supply and demand comes in to play. The more supply (i.e., people or companies doing what you do), the less you will be able to charge for it; the less supply (assuming it is of sufficient benefit to generate demand), the more you can charge.

"Why me?" is actually one of the best questions you can ask if you want to make more money—and as with all questions, it works best if you keep asking until you get an answer.

3. Reveal the best kept secret in marketing

What's the best kept secret in marketing? Far too often, the only real answer is you!

How many people actually know what it is that you do? Ten? One hundred? One thousand? How many of them have actually experienced it for themselves?

No matter what your field, the numbers speak for themselves:

**The more people who know what you're up to,
the more of them will be buying whatever it is you're selling!**

But even when you're reaching a lot of people, you may not yet be making the amount of money you want. This is where perception comes into play. . .

4. Tell a better story

If you want to make more money, you need a better story—one that conveys both the value of what you're offering and the values of the person who is offering it. Practice your story with everyone you can—you'll know you're on the right track when the people who hear it go "Wow!" and you'll know you've got it really right when they start to take out their wallets!

The following exercise will help you get started on putting these four strategies to work for you. . . .

From theory to practice. . .

The Value Snapshot

1. Use the questions above to rate your current product or service on a scale from 1–10 in relation to benefit, uniqueness, visibility, and story. Add up your four scores for a quick "value snapshot."

2. Brainstorm as many strategies as you can to increase your score by ten points over the next month.

3. Take the next step—put your favorite strategies into action!

The "Freedom Fund"

"The difference between poor people and rich people is
that poor people spend money and save what's left;
rich people save money and spend what's left."
— Jim Rohn

Once you begin increasing your income and "money as security" becomes less of a driving force in your life, a whole new set of "Wow!" wants tends to emerge. In fact, one of the most common reasons people hire me as their coach is to assist them in leaving the not-so-secure security of their jobs and making the leap of faith into the world of self-employment or entrepreneurship.

What generally throws them for a loop is when I encourage them to become self-employed *before* they leave their jobs.

Let me explain what I mean . . .

The employer/employee relationship can generally be described as being based on an energy exchange—I agree to give you a certain amount of money, in exchange for which you agree to do whatever I say (within reason or not, depending on your job and your point of view!).

Being self-employed means that you are in the employ of yourself, which is to say you agree to give yourself a certain amount of money, in exchange for which you agree to do whatever you say (again, within reason or not, depending on your job and your point of view!).

How can you become self-employed before leaving your job? By following four simple steps:

1. If you don't already have one, open a high-interest instant access savings account and a regular current account.

2. From now on, arrange to have every paycheck, commission check, interest check, etc., go directly into your savings account.

3. Ask yourself how much money you need each month to live a "comfortably frugal" lifestyle. This number will become your new monthly self-employment salary.

4. Once a month, pay yourself your agreed-upon salary from your savings into your current account. If you want to have a separate account for taxes and other periodic expenses, you can make a payment into that account as well.

The difference between what your company deposits into your savings account and what you pay yourself into your current account is the beginning of your "Freedom Fund"—from six to twelve months of comfortably frugal living expenses, allowing you the freedom to make nonfinancially motivated choices about what to do next in your working life. (If you're feeling particularly daring, most banks will actually be willing to print "Freedom Fund" right on to your deposit slips.)

Once you are truly self-employed, you become disconnected from the financial control of your company. Since they don't pay your salary anymore (although they do of course continue to contribute to your Freedom Fund for as long as you work there), you are not beholden to them in the same way.

In fact, once you are no longer financially dependent on your job, you may decide to stay right where you are. The lure of self-employment is often really a craving for freedom, and once your job turns from a "must" into a "could" you are free to enjoy it, sometimes for the very first time.

For the rest of you, your Freedom Fund will become a gateway to a world of possibility, where pursuing your "Wow!" goals is not so much a leap of faith as a parachuted descent into the life of your dreams.

What if I'm already self-employed?

If you're already self-employed, this system works even better. Just follow the same four steps, and look forward to finally stepping off the financial roller coaster. The only downside to this system is that you don't get to spend more when you get a big payday—you will have the same amount to spend each month, regardless of how much you are actually earning.

The key to making this work for you is to personalize it. Tune into what feels joyful and alive to you and what level of reserve you really want to aim for. Most self-employed people are so used to living from job to job that having six months" salary in the bank may seem an unnecessary luxury. For others, years of worrying about making ends meet have contributed to huge patterns of worry and fear, and anything less than a year doesn't feel like enough.

Here's a letter from a reader of my weekly tips whose family set up their own Freedom Fund with fantastic results:

Dear Michael

Just a quick note to say thanks for the great tips you send out each week. One of the first I received was the Freedom Fund experiment. My wife and I tried it and set a target of six months' salary for the "reservoir." We worked out that it would take 12 to 24 months.

We did it in 2 months!!!! And now, another 2 months later we have 2 years salary in the reservoir (earning 4% interest per month!!), I have quit my stressful executive job and have my own corporation, we have no debt outside the mortgage, I have time for my family, we go to the gym every day and we feel like we are really living.

When we first set the target we did not realize how powerful it is to be able to make non-financially-motivated decisions. THANKS!!

Nick, Joanna, & Lisa (age 6) Halsey
Worcester, UK

While their results were particularly impressive, this process does have a tendency to work much faster than you think. One of the reasons for this is that it taps into some fundamental human psychology. Let's face it—would you rather have money taken away from you each month "for your own good," or to get to decide each time you're thinking about spending money on something how much extra you want to keep?

As you watch your Freedom Fund grow, your natural "where there's a way, there's a will" motivation kicks in and you will surprise yourself with how many creative ways you find to fill it to overflowing!

From money to wealth

"Wealth is a measure of access to resources."
— Sanaya Roman

Up until now in this chapter, we have been focusing exclusively on money—and as we've discussed, I believe that when appropriately contextualized, having more money is an extremely worthy goal.

However, in my experience it is almost never a lack of money that actually stops us from achieving our goals, but rather our inability to harness the full complement of resources available to us at any moment.

One of the models I have been using and sharing with my clients for over a decade is what I call "the Resource Bank"—a way of cataloging and utilizing resources that you may never have previously considered as part of your abundant wealth.

From theory to practice . . .

The Resource Bank

1. Begin by taking stock of all the resources you have available to you in your life. For ease of access, we will divide them into four categories ranging from the most renewable (i.e., things that the more you use them the more you have) to the least renewable (i.e., things that the more you use them, the less you have).

Category One: Your Genius
What are the qualities, skills, gifts, and talents you bring to the world?
Don't worry if you can't think of how they could ever be useful—just list as many of them as you can. . . .
Examples:
Loving, kind, a great dancer, a good negotiator, funny, can drink an entire pitcher of beer without swallowing, etc.

Category Two: Your Contacts
Who do you know? Who else? Who else? Who do they know?
They say that every person knows on average at least 250 other people. That gives you direct or direct referral access to up to 62,500 people, each of them with access to a resource bank of their own!

Here are some categories you can use to generate names for your list:

• People you work with
• People you work for
• People who work for you
• Family
• Friends
• Neighbors
• Your "fan club"
• People you went to school with
• People you used to work with
• Customers/clients

Category Three: Your Money
How much money have you got—current account, savings, investments, etc.? If you cashed out of your home and/or business tomorrow, how much cash could you raise?
Even though money isn't your only source of wealth, it's still a good one. Some problems actually do go away when you throw money at them. (For everything else, there's the rest of your Resource Bank!)

Category Four Your Stuff
What do you own? What stuff of other people's do you have access to?
In addition to the stuff we use in our day-to-day lives, most of us have hoarded far more things than we need in our lives. Before

you empty out your garage, basement, or closet, take a quick look through your stuff and make note of anything you've got that you or somebody else might want or need.

Examples:

House, computer, car, fax machine, photocopier, desk, chairs, etc.

2. Now, choose a problem, goal, or any area of your life where you are feeling stuck. Hold the problem or goal in your mind as you go back through all the items you wrote down in your Resource Bank. What you're looking for is new connections—mini "aha" insights into ways of hooking up resources that you may never before have considered. As ideas pop up, make a note of them or put a star next to that item in your Resource Bank.

3. Take action on your new ideas. Put your gifts into action, make some calls, spend some money, use your stuff, and prepare to be amazed!

Here are some of the ways you can put the Resource Bank to work in your own life:

- Making more money
- Finding new clients
- Generating new marketing or business ideas
- Dealing with difficult people or conflicts at home or at work
- Making more of a difference in the world.

Here's why it works so well . . .

Most of us rely on the same one or two resources to bail us out of trouble or propel us forward toward our goals again and again and again. When we get stuck, it's not because we've *really* run out of options, but rather because our habitual "knights in shining armor" aren't working or available to us in this particular situation.

What makes the Resource Bank such a powerful tool is that it forces us to expand our thinking outside our traditional comfortable confines. And when you take a trip down to your personal Resource Bank, you may be pleasantly surprised to discover how much is in your account!

From wealth to abundance

"With money in your pocket you're
handsome, funny, and you sing nice too."
— Old Yiddish Proverb

When I was studying acting in London, I had a part-time job working in a New Age bookstore. One day, Robert Plant, the lead singer for Led Zeppelin, came into the store and walked up to the owner. "What have you got that's good?" he asked. After a few moments' thought, the owner walked over to the shelves and handed him one of our most popular items—a subliminal "Abundance" tape that promised to "condition your mind for wealth." Plant looked at the tape in amusement. "Actually," he said, "I think I've got that one covered. What else have you got?"

As we bring this chapter to a close, I want to share with you a third way of thinking about money—for beyond money or even wealth lives the possibility of true abundance. And when you take the journey from money to wealth to abundance, adventure awaits you at every turn!

My own journey began when I first started interviewing authors for my radio show and I noticed a very peculiar phenomenon. Whenever I was interviewing an author who I thought was "above me," I felt nervous and inhibited; when I was interviewing an author who I thought was "beneath me," I felt easy in myself and able to perform freely. On closer examination, I came to realize that the fundamental difference was less to do with the relative status of the author than it was to do with a fundamental difference in my approach.

In the first set of interviews, I was coming from a sense of lack and focusing on what I wanted to get; in the second, I was coming from a sense of abundance and focusing on what I was able to give.

This is the first of three keys to experiencing the freedom that comes from living from abundance in your own life:

Key Number One—
Focus on What You've Got to Give, Not What You Want to Get

Are you going into business because you need the money?

Then you are focused on your lack—on what you feel you "need" to get in order to make your endeavor worthwhile.

Imagine, on the other hand, going into business because you have something incredible to contribute. Are you liable to walk out with money?

What if you're in sales—will you do better calling a prospect to sell them something (coming from lack—you "need" their money), or calling a prospective client from abundance—because you have something wonderful to share with them?

How about in the area of your intimate relationships?

Most people say they want to be in a relationship because they want love. But entering into a romantic partnership to get love is like going into a bank to borrow money—you might be able to get some, but if you're not careful you can get into some serious debt—and the interest rates are subject to fluctuation!

If, on the other hand, you enter into a relationship with an abundance of love already in your heart, that's like going into the same bank to make a hefty deposit. You'll be wined and dined by the bank manager, because they know there are plenty of other banks who would love to get their hands on what you have to offer. Because you have come to them from a place of abundance, they know your account will always be in credit, and they'll always be glad to see you.

Key Number Two— Cultivate an Abundance of Well-being

Have you ever seen a champagne waterfall, where one glass is placed atop three glasses balanced atop five glasses and so on down to the linen tablecloth?

As the top glass fills to overflowing, it naturally fills all of the glasses beneath it, and on and on the flow of abundance goes all the way down to the bottom.

One secret to living from abundance is to begin filling your own glass by connecting daily with your own inner love, freedom, energy, and power. As you fill yourself to overflowing, you will naturally share the best of what you have with those around you.

Key Number Three— Bless the Abundance of Others

According to Huna teacher Serge Kahili King, a blessing is "a compliment phrased like a promise." Because energy flows where attention goes, whenever we take the time to appreciate and acknowledge the success, wealth, and happiness of another, we create an abundant blessing—more than enough "good vibes" to assist both the receiver and ourselves.

This is the basis for our final financial experiment . . .

From Theory to Practice . . .

Abundance!

1. Throughout the day today, notice if you are coming from a place of abundance or one of scarcity. When you notice yourself focused on your own lack, ask yourself any of the following questions:

   • What is it that I most want to give in this situation?

   • How much do I already have in this area of my life?

   • What is it about being in this situation that I am most grateful for? What is it about that which "makes" me feel grateful?

   • What is it I want? What would it be like if I already had more than enough of it?

2. Look for people in your life who are "heroes of abundance." Be sure to take time to bless their success, and where appropriate, allow your cup to be filled in their presence.

3. Consider beginning each day by filling yourself up with good things. Read from books or e-zines that inspire you. Make a journal note about all the good things in your life. Meditate on the infinite goodness that surrounds you.

   You will know that you are done when you feel an inner "fullness"—often a feeling of deep contentment and satisfaction characterized by gentle tears of gratitude. Over time, you will find that although your capacity for experiencing good and living from abundance increases, it takes less and less time to fill yourself to overflowing.

Coming face-to-face with the wall

As we continue on through our obstacle course to success, one final obstacle awaits—and as with most obstacle courses, it is for many of us the most fearsome of all. . . .

CHAPTER 16

FEAR

Information	Skill	Belief
Well-being	Other people	Motivation
Time	Money	**Fear**

The snake in the corner of the room

*"Ultimately we know deeply that the other side
of every fear is a freedom."*
— Marilyn Ferguson

IMAGINE YOU ARE LIVING in a dark room, terrified night and day by the presence of a large and deadly snake who lives coiled in the corner. You do whatever you can to avoid that corner of the room, a part of your attention forever focused on the snake in case it decides to slither away from its preferred resting place.

Now, imagine that for one full minute, all the lights come on in the room. Allowing your curiosity to overcome your fear, you look over to the snake only to find it was nothing more than a bit of coiled rope with a frayed end—no more daunting or dangerous than an oversized piece of string.

Even if the lights went back out, you would never again be frightened of that piece of rope in the same way. Because you had seen for yourself what it actually is, you could never again fall victim to the illusion.

In Zen Buddhism, this temporary experience of "the lights coming on" (i.e., "enlightenment") is called Kensho. While the experience may fade, the insights received from the experience are yours to keep always.

Here are some of the typical mini-enlightenment experiences my friends and clients have shared over the years:

- *Finally having that conversation you've been avoiding, only to discover that it was no big deal and that the relationship you were worried about destroying is now stronger than ever.*

- *Coming out of the closet about your deepest, darkest secret to find that everybody already knew and/or nobody really cares!*

- *Finding out that the person you were so jealous of or frightened by was actually jealous and frightened of you.*

- *Finding yourself face-to-face with what you most fear and realizing that what made it so scary was the story you'd been telling yourself about what it would mean about you or your life if you "got it wrong."*

One of my own most recent Kensho experiences came while sitting in the "comfy chair" section of my local bookstore. I have long had a fear of verbal confrontations with strangers, believing that I would either come on too strong and really hurt someone, thereby "proving" my secret fear that I was an insensitive jerk, or back off too quickly and "prove" my secret fear that I was a wimp and a loser and a walkover.

Just as I settled into browsing through a pile of books I'd lovingly collected off the shelves, the woman in the comfy chair next to me took out her phone and began a series of extremely loud phone calls to, among other people, her boyfriend, her gynecologist, and a woman named Marni who was clearly not being as supportive as she would have liked.

Ordinarily, I would have sat there quietly seething in my seat (fright), made a righteously indignant request that she put away her phone (fight), or simply got up and walked away (flight). For some reason, on this occasion I did something completely different. I asked her if she would mind putting her phone away.

What shocked both of us was my complete lack of righteousness. She was so prepared for a battle that my lack of fight completely flummoxed her. She hung up her phone and walked away, leaving us both slightly puzzled as to what had just happened.

On reflection, I realized what I'd realized—that I could just ask for what I want without having to make up a story to justify it (and thereby "prove" that I was still a good human being and wasn't being unreasonable).

The essence of Kensho is this:

**■ often takes only one glimpse of freedom
to eliminate the fear forever.**

In order to "turn on the lights" and experience greater freedom in your own life, let's take a closer look at what fear is, how it works, and where it comes from. . . .

What are you so afraid of?

"Do the thing you fear and the death of fear is certain."
— Eleanor Roosevelt

Many years ago, I appeared on a UK TV program called *Put It to the Test*. My challenge was to put the NLP Fast Phobia Cure to the test on national television. Three arachnophobics joined me in the studio, hooked up to EEG and EKG machines by electrodes and monitored by two medical doctors.

During the show they were shown a clear container that contained several tarantulas, and sudden increases in heart-rate variability and electrical activity in the brain spiked off the monitors. I worked with them for approximately 30 minutes, at which point they were returned to the studio, reconnected to the equipment, and once again exposed to the tarantulas. This time, their heart rate and brain activity remained near normal, even when the spiders were brought directly in front of their faces.

Despite the medical doctors' amazement at the results, I wasn't particularly surprised as I had seen the technique work hundreds of times before. What I found most interesting about the day was what happened before we began filming. . . .

A few hours before we were due to go before the cameras, the volunteers were hooked up to the monitors for a dress rehearsal. A stage manager brought in the empty container in which the spiders would eventually be placed. As soon as the volunteers saw the empty container, their heart rates and brain activity spiked *exactly as if the real spiders had been brought into the room*. What was suddenly obvious was that they were not afraid of spiders—they were afraid of what they made up in their minds and bodies when they *thought* about spiders.

What I have come to see in my own experience and that of my clients is that this is not just true of phobias but of all fears:

**You aren't afraid of what you think you're afraid of—
you're afraid of what you think.**

Since the source of 99% of fear is in your thinking, you can quickly and easily release your fear (once you know how) without anything having to change in the world.

From theory to practice . . .

TiVo® for Your Brain

(Run through this exercise with things that are just a little bit scary until you get comfortable with it. As your skill increases, you can play with more fearful situations. . . .)

1. Imagine you are sitting at home in your favorite place to watch television. By your side you have a special remote that lets you stop, rewind, fast forward, and play with the images on the screen.

2. As you flick through the channels, you will find a blank screen. This is a special channel that broadcasts only shows about breaking through old fears. In a moment, they will be showing an old black-and-white movie featuring an actor/actress who looks and sounds remarkably like you in a situation not unlike one you may be facing soon.

3. As the movie begins, take a closer look at your remote. This time, you may notice some extra buttons that give you an even greater degree of control over what is happening on the screen:

   Brightness—turns the brightness up and down until it's comfortable to watch

   Color—allows you to change the movie back and forth from b&w to color

   Size—makes the images larger or smaller

   Distance—brings the images closer or pushes them farther away

   Volume—turns the volume up or down

   Temperature—turns the temperature in the room up or down until it feels "just right"

   Cartoon—turns the movie from live action to cartoon and back again

> **Alternate Ending**—as with many DVDs, this button allows you to view the movie with as many alternate endings as you would like to see
>
> **Interactive**—allows you to interact with what is happening on the screen, including switching the point of view, adding or changing the soundtrack, and adding captions or thought bubble for what is happening.
>
> 4. Run through the movie as many times as you like. If there are any moments you find particularly uncomfortable, play with the different options on your remote until the movie is just the way you like it and you can watch it with feelings of ease, comfort, and well-being. (Running it backwards with circus music on the soundtrack tends to work remarkably well!)

The origins of fear

As children, we are taught to fear things in order to keep us safe. Rather than take the time to explain the dangers and subtle nuances of a vast uncharted world, our well-meaning parents and guardians pass on a sort of "shorthand of fear" in an effort to ensure our survival. Because we are conditioned to think our fear will keep us safe, we often treat it as a "red light"—a signal from our bodies that we should stop.

But as Zen teacher Cheri Huber points out:

"Intelligence is what keeps us safe . . . what would be helpful is for someone to explain i all—not as if the child is stupid or careless or headed for disaster—but simply by way of giving information to someone who doesn't have it."

I remember the first day this really made sense to me on a visceral level. I was waiting to cross a busy road, stepping back involuntarily whenever a car whizzed by, when I realized I didn't have to be afraid of being hit by a car to not step out into the road. I could take care of myself in this way simply because I wanted to and knew how to—I no longer needed fear to help me do it.

Former US Navy Seal Richard Machowicz puts it like this:

"Fear is not a true indicator of danger, evaluated experience is. . . . It's a given that fear exists for every one of us. But never for a moment think that if you're afraid of something, that fear is somehow a warning and will save you. Good evaluation of past experiences makes for good decisions, period. And it's good decisions that will save you."

The next time you are thinking about doing something and fear arises, ask yourself the following three questions:

1. *What's the worst that can happen if that which I fear came to pass?*
2. *What's the best possible outcome for me or for others if I "felt the fear and did it anyway?"*
3. *What's more likely to happen than either of those two things?*

Each time you ask and answer these questions, you will find yourself able to make better and better decisions, even in the face of a seemingly frightening situation. What can make evaluating your experience even easier is to know that you don't have to go through it (whatever it is) yourself.

Imagine having someone in your life who would walk with you every step of your path, love you unconditionally, and support you no matter what, even when you were "wrong." Now, imagine this person makes you feel absolutely safe and cared for—loved, approved of and watched over.

Do you feel more willing to take on a challenge when you are with them? Do you feel more willing to take on the world?

How about just more willing to take on your life?

Fortunately, there is a part of you that is always present, always loving, always kind, and always there for you. If you haven't met that part of yourself yet, take a few moments now to guide yourself through this exercise. . . .

From Theory to Practice . . .

Meeting Your Inner Guide

1. Relax your body and allow yourself to become fully present—seeing these words, hearing the sounds around you, and feeling what you feel.

2. Now imagine you are sending love into every part of your body—your toes, your eyes, your thighs, your nose—go through every part of your body until you are tingling from head to toe.

3. The part of you that is able to give yourself love is your inner
   guide. Ask that part of you for any guidance it can share with
   you about how to move forward in the face of your fears.

As you practice spending time with yourself in this way, you will
find your fear begins to disappear and new possibilities become
available to you. Love conquers fear, every single time—and the
source of the love is inside you.

Overcome your fear of rejection

"All actors search for rejection.
And if they don't get it, they reject themselves."
— Charlie Chapin

In 1977, an oft-quoted survey was published in *The New York
Times* that revealed that a larger percentage of respondents feared
public speaking than death.

While this makes a kind of logical sense (more of the people
involved in the survey had experienced public speaking than
death), it has always seemed to me that the most crippling fear
many of us face is our fear of rejection.

Whether it stops us from making a sales call, asking someone
on a date, or pursuing the life of our dreams, our survival-based
fear of rejection is activated any time we make (or think about
making) a request from anyone.

This is largely because the possibility of being rejected is
generally real. The person we are selling to may decide not to buy,
the person we are asking out may indeed say no, and the road to
the life of our dreams may well be paved with rejection.

When I was acting full-time, my friends and I faced rejection
on a daily basis. And like anyone else who sells their product or
services for a living, if we didn't collect enough rejections we were
unlikely to make any money. In fact, an actress friend recently
pointed out that if she wasn't getting rejected at least ten times a
week, she began to panic about how slow things were!

Several years ago, I came up with a simple trick that works
wonders in easing the fear of rejection and allowing us to put our
best foot forward when we are faced with the possibility of rejection.

You can use it the next time you're feeling nervous before a
sales call, job interview, meeting, or even a blind date. . . .

From theory to practice . . .

Bringing Your Tribe along with You

1. A few minutes before your meeting/phone call/request/interview, begin to focus on the people in your life who love you. If you are religious, you can also focus on God's love for you; the more humanistically inclined can add in the love of a child, a partner, or a pet.

   (If you can't think of anybody or anything who loves or has loved you, there are probably more important things for you to work on in your life than getting better at making sales calls!)

2. Continue to focus on the awareness (and the associated feeling) that you are loved and begin to think about the impending event. Notice that you may still want what you want from the other people, but you do not need them to love or approve of you. You are already loved, accepted and approved of.

3. Bring this awareness and feeling with you into your meeting. If at any point during the meeting you begin to feel unduly nervous, you can simply go back to this awareness and feeling of being loved.

Why does this work so well?

It goes back to what we spoke about in Chapter 5—our biological predisposition toward safety or security. By calming this ancient part of our brain (by flooding it with the feeling of connection and belonging that comes with the awareness of being loved), we are better able to tap in to the full resources of our mind.

It is almost like sending a message to your brain that says, "Don't worry if this person or tribe does not accept you—you are already safe!"

Lions, tigers, and babies

One of the funniest things that happened while my wife was in labor with our first child (a time she is quick to point out was not replete with comic moments) occurred around 6 A.M. on the third morning of a 57-hour labor. In the midst of her pain and suffering, the attending midwife finally managed to get an anesthesiologist down to the delivery room to administer the epidural, a kind of intensive pain killer that's designed to totally numb your lower body to the point where you have to be told when you're pushing out the baby.

Well, in moments, the transformation that came over my wife convinced me that I should be investing our nest egg in the manufacturer of epidurals. Whereas seconds earlier she had been howling in the kind of agony that would've gotten her noticed on the set of *Saving Private Ryan*, suddenly she sat up, happy as could be, and asked me to pass her the Sunday papers. For the next five minutes we sat together, chatting and reading as if this "giving birth thing" was no more difficult than a simple annual checkup.

And then it happened—the next contraction began, and it became instantly clear that the epidural hadn't worked at all and the ease and relief my wife had just experienced was caused not by drugs but by the placebo effect of her own expectations during the lull between contractions.

Six hours, seventy-two contractions, and one unofficial purple heart later my wife gave birth to a healthy baby boy named Oliver, who has brought enough joy into our lives in the intervening years to justify the 57 hours of pain and suffering he caused coming into the world. (Well, to me anyway. You'd have to ask my wife how she feels about it . . . did I mention it was a 57-hour labor?)

What was also born that day was a great way to deal with pain and fear, that has been tested in the frying pan and fire of everyday life by myself and hundreds of my students, not to mention by a few thousand Zen masters in days gone by. What I learned from watching my wife ' trick herself" into feeling better in the midst of exhaustion, fear, and pain, was that no matter how bad or painful we think something is going to be, life is almost always all right in the present moment.

For much of our lives, what causes our pain and fear is in fact our expectation of further (and worse) pain and fear in the future. By checking in with ourselves in any moment to see if it is all right now we discover that invariably the answer is a resounding yes!

In other words unless you are reading this while plunging 60 miles per hour headfirst into a giant threshing machine, chances are that everything is fine right where you are sitting now.

From theory to practice . . .

Is It All Right Now?

1. Choose an activity that you either want or have to do, but you dread doing it.
   Examples:
   Going to the dentist; phoning up that beautiful person you met in the bar last night and asking them for a date.

2. Schedule a specific time to do it.

3. In between now and then, you are liable to experience moments of anxiety(!). Whenever you find yourself beginning to feel afraid, ask yourself, "Is it all right now?"

   If your answer is No! check again. Any lions, tigers, or bears? If you knew that you wouldn't really have to do what it is you fear, would you feel all right now?

4. Repeat step three as often as necessary.
   Example:
   Going to the dentist. I feel frightened when I read an article about root canals gone wrong. Is it all right now? I take a deep breath and look around and see that I am sitting in my living room, reading. No lions, no tigers, no bears. Yes, it is all right now.

   Example:
   Making an important phone call. The time for the call is approaching, and I feel sick to my stomach. It's not worth it! I'm not going to call . . . is it all right now? Well, my heart is racing. It doesn't feel all right. But I know that if I let myself off the hook and decided not to call, it would be fine. . . . I'll make that decision later. No lions, no tigers, no bears. Yes—it's all right now.

5. When the scheduled date and time arrive, begin to do what it is that you feared doing. Keep checking in at every step of the process, and notice how much of the time it is (you are) actually all right now.
   Example:
   At the dentist's office. It's all right sitting in the waiting room. And it's still all right lying in the dentist's chair while we chat. It's even all right as I sit peacefully and listen to the drill come toward me. Oh no, it's going to touch my teeth. . . . it's touching my teeth! It's touching my teeth! Aaargh! Is it all right now? Embarrassingly enough, it's fine. Sorry, Doc!

> *Example:*
> *Making the call. It's all right looking up the number. It's all right picking up the phone. It's even all right listening to it ring. Uh, oh, someone's picking up. It's them! They're saying "Hello!" They want to know who it is! Aaargh! Aaargh! Is it all right now? I take a deep breath and begin to look around as we continue speaking. No lions, no tigers, no bears. Yes, it is all right now.*

The root of all fears

"No-one is truly free who is afraid to die."
— Martin Luther King, Jr.

On most people's list of empowering beliefs to live by, "We're all going to die" doesn't make the top ten, or even the top fifty. Yet for me, this is one of the most motivating and inspiring concepts in the world.

You see, if we're all going to die (and we don't know when), then it would only make sense to live each moment fully. If we're all going to die (and we don't even know where), then what would be the point in engaging in activities that brought us no rewards along the way but might one day get us something that we want? If we're all going to die (and none of us knows exactly when that will be), wouldn't it naturally follow that we would want to make provisions for our loved ones and family?

Several years ago, I stood atop one of the tallest buildings in the world and got a terrifying jolt of vertigo. I closed my eyes, took several deep breaths, and reminded myself that I was going to die anyway—the only question was when. Bizarrely, rather than increase my fear, reminding myself of my own mortality completely eliminated the fear. From that point on, I was able to walk around the observation deck and look out over the city with a feeling of ease and grace.

In some ways, all fear stems from the fear of death. Follow the "ladder of fear" down rung by rung (. . . *and what are you afraid would happen if your fear came to pass? And what are you afraid would happen if that came to pass?*) and you will inevitably find yourself bumping up against your own eventual demise.

By making peace each morning with the fact that today might be your last, you ironically free yourself up each day to truly live.

I will always remember my very first parachute jump. On the day of the jump, we went down to the aerodrome, had two minutes of basic training, two hours of waiting, and then clambered into an open-bellied plane. As we gradually climbed higher and higher to our cruising altitude of 10,000 feet, it occurred to me that although what I was about to do was considered "risky," I had probably never been safer in an airplane before. (Usually the parachutes are stowed underneath your seat—this time one was already on my back!)

It wasn't until the moment of jumping, as I looked out of the plane at the vast expanse of unknown sky and cloud below me, that I realized that this was not a new experience for me—that in some ways, jumping out of airplanes was something I've done my whole life. Sure enough, there was that familiar jolt of adrenaline as I considered what I was about to do, followed by the almost invisible moment of decision. Next came the headlong rush toward the edge, and then half-jumping, half-falling headfirst into the void.

Once I got used to the speed of freefall the parachute kicked out, and soon I was able to control my descent, aim for the landing site, and enjoy the view as I floated effortlessly toward my target. I also had time to reflect on the experience. As my mind began to wander, I remembered one of my favorite stories. . . .

More Curious Than Afraid

In 1911, for reasons no one has ever been able to ascertain, a man appeared, naked and alone in the foothills of Mt. Lassen in Northern California. With the help of two anthropologists from Berkeley named Thomas Waterman and Alfred Kroeber, it was learned that he was the last remaining member of a once strong tribe of Native American Indians known as the Yana. Although accepting the friendship of the Westerners who took him in and gave him a home at the local University, he would never share his real name, and he became known as "Ishi," which translated simply as "man."

Having never before lived in what his benefactors called "civilization," he was continually being introduced to things he had never before experienced. On his first visit to San Francisco, Ishi was taken to the Oroville train station. When the train approached, he walked quietly away from his traveling companions and stood behind a pillar. When they beckoned for him to join them, he strode forward and boarded the train.

Back at the University, he was asked by Kroeber about his strange behavior at the train station. Ishi told him that when he was growing up, he and the members of his tribe would see the train pass through the valley. Watching it snaking along and bellowing smoke and fire, they thought it was a demon that ate people.

Amazed, Kroeber asked, "How did you find the courage to get on the train if you thought it was a demon?"

Ishi replied, "My life has taught me to be more curious than afraid."

By taking time every day to do at least one thing that is a little bit scary for us, we recondition our minds and begin developing our courage—the muscle of the heart.

We are then free to follow the advice of Sir Laurence Olivier, who responded to a young Albert Finney's question of how to deal with nerves by saying:

"Do what ' do, dear boy—amaze yourself with your own daring!"

Living beyond fear

Perhaps the most powerful tool I know for dealing with fear doesn't actually deal with fear at all—it simply presupposes that being human, we're liable to be afraid, and asks us to imagine how life would be different if we weren't.

A few years back, I was about to sign a contract to work exclusively for a very successful training company when I broke out into a cold sweat. This "subtle physiological clue" tipped me off that even after nearly 15 years as a professional coach, trainer, and speaker, I was still experiencing some hidden fears to do with my career that might be holding me back.

While observing, analyzing, transforming or even pushing through the fear would all be reasonable responses, a question popped into my head I had never asked before:

What would I do if I wasn't afraid?

The answers came so quickly and easily that at first I was overwhelmed. But I kept asking. And even without taking a single action, I began to feel a sense of freedom and ease that was both foreign and familiar, like coming home to a brand-new house.

I started asking the question regularly, in a variety of situations, and quickly came to realize that even though most of the time I wasn't feeling fear in my body, I was invariably allowing fear to hold me back in my life.

Therein lies the problem with the whole "feel the fear and do it anyway" philosophy—in order to live it, you actually have to feel the fear first, and most of us have so efficiently designed our lives around avoiding what we fear that we don't even know we fear it. But if you know in your heart what to do to reach one of your goals and you're still not doing it, chances are you're afraid of something.

From theory to practice . . .

Living Beyond Fear

1. Choose any area of your life where you'd like to have a breakthrough, in terms of your results or the quality of your experience or both.

2. For each life area, complete the sentence starter "*If I wasn't afraid, I would . . .*" as many times as you can (aim for at least ten completions). These sentence completions are not a new to-do list. You'll know which (if any) of your ideas to act upon because you'll find yourself acting upon them!
   Example:
   Life area—My relationships.

   If I wasn't afraid, I would . . .
   - *tell the truth more often*
   - *take time for myself even when my partner didn't like it*
   - *make them the most important person in my world*
   - *ask for sex when I wanted it and just say no when I didn't*
   - *commit more deeply to my partner*
   - *just love them completely without holding back and see what happened*

3. Repeat this exercise often, with as many different areas of your life as you can think of—I recommend at least once a day, though doing it more frequently seems to accelerate the process. Notice how quickly you experience more freedom, progress, and joy.

The fact is, there is a tremendous difference between simply not feeling fear and the freedom that comes from finding that space in yourself which is actually beyond fear. And the more time you spend living beyond fear, the sooner the answer to "What would I do if I wasn't afraid?" will become "Exactly what I'm doing now."

HOW TO HAVE A WONDERFUL LIFE

"What is it you want, Mary? What do you want? You want the moon?
Just say the word and I'll throw a lasso around it and pull it down."
—Jimmy Stewart, in the movie *It's a Wonderful Life*

I was having coffee with a prospective client recently and mentioned that although I spend much of my time coaching, teaching, and writing, I don't really consider myself to be a coach, teacher, or writer. When he asked me what business I do consider myself to be in. I really had to think about it.

"I'm in the 'having a wonderful life' business," I finally replied.

Everything we have talked about in this book, from creating a life that makes you go "Wow!" through each of the nine major life obstacles, is really about having a wonderful life. In fact, I have never met a single person who doesn't want to have a wonderful life, even if they define what would be wonderful in very different ways.

Which brings us to what is perhaps the most important question in the whole book:

If a wonderful life is the sum total of a whole lot of wonderful days, what can we do to ensure we have as many wonderful days as possible?

Here are my top ten tips . . .

1. Decide to make today a wonderful day

As simple as it sounds, I suspect one of the main reasons people don't have more wonderful days is they've never decided to have them. They assume "wonderful days" are like the weather—possible to predict in the short term but impossible to control. Think again. With a whole lot of intention and a little bit of skill, you can create your very own micro-climate of fun and carry it with you wherever you go.

Your experiment?

Decide to make it a wonderful day!

2. Expect wonderful things to happen

Best-selling author Brian Tracy begins every morning telling himself repeatedly, "Something wonderful is going to happen to me today." Invariably, it does. The first week I experimented with saying it, I got three acting jobs, a new coaching client, and a refund from the gas company.

All together now . . .

> "Something wonderful is going to happen to me today.
> Something wonderful is going to happen to me today.
> Something wonderful is going to happen to me today!"

3. Give yourself something to look forward to

Today, it was sushi for dinner. Tomorrow, an afternoon nap. Tuesday night, a baseball game. Wednesday, my latest books should be arriving from Amazon. Thursday, I get to cash a great big check. Friday, I'm off to the movies with Nina and the kids. Sounds like a pretty wonderful week to me!

4. Cut the world (and yourself) infinite slack

There is a story that the great 19th-century French actor Coquelin called his company together before a show one summer's evening to tell them he could not go on. When they asked him why, he replied, "I just don't feel like upsetting myself today."

Why not take a day off from upsetting yourself today? You can continue to do as much or as little as always to make your life the way you want it—just step off the emotional rollercoaster and carry your life with ease and grace.

5. Do wonderful things

There are essentially three categories of wonderful things to do:

A. Things that feel wonderful while you do them.
B. Things that produce wonderful results.
C. Things that feel wonderful while you do them and produce wonderful results.

To have a wonderful day, make sure your to-do list is filled with As, Bs, and Cs!

6. Spend time with wonderful people

Want to have a wonderful day, one day after another? Make a list of the most wonderful people you know and resolve to spend time with at least one of them, every single day, starting today.

7. Eat wonderful food

Remember the experiment done in the 1930s where tiny children were allowed to choose their own diet for a period of a month? Well, if a group of two-year-olds could stumble their way onto a balanced diet, why not you?

Just for today, rather than trying to decide what to eat based on one of the over 7,000 diet books listed in *Books in Print,* choose your food by how wonderful it makes you feel to eat it!

8. Read wonderful books

In *The Power of Myth,* Bill Moyers recounts the story of one of Joseph Campbell's university students complaining at the phenomenal amount of reading he had put on the reading list for his courses. Campbell replied, "I'm astonished you even tried— you've got the rest of your life to read those books!"

My own theory (and I read two or three books a week) is that even if I read 16 hours a day, seven days a week, I would have only scratched the surface of what's out there—so there's really no need to ever read a book that's less than truly wonderful.

(I've put a list of some of the most wonderful books I've read to date in the "Want to learn more?" section on my website— you'll find the link at the end of the book.)

9. Remember the wonderful things in the evening

Wouldn't it be awful if you had a really wonderful day and didn't even notice? Take some time out this evening to reflect on all the wonderful things you did and all the wonderful things that happened to you today, and watch the law of attraction take action—the more you look, the more there'll be to find!

10. A wonderful day is a day filled with wonder

High on my list of classic movie miscasting is John Wayne playing a Roman centurion in John Huston's *The Greatest Story Ever Told.*

Wayne's pivotal line, "He truly is the son of God," was apparently not being delivered with quite the gusto Huston had envisioned. "It needs more awe," directed Huston, to which Wayne replied in his famous drawl, "Aww . . . he truly is the son of Gawwd."

Spend some time today contemplating the mysteries—marvel at the beauty of a butterfly, try and feel the earth spinning beneath your feet, or look deep into the eyes of your children and wonder how in the heck they got here.

**Have fun, learn heaps and remember—
every time you have a wonderful day
another angel gets its wings!**

Until we meet,

Michael Neill

WANT TO LEARN MORE?

Visit **www.geniuscatalyst.com/learnmore.php** for a list of resources.

Your secret password is:
BGL21292

ABOUT THE AUTHOR

MICHAEL NEILL is an internationally renowned success coach and a licensed master trainer of Neuro-Linguistic Programming (NLP). His weekly coaching column is syndicated in newspapers and magazines worldwide, and he's the host of *You Can Have What You Want* on Hay House Radio.

Website: **www.geniuscatalyst.com**

We hope you enjoyed this Hay House book.
If you'd like to receive a free catalog featuring additional
Hay House books and products, or if you'd like information about the
Hay Foundation, please contact:

Hay House, Inc.
P.O. Box 5100
Carlsbad, CA 92018-5100

(760) 431-7695 or **(800) 654-5126**
(760) 431-6948 (fax) or **(800) 650-5115** (fax)
www.hayhouse.com® • **www.hayfoundation.org**

⸻

Published and distributed in Australia by:
Hay House Australia Pty. Ltd. • 18/36 Ralph St. • Alexandria NSW 2015 •
Phone: 612-9669-4299 • *Fax:* 612-9669-4144 • www.hayhouse.com.au

Published and distributed in the United Kingdom by:
Hay House UK, Ltd. • 292B Kensal Rd., London W10 5BE •
Phone: 44-20-8962-1230 • *Fax:* 44-20-8962-1239 • www.hayhouse.co.uk

Published and distributed in the Republic of South Africa by:
Hay House SA (Pty), Ltd., P.O. Box 990, Witkoppen 2068 •
Phone/Fax: 27-11-706-6612 • orders@psdprom.co.za

Distributed in India by:
Hay House Publications (India) Pvt. Ltd., Muskaan Complex, Plot No. 3, B-2,
Vasant Kunj, New Delhi 110 070 • *Phone:* 91-11-4176-1620 •
Fax: 91-11-4176-1630 • www.hayhouseindia.co.in

Distributed in Canada by:
Raincoast • 9050 Shaughnessy St., Vancouver, B.C. V6P 6E5 •
Phone: (604) 323-7100 • Fax: (604) 323-2600 • www.raincoast.com

⸻

Tune in to **HayHouseRadio.com®** for the best in inspirational talk radio featuring
top Hay House authors! And, sign up via the Hay House USA Website to receive the
Hay House online newsletter and stay informed about what's going on with your
favorite authors. You'll receive bimonthly announcements about: Discounts and
Offers, Special Events, Product Highlights, Free Excerpts, Giveaways, and more!
www.hayhouse.com®